Memories of (

ALSO EDITED BY PETER SEKIRIN

Americans in Conversation with Tolstoy: Selected Accounts, 1887–1923 (McFarland, 2006)

The Dostoevsky Archive: Firsthand Accounts of the Novelist from Contemporaries' Memoirs and Rare Periodicals, Most Translated into English for the First Time, with a Detailed Lifetime Chronology and Annotated Bibliography (McFarland, 1997)

Memories of Chekhov

Accounts of the Writer from His Family, Friends and Contemporaries

Edited and Translated by PETER SEKIRIN

Foreword by ALAN TWIGG

McFarland & Company, Inc., Publishers

Jefferson, North Carolina, and London

LIBRARY OF CONGRESS CATALOGUING-IN-PUBLICATION DATA

Memories of Chekhov : accounts of the writer from his family, friends and contemporaries / edited and translated by Peter Sekirin ; foreword by Alan Twigg.
    p.   cm.
Includes bibliographical references and index.

ISBN 978-0-7864-5871-4
softcover : 50# alkaline paper ∞

1. Chekhov, Anton Pavlovich, 1860–1904.
2. Chekhov, Anton Pavlovich, 1860–1904 — Family.
3. Chekhov, Anton Pavlovich, 1860–1904 — Friends and associates.
4. Authors, Russian —19th century — Biography.
I. Sekirin, Peter.
PG3458.M43   2011
891.72' 3 — dc23
[B]   2011033685

BRITISH LIBRARY CATALOGUING DATA ARE AVAILABLE

Front cover image: Anton Chekhov, 1901

Manufactured in the United States of America

McFarland & Company, Inc., Publishers
  Box 611, Jefferson, North Carolina 28640
  www.mcfarlandpub.com

Table of Contents

Table of Contents

Five. Chekhov and Theater

Six. Chekhov in Yalta: 1898–1904

Foreword
by Alan Twigg

One can argue Anton Chekhov is the second-most popular writer on the planet. Only Shakespeare, in 2011, outranks Chekhov in terms of the number of movie adaptations of their work, according to the movie data base IMBD. The rankings are William Shakespeare (836 titles); Anton Chekhov (324 titles); Alexandre Dumas père (245 titles); Edgar Allan Poe (243 titles); Agatha Christie (126 titles).

This will be news to most North Americans.

We generally know less about Chekhov than we do about the mysterious Shakespeare, even though Chekhov died, at age 44, in 1904, just over 100 years ago.

* * *

All the more reason to welcome *Memories of Chekhov*— a groundbreaking work for several reasons:

Here is a "documentary biography" that provides intimate knowledge of Chekhov from more than 100 people.

Nearly all of the material in *Memories of Chekhov* appears in English translation for the first time.

And here, as well, for the first time, we are introduced to Chekhov the playwright and short story master combined with Chekhov the man. Until now, the English-speaking world has had no idea about the richness of Chekhov's personal life.

* * *

By their actions ye shall know them.

By most accounts, Chekhov was an exemplary person. "This was a wonderful secret that Chekhov took to his grave," wrote Grigory Rossolimo, "how to charm people from your very first encounter."

1

Now diverse memories of Chekhov's behavior constitute proof positive that the adjective Chekhovian is more complex than Orwellian, Tolstoyan or Kafkaesque. A medical doctor who preferred not to charge for his services, Chekhov, the grandson of a serf, has been revealed by Sekirin's sleuthing in Russian archives to have been an apolitical figure who balanced compassion, humor, conviviality, charity and estrangement, never making a show of his genius.

As a literary man, according to Tatiana Shchepkina-Kupernik, "Chekhov never felt professional jealousy towards others." He gave advice to every fledgling author. "Chekhov was very humble," according to Vassily Maklakov, "and he never showed himself to be an important man."

But for all his reported charm and gregariousness and humility, there was a seldom-recognized side of Chekhov's character — the loner — that is best summarized by Ignaty Potapenko:

> The process of creation for Chekhov could not tolerate the intrusion of others into his inner world, not even his friends. I could even say that — if we were to speak completely truthfully and honestly — that Chekhov did not have any friends at all. Many people considered themselves to be Chekhov's friends, especially after his death. I am sure they confided their deepest secrets to him with sincerity. However, he never revealed his secret life to anyone else at all.

Chekhov's life was a feast of diversity, empathy and observation. *Memories of Chekhov* variously unveils Chekhov's hard times as a child (Maria, Nikolai, Ivan and Alexander Chekhov); his love for nature and gardening (M. Chekhov, A. Khotiaintseva, T. Shchepkina-Kupernik, V. Veresaev, A. Kuprin, J. Avdeev, A. Hotiaintseva); and his passion for fishing (I. Belousov, I. Braz, A. Serebrov). "I think some of the best creations of the Russian literature were thought over and were created during time spent fishing," he wrote.

We learn of Chekhov's interest in visual arts and his friendship with painters (M. Nesterov, A. Khotiaintseva, V. Simov, N. Panov, I. Repin) and trip to Sakhalin Island and Siberian prisons (A. Roskin, A. Koni, A. Suvorin, A. Chaikin). "Sakhalin had ten thousand people," writes Roskin, "and Chekhov filled out ten thousand census cards in his handwriting."

Chekhov the humanitarian worked for free as a doctor for several years (Z. Pichugin, G. Rosslimo, V. Giliarovsky), had a sometimes stormy personal life (L. Avilova, A. Suvorin, E. Shavrova-Just, T. Tolstaya) and he enjoyed drinking good wine with friends (S. Podiachev, E. Karpov, E. Yasinsky), playing cards (N. Teleshov, Z. Pichugin) and attending night clubs and parties (V. Simov, A. Glama-Mesherskaya, E. Yasinsky, S. Sobolevsky, N. Teleshov). "He was a stickler for having good manners all the time," records Ignaty Potapenko. "No matter what."

Chekhov built village schools and libraries with his own money and organized a cholera epidemic medical station (M. Plotov, A. Kazan, I. Bunin, N. Drozdova, T. Kupernik, J. Avdeev, G. Rossolimo). His altruism extended to passionate support of university students and aspiring writers (V. Korolenko, E. Shavrova, S. Podiachev, A. Lazarev-Gruzinsky, A. Yakovlev, K. Korovin).

Tolstoy dismissed Chekhov's plays but nonetheless gained his complete adoration as a father figure and novelist. "Leo Tolstoy loved Chekhov as a father loves a son," observed Maxim Gorky. Chekhov's friendships with Tolstoy and Gorky were well-known; his affairs with countless women are not.

According to two volumes of Chekhov letters, published in 2004 and 2007 in Moscow, the writer's sister Maria (the long-time director of the Chekhov Archive) kept his most intimate confessions (mostly made to his friend and publisher Alexey Suvorin) hidden from the public; she even used black ink to delete some "sensitive" lines, to paint him as "a good brother" and an ideal family man.

According to these letters, Chekhov had more than 30 (documented) steady girlfriends during the last fifteen years of his life.

Here are some snippets from Chekhov's letters to Suvorin:

"The sofa is no good when it comes to love-making: I have not once seen a single apartment — in the homes of decent families, of course — with furniture that would permit you to take and use a fully dressed woman, and I curse all sofas for this deficiency...."

"An affair with a woman from a respectable family is going to take far too much of your time.... First, you need to do this at night. In the hotel room, your lady will fall into a fit of terror, trembling and exclaiming: 'Oh my God, what am I doing? No, no.' Then it will take you another hour to undress her and to talk her through it, and on the way back home, she will look at you as though you have raped her, and mumble all the way home, 'No, never, I will never forgive myself for this.'"

"I have known many dissipated women, and have sinned on numerous occasions."

In the course of his travels around the world, Chekhov met a Japanese geisha and a beautiful Hindu woman. Evidently he took some pleasure in describing his sexual experiences: "Here in Paris, I make daily sacrifices to the goddess of love. My French girl-friend is well-built, but I am a little bored by all this, and want to go back home to Russia."

Chekhov's most intimate letters were only recently published by the Voskresenie Publishers in Moscow in 2008 (A.P. Chekhov, *Complete Works in 35 Volumes*). One can anticipate a sequel to *Memories of Chekhov* from Sekirin, if this volume finds an audience.

*　　*　　*

Chapters about Chekhov's theatrical career provide some of the most fascinating material. Towards the end of this book, Chekhov's wife-to-be Olga Knipper and her fellow actress Maria Chitau vividly recall contradictory responses to Chekhov's second play, *The Seagull*. Although *The Seagull* was to become the most popular of Chekhov's plays during his lifetime, its premiere in St. Petersburg was fraught with anxiety and public disaffection. "We had never heard so much booing," wrote Chitau, describing opening night. "For as long as I remember, no other performance in the history of our theatre had ever failed so completely. By the middle of the performance, the actors realized it would be a complete disaster."

The response was so severely negative that Chekhov left both the theatre and St. Petersburg immediately. Oddly, the following night was different. "During the third act," Knipper recalls, "there were several protests in the theatre hall. Everything seemed new, and hard to explain—such things as complete darkness in the theatre; the fact that the actors were sitting with their backs to the public during the play itself.

"We were waiting for the last act. When the play was over, there were a few moments of complete silence. Then it seemed that a huge water current has destroyed the dam that was holding it back. We could not understand what was happening—it was complete madness, and a total triumph.

"Both the theatre viewers and the actors were united in one body. We were standing, embracing each other, and kissing, hugging and cheering. There was a seemingly endless ovation. Some of the public were in tears. We requested that a telegram should be sent immediately to Chekhov in Yalta, informing him that both the play and the playwright were a complete success."

*　　*　　*

Although Maupassant preceded him, as did Poe, Chekhov is often described as the father of the modern short story. Chekhov's beguiling plays, with their "theatre of mood," most notably *The Cherry Orchard*, *Three Sisters*, *The Seagull*, *Ivanov* and *Uncle Vanya*, are still produced widely all over the world.

How many other great writers have ever been so extraordinary on the stage *and* on the page *and* in the realm of personal intimacy?

What compelled this apparently dutiful fellow named Chekhov—a relatively poor provincial raised far beyond Moscow or St. Petersburg—to write his remarkably diverse short stories and to create provocative, transformative works for theatre? Chekhov asked himself this question. "For whom do I write?" he wrote to Suvorin in December of 1888. "For the public? But I have never seen the public. For the money? Is it the money that I want? But I have never seen the big money, and therefore, I am quite indifferent to it."

Equally unanswerable is why we *like* Chekhov? Richard Ford has pondered the mystery of Chekhov's appeal in his foreword to *The Essential Tales of Chekhov* (Ecco Press, 1998). "There is, of course, no typical Chekhov story, a fact that by itself should please us, and makes the pseudo-critical shorthand of 'Chekhovian' essentially pointless."

Ford and Sekirin have both identified "The Lady with the Dog" as their favorite or quintessential Chekhov story. Letters have revealed it to be autobiographical; the story of a dalliance that turned into an affair that turned into an obsession. Why did this happen? Chekhov apparently didn't know either. And he didn't attempt to explain, apologize or supply an ending. Instead he records: "Anna Sergeyevna and he loved each other," he writes in the story, "like people very close and akin, like husband and wife, like tender friends; it seemed to them that fate itself had meant them for one another, and they could not understand why he had a wife and she a husband; and it was as though they were a pair of birds of passage, caught and forced to live in different cages."

The prototype for Anna was Elena Shavrova. She was 15 and Chekhov was 29 when they met for the first time. She brought him the manuscript of her first short story, and instantly fell in love with him. By the age of 20, she understood that she had no chance with him, after approaching him many times, so she got married, without thinking much about her choice, to a civil servant, Mr. Youst. In 1897, when Chekhov was 37 (and she was 23), they met in Moscow briefly, and instantly fled together to Yalta. Around 1898–99, when "Lady with the Dog" was published, they parted — never to meet again.

Eventually Chekhov met his future wife, Olga Knipper. Chekhov wrote 68 letters to Elena/Anna, more letters than to any other woman (except for his wife). Meanwhile three other women — Ms. Podgorodnikova, Ms. Vasilieva, and Ms. Tsingovatova (or their friends) — stated they were the female prototypes for the story. Evidently there was no shortage of women who wished to be associated with Anton Chekhov.

The recently published material about Chekhov's love life reveals that he was neither a vile seducer nor a paragon of virtue (within the Christian ideal of a devout family man). Instead, Chekhov was a deeply wise man who took the necessary risks to learn what it means to be deeply human.

Anton Chekhov once told Evgeny Yasinsky that if he (Chekhov) had not been a writer, he would have become a doctor specializing in the new field of psychiatry. And according to Konstantin Korovin, Chekhov once said, "I have neither ideas, nor messages." Chekhov stated in one of the letters, "I am neither a liberal, nor a conservative; neither a reformer, nor a monk; and I am not indifferent to life.... My holy of holies are the human vessel, health, intellect, talent, inspiration and, of course, love and freedom."

Anton Chekhov does not tell us how to live.

Rather his work encourages us *to* live.

* * *

Famous Russians such as writers Ivan Bunin and Maxim Gorky, theatre director Konstantin Stanislavsky, composer Pyotr Tchaikovsky and the poet Tatiana Kupernik have left vast and reliable accounts of Chekhov, but the majority of Sekirin's research materials were retrieved, one at a time, from obscure sources. Over a ten-year period, Sekirin uncovered numerous now-extinct periodicals and newspapers, with tiny circulations, from Siberia and Ukraine.

Approximately two-thirds of the material in Sekirin's *Memories of Chekhov* does not appear in the Russian volume that inspired it. Peter Sekirin's "documentary biography" develops this genre even further. The thoroughly engaging material in *Memories of Chekhov* is a triumph of diligence and curiosity.

Alan Twigg has written 15 books and produced six documentaries, and is the editor and publisher of *BC Bookworld*, one of Canada's major book review magazines.

Preface

Memories of Chekhov is the first book on Anton Chekhov to be based entirely on primary sources: the letters, diaries, essays, and memories of Chekhov's family, friends and contemporaries. Extant biographies of Chekhov do not emphasize this firsthand, documentary evidence, yet those who knew him left more than a hundred reminiscences scattered in rare periodicals and archival sources from the 1880s to the 1930s.

These materials pose major research challenges: First, they are scattered in extremely rare sources. Second, not all surviving accounts are historically valid: several journalists from Odessa who never met Chekhov nonetheless wrote detailed accounts of their alleged "interviews" for the *Odessa News*; Veresaev mentions a trip that Chekhov never made. Validity, therefore, was the major criterion for the selection of the material for this volume. Such famous Russians as Ivan Bunin, Maxim Gorky, Konstantin Stanislavsky, the poet Tatiana Kupernik, and the lawyer Anatoly Koni left vast and reliable accounts; here the challenge was to let those voices tell their stories of a great storyteller.

Memories of Chekhov consists of six chapters. Four cover distinct chronological periods: his early childhood in Taganrog in the 1860s and '70s; the literary scene in Moscow in the 1880s; life in Melikhovo in the 1890s; and life in Yalta in the early 1900s. Since most of the friends who left memories were either authors or theatrical people, two additional chapters focus on these aspects of his life. Most memories appear in order, but a few range over wider tracts of Chekhov's life. Each chapter is introduced by a series of the most significant short quotations from letters, diaries and other firsthand documents relating to this period. The body of the chapter juxtaposes the longer narratives of Chekhov's friends, colleagues, and relatives.

Most material was selected from contemporary periodicals — newspapers, magazines, and collections of essays — which are now bibliographical rarities. I am grateful for the assistance of the Library of Congress, the New York Public Library, the Russian National Library in Moscow, the University of

Illinois in Urbana–Champaign Library, the Ukrainian National Library in Kiev, and the Chekhov Museum and Archive in Moscow and in Yalta. There are too many librarians, editors and curators who contributed to the research on this book to mention here, yet I would like to express my deepest and most sincere thanks to Mrs. Helen Sullivan from the University of Illinois at Urbana Slavic Reference Library, Mrs. Liudmila Riazanova from the Russian National Library, and Mr. Edward Kasinec from the Slavic Collection of the New York Public Library. I am also grateful to Kim Yates and Chet Scoville from the University of Toronto, as well as Karla Lees and Marina Kudrow, who read the manuscript at different stages, and made valuable suggestions on how to improve it. Special thanks to Alan Twigg for his Foreword.

All of this material appears here in English translation for the first time. Approximately a third was originally collected in the Russian edition, *Chekhov v vospominaniakh sovremennikov* (Chekhov in the Memoirs of His Contemporaries). With five successful editions of over 100,000 copies each published in Moscow in 1947, 1952, 1954, 1960 and 1986, that volume inspired this research. *Memories of Chekhov* assembles the accounts of over a hundred men and women who knew Chekhov and recorded their most intimate and precious memories.

Numerous questions remain. What was the exact date of Chekhov's birth? The official records do not coincide with dates from the personal letters. What was the exact date of his first publication? Most of these early works were published in small periodicals which did not publish the date of issue, just the year and the number.

What was the nature of Chekhov's rather stormy but highly secretive personal life? When the Russian archives opened recently, we learned that Chekhov was an active womanizer; a few of these ladies appear here, including Tatyana Tolstoy, Lydia Avilova, Elena Shavrova, several female writers and actresses, and even a Japanese geisha. Instead of emphasizing such revelatory material, I have chosen to present a well-rounded presentation of Chekhov's activities and character. A great deal more emphasis has been afforded to Chekhov and theatre. There is a risk that sensational material on Chekhov's hitherto unknown sex life could make for a lopsided portrait and, more likely, a distorted view of the book and its subject. It is the overall view of Chekhov's complexity that must come first.

Exciting new discoveries about Chekhov's literary and theatrical life continue to turn up in recent research. Most of the material will appear for the first time in manuscript form, except for memories by Maria Chekhova, Alexander Chekhov, Maxim Gorky and Ivan Bunin. The other materials — memories by personal friends, aspiring authors, painters and architects, actors, theater directors — will be a real discovery both for Chekhov scholars and for Chekhov lovers.

My favorite discovery was a rare editorial by Chekhov in *Russian Thought* dedicated to the life of Nikolai Przhevalsky, a famous Russian geographer. At the very end of the 19th century Chekhov wrote, "Reading this biography, we do not ask: 'Why did he do this?' or 'What did he accomplish?' but we say, 'He was right!'" These words also describe Chekhov's own life.

I hope the reader will conclude *Memories of Chekhov* with the same sense of admiration. It is hoped the material in this volume will provide additional stimulus for future Chekhov scholarship — including my own.

CHAPTER ONE

Childhood and School Years: 1860–1879

Introduction

As a child, Anton Pavlovich was a healthy, energetic and lovely young boy with a large head. He liked to make jokes and play children's games. Of all his brothers, Anton had the best imagination. He was always re-enacting major roles from the theatre, or imitating others.

It was hard to imagine a more lively and good-humored boy than Anton Pavlovich as he grew into a teenager. He was always organizing amateur plays at home.

— Mikhail Chekhov. "Anton Chekhov and His Plots"

According to the memories of M.A. Rabinovich, who was Chekhov's schoolmate, student Volkenstein was expelled from the school, after slapping another student for calling him "a Jew."

Chekhov convinced his school-mates to sign a petition that the entire class would drop out of school if Volkenstein will not be re-instated. The principal yielded to popular demand and allowed Volkenstein to resume studies.

— Mikhail Andreev-Turkin. "Chekhov in Taganrog," Rostov, 1935, pp. 38–44.

No one noticed Anton Pavlovich Chekhov as a high school student. "He was a good student, but he was more or less like the others," Mr. Filevsky, the math teacher, wrote. However, Stefanovsky, the teacher of literature, mentioned at the teachers' meeting the great literary skill and depth of thought in the literary compositions of the high school student Anton Chekhov.

— A. Tan-Bogoraz. "At Chekhov's Hometown"

In the 1890s, while reminiscing about his old school days, Chekhov told his school-mate L. Volkenstein the following: "Recently, looking through my papers, I found one of my sixth grade essays. I think that even now I would not write a better essay on his topic."

— Leonid Volkenstein. "About Chekhov." *Illustrated Russia*, 1934 (7 July) Nu. 28.

Every day, the Chekhovs were occupied with something. All the boys got up early, went to school, came home and did their homework. Then, they were engaged in the activities which corresponded to their interests: elder Alexander made electric batteries, Nikolai painted, Ivan made small books, and the future writer Anton would write. The major feature of the Chekhov family was how they used to sing and pray together.

— Mikhail Chekhov. "Around Chekhov"

Our father was very demanding and strict. If the brothers disobeyed him, or did something wrong, he might give them a good beating. Little Anton also was punished from time to time.

— Maria Chekhova. "My Memories"

Our mother, Evgenia Yakovlevna, was different from our father. She was a soft and quiet woman. She had a poetic nature. By contrast to the father, who seemed very strict, her motherly care and tenderness were amazing. Later, Anton Pavlovich said very truly: I have inherited the talent from the father's side, and the soul from the mother's side.

— Alexander Chekhov. "From Chekhov's Childhood"

If you see my father, please tell him that I received his nice letter, and I am thankful to him for it. My dad and mom are the only two people on earth for whom I would sacrifice everything I have. And if ever I should achieve something good in my life, it is due to them. They are very nice people, and their limitless love for their children places them higher than any of my praises.

— Anton Chekhov. "Letters." His letter to
M. Chekhov, July 29, 1877

Mikhail Chekhov. "Around Chekhov"

As far back as I can remember, even when Anton was in high school, he loved to flirt with the female students, and he related his love affairs to me as stories bursting with optimism. When he was at University and I was still in high school, he often would tug at my sleeve, and, with a nod toward a young lady who was passing, he would tell me,

"Run! Go after her, quickly! This is a real discovery for a high school student."

Later, Alexy Suvorin told me a story from my brother's life that Anton had told him, in his very words.

One day, when Anton was still a high school student, he was standing near a well out in the middle of the steppe, contemplating his reflection in the water. A girl, about fifteen years old, came to get some water. She was so pretty, and he was so instantly infatuated, that they started to kiss and embrace at once. Then they both stood for a long time by the well, gazing in silence at their reflections on the water's surface. They did not want to leave, and she completely forgot about the water she had come to fetch.

Anton Chekhov told this story to Alexey Suvorin much later, when he had become a very famous writer, in the course of a conversation about similar wavelengths and love at first sight.

Mikhail Chekhov. "Anton Chekhov During His Summer Vacations"

The Chekhov family emigrated from Taganrog to Moscow in 1876, but Anton Pavlovich stayed behind until 1879 in order to finish high school and get his diploma. At the time, no one in Taganrog had summer cottages, and during summer vacation people simply stayed in town.

The Chekhovs also stayed in the city, five brothers and one sister. School had just let out and the children, together with their schoolmates and the neighboring boys, spent their summer vacation together. The days were dry, and they walked outside barefoot. It was impossible to sleep inside the house because of the heat, so they made several beds in the backyard and a small tree house in the garden, where they spent their nights.

Anton Pavlovich, still a high school student, had made a bed on the ground under a wild vineyard in the backyard, and he called it "Job's house under the fig tree." Sometimes he wrote poetry, and once he even created a fairy tale that he wrote down and read to us.

We woke very early as a rule. Sometimes our mother, Evgenia

Chekhov in October 1893. Autograph dated March 1894. "To Varvara Kharkevich for Good Memory. March 1894. A. Chekhov." Kharkevich was the principal of a girls' high school where Chekhov was a trustee.

Yakovlevna, asked our brothers to go and get something to eat at the local market in the city square. I went there with them sometimes. One day, Anton bought a live duck. As we walked home, he kept pulling the duck's tail feathers to make it quack.

"Let the people of the town know that we are rich enough to eat a duck for dinner," he said.

He liked to look at different birds at the market, and he became a real expert in them.

Every day, we went swimming in the sea. As a rule, we invited several boys from neighboring houses, and we were quite a big company when we came to the seashore.

Usually we went to the public beach. It was a very shallow place, and in order to get up to your neck in the water you had to walk for half a mile. Very often we went fishing. When that was the case, we went to the seaport on the other side of the city. The port was bounded by piles of huge, sharp stones stacked on top of each other. We used to catch the little fish: bullheads or gobbles. One day we caught 365 bullheads, one for each day of the year.

Between fishing, we swam, even though the bottom was covered with very sharp stones. One day, Anton dived into the water headfirst and hit his head on a rock. It injured his forehead, and he had a scar on his hairline for the rest of his life. This scar was recorded as a distinguishing mark in his passport when he finished high school and traveled from Taganrog to Moscow to attend university.

Very often we went to the City Park, and sometimes we had picnics outside of the city. I remember that Anton used to make a fire, and Nikolai would lie down on the grass staring at the flora and fauna, and Ivan would sniff and slowly change his boots. Then we would arrange for a bed for the night at a local peasant's house, and early in the morning my brothers would go fishing.

One day, they caught five small pikes and over a hundred crabs, and our mother made a wonderful dinner. I remember those dear days very clearly.

Ivan Chekhov and Leonid Sulerzhitsky. "Memories of Chekhov"

Chekhov was interested in the theater from an early age.

It was usually the two of us, as a rule. We would buy the cheapest tickets to our local drama theater, sitting in the upper row, to the right, the seats closest to the ceiling at the very back. These rows did not have numbers, so in order to get decent seats, we needed to arrive long before the beginning of the performance.

We usually did not even know what they were being performed on any given night. We were interested in everything — whether drama, opera, or musical comedy.

After the performance, we would walk home, conversing loudly about what happened in the theater that night. And surely, on the next day, Anton Pavlovich would perform all these in roles.

Maria Drossi and Alexander Roskin. "Chekhov's Young Years"

The students of the Taganrog were not allowed to visit the local theater without parents. We knew that the teachers from our school would check out the theater during the performance. So in order not to be recognized, we used to put some make-up and disguises on.

It was strange to see ourselves, young men that we were, with added fake beards, whiskers, and black sunglasses. We would sit in the farthest seats in the back of the theatre, dressed up in our fathers' huge clothes....

Thanks to some assistance of Chekhov's friend's father, Mr. Yakovlev, who worked for several years at the local theater, we would be allowed access backstage to meet and talk with the actors. It was there that we had our first meeting with the famous actor Solovtsov.

The Taganrog Drama Theater had a troupe full of great actors at the time, such as Yakovlev, Novikov and Solovtsov. It was easy to fall in love with the theater. With Yakovlev's help we actually built a theater scene in one of the abandoned barns, where Anton Chekhov would perform short one-act plays in front of his friends with a great success.

We went to the theater on a regular basis when we were kids. In 1898, when Chekhov visited Taganrog as an adult, he wrote to his sister Maria,

"I write this letter to you from the theater, sitting at the back bench, in a winter overcoat. A very cheap orchestra and the back bench at the theater remind me of my childhood."

Alexander Chekhov. "From Chekhov's Childhood"

"I have a lot of schoolwork to do," says Anton Chekhov.

"You will do your homework at the general store. Go there! You will have to supervise! Hurry up!" replies his father.

Anton throws away his pen in disappointment, closes his textbook, picks up his winter coat uniform, puts on leather boots with worn-out soles, and goes to his father's general store.

The store is located on the ground floor of their house.

He is not really happy to be there. It is very cold inside.

The two boys who are working there, Andrew and Gabriel, are freezing from cold. They have blue hands and red noses, and they stamp their feet on the ground, hunching their backs against the cold.

His father gives a new order to Anton,

"Sit at the cash desk!"

Then he leaves.

The boy climbs onto a big cardboard box, and from there, to a tall chair behind the counter of the cash desk. He resumes his schoolwork at the store. He sits there for at least three hours. He knows that his father, Pavel Egorovich, will not return for a long time.

Anton sits there, thrusting his hands deep into the pockets of his coat like Andrew and Gabriel. He cannot complete his homework in this cold place, and tomorrow his father will scold him for bad marks at school.

Very few of the readers and admirers of Anton Pavlovich Chekhov know that, in his early boyhood, he worked at a very small, cheap general store, helping his father. His impressions of carefree childhood were based on observations made from a distance. He never experienced these happy years, filled with joy and pleasant memories. He did not have a chance to play with his friends, or simply sit around. He did not have time to do this because he spent most of his free time at his father's general store. Besides, his father had rules and prohibitions regarding everything.

He could not run around because, as his father told him, "You will wear out your boots." He could not jump because "only street bums hop around." He could not play games with other children because "your peers will teach you bad habits."

"Do not hang around outside! Get inside the store and stay there! You have to learn the trade!" Anton Pavlovich used to hear this from his father all the time.

That store... While his friends were fooling around, having a good time, the hours and years of his childhood trickled away, as he sold goods for pennies under his father's relentless eye. Anton Pavlovich was forced to do this throughout most of his school years, starting when he was a little boy. When he was older, he would tell his friends and relatives,

"During my childhood, I did not really have a childhood."

Alexey Dolzhenko. "Memories of Anton Chekhov"

Two sisters, Evgenia Yakovlevna and Feodosia Yakovlevna, were married in the same year in Taganrog. The elder sister Eugenia married Pavel Egorovich Chekhov; and had six children including Anton Chekhov.

Feodosia, the younger sister married Mr. Dolzhenko and had an only son, Alexey [*Anton's cousin and the author of this memoir — P.S.*].

When I was a little boy, I lived in Taganrog with my parents. The Chekhov family often visited us. We children liked to play together, and often stayed overnight or on longer visits, for the whole week. I remember how we as boys had many pillow fights in the bedroom. Anton and Alexander were always the winners, with the rest of us cheering them on.

One day, the Chekhovs visited on my birthday. Everyone gave me a gift. Anton read out loud a poem that he had written, Nikolai gave me a painting he had made, Alexander gave me a children's book, and Ivan gave me a set of coloring pencils. We sat around the table and had a great time.

Soon after my birthday, disaster struck our family. My father became sick, and after a brief illness he passed away, leaving my mother and me without any financial support. Things grew so hard that we moved in with our in-laws, that is, into the Chekhov house.

We had a little room in the basement, the store the Chekhovs ran was on the ground floor, and the Chekhov family lived on the second floor. We lived on different floors, but remained close, like one extended family. Anton had a large head when he was a little boy, so we gave him the nickname "the bomb."

The windows of the house faced the Azov Sea, about two kilometers away. From the windows, we could see the sea very clearly and spent hours watching the sails of the local fishing boats, and the bigger steamships that crossed the sea at the horizon.

We used to play together at the seashore. One day, we went walking along the coastline and without knowing it, we were actually walking out into the sea due to low tide. Suddenly, the wind started blowing in the other direction, and the high tide began to come back in. We hurried to climb on the top of an old wrecked sailing boat that was lying upside down. We were cut off from the shore. The white water became deeper, with the waves swirling and getting stronger. Then the little boat started moving and floating. We grew very scared.

Anton Chekhov was the only brave one of the bunch, and he was laughing at us. I don't know what could have happened, but some sailors noticed us from the distance and rescued us.

When Anton was a high school student, he loved fishing. Four of us boys always went fishing together — Anton, Nikolai, Ivan and me. Anton was always the best fisherman among us, as he always caught more fish than the rest of us.

He invented a special float for his fishing rods, in the form of a little man carved from a piece of wood. As soon as a fish latched on to the hook, the little man raised his hands. He could also indicate what size of fish it was. If it was a big fish, he raised his hands higher.

When we used to go fishing, we took all necessary cooking utensils: a frying pan and spices; sometimes Anton brought wine. We cooked the fish on the seashore so that Pavel Egorovich, the father of the Chekhov family, did not know what we were doing there.

Pavel Egorovich was the owner of a general store in Taganrog. When he declared bankruptcy, the family moved to Moscow.

Maria Chekhova. "My Memories"

I spent my childhood in the city of Taganrog. I was the only daughter in a family with five boys. Ours was a rather strict family, but I have good memories of my childhood. We spent it playing games, joking around and having a good time.

My brother, Anton, played the chief role in our games and performances. Our childhood passed with him in the midst of it.

When I was in the second year of elementary school, my father went bankrupt. He had never been a very good merchant. In his heart, he was an artist, and he could not organize his business, a small general store. He announced bankruptcy, halted his trade, and moved to Moscow. At the time, my two oldest brothers had just entered their first year of university. In the summer of 1876, my mother, my younger brothers Mikhail and Ivan, and I joined our father in Moscow. Anton remained alone in Taganrog to finish high school.

In Moscow, we lived in poverty. We had material problems; often we did not have enough food to eat, and if we did, there was always an over-whelming number of issues to occupy our lives. My happy childhood was over. A more serious, difficult life had begun for me; after the trauma caused by my father's bankruptcy, my mother was often sick, and I had to take charge of our household.

In 1877, my brother visited us briefly. Upon seeing our hardships, Anton returned to Taganrog and began sending us a part of the money he earned from tutoring, even though he himself lived from hand to mouth. From his youth, Anton had a sensible and responsible attitude towards our family, and he supported us by any means possible. Immediately after graduating from high school, he moved to Moscow, entered the university and became the chief provider for our family.

After his arrival to Moscow, our friendship became even stronger. Our lives improved because of him. He was a student in the Faculty of Medicine of the Moscow University, but at the same time, he had a comfortable income from his literary work. I was very proud and grateful for his literary success, and for those first three- and five-ruble royalties made by my brother, the writer "Antosha Chekhonte."

After I finished high school, my brother paid for me to take Ladies' Teachers Education Courses, a kind of teaching program.

In the fall of 1883, Anton Pavlovich was in his last year of university. At the same time, he had become an acclaimed author of humorous short stories in illustrated magazines. Our bustling life was full of humor and laughter. Our house always had visitors, including numerous friends from my courses.

Shortly after, Anton Pavlovich graduated from university and a sign appeared by our entrance that read, "Doctor A.P. Chekhov." *[This sign is now at the entrance of the Chekhov Museum in Moscow.— P.S.]*

By the time he had gotten his doctor's diploma, he had already been the unofficial head of the family and our major provider for some time. As a result of his hardworking character and his literary talent, we had left behind our life of poverty, and now lived a normal life. Anton Pavlovich worked without pause, and we all wished to be of some help to him.

After completing the Teachers Courses, I got a job as a history and geography teacher at a private

Maria Pavlovna Chekhova, the writer's sister, Moscow, 1899.

school in Moscow. At the time, we lived on Sadovaya Street in a small, two-story house that Anton Pavlovich called "a wardrobe," because, in his opinion, it looked like one. This period of my life brings back many bright and happy memories. My brother was now a popular writer. He received letters from two famous writers, Grigorovich and Pleshcheev, recognizing his great talent. A little later, a collection of his short stories was awarded the national Pushkin Prize, a prestigious literary award.

I remember that Pyotr Illych Tchaikovsky once visited our house, and spoke with my brother; Anton Pavlovich greatly admired the talent of this composer *[He went on to dedicate "Gloomy People," a collection of his short stories, to Tchaikovsky — P.S.].* They exchanged autographed photographs. Then Tchaikovsky began discussing the possibility of Chekhov's participation in his new opera *Bella,* after the poem by Lermontov. The composer asked my brother to write a libretto for the opera. Sadly, this project was never completed, since my brother had planned a trip to Sakhalin Island in Siberia, and Pyotr Illych died in 1893.

Sergei Yakovlev. "Memories of A.P. Chekhov"

My brother and I sat listening to Mr. Jacque, our French tutor, stressing the importance of grammar. Then, our father came in. A young and very poorly dressed man followed him into the room.

"Here is your new tutor in Russian, and here are your new students," said my father. The young man appeared confused. He stretched out his hand and introduced himself,

"My name is Anton Pavlovich Chekhov." He was very tall and thin, with a tender and gentle smile. Without reading us lectures on how to behave, or punishing us, he taught us real lessons about the Russian language, which we enjoyed immensely. In several months, during one of our family dinners, my father said to one of our guests,

"Yes, I agree completely with you. Chekhov has great talent. His books are well-read, and he will be a great figure in literature one day."

Thus we found out that our tutor was a writer. From that day on, we began treating him with more respect, and did all our homework. Chekhov noticed this change immediately. He asked us,

"Why have you changed your attitude? Why do you think that my lessons are so important now?" We told him what we had heard. Chekhov said in a calm voice,

"My friends, your father is giving me undeserved praise. I do not have any talent, and I write books because otherwise, your teacher would have nothing to eat, and he wants to eat every day. What do you think?"

We agreed with him.

"Thankfully there are good editors who like to pay me, and agree to publish my books under the name 'Antosha Chekhonte.'"

We met Anton Chekhov later, under very special circumstances in 1897. I was a member of an amateur theater, and we had to perform in a distant Moscow suburb. Before the performance began, I went to the cash desk to see how ticket sales were going. A tall man with eyeglasses stood there. His face was familiar, but he had a small beard. In a moment, I recognized my former Russian teacher and introduced myself. He smiled at me and we embraced each other. I found out that Anton Pavlovich worked as a trustee at a local school. Chekhov invited me to his house, saying,

"Now that I am no longer your tutor, but a landlord myself, can you promise me that you will visit me at my Melikhovo estate?"

After the performance, we went to a local restaurant, where Anton Pavlovich treated us to a wonderful dinner. I was planning to visit Melikhovo in a few weeks, when I received a rather sudden letter from Chekhov. He wrote,

"I'm writing this letter from a bed. I am a little bit sick, so the doctors have arrested me and put me in the hospital. I would like to see you, so please pay me a visit."

On the next day, I went to see Chekhov at the hospital.

"Can I see Anton Pavlovich Chekhov?" I asked the nurse after introducing myself.

"Anton Pavlovich is not well, so please do not stay for more than ten minutes, and do not allow him to speak. Leo Tolstoy has just been here. He spoke to Chekhov for half an hour, and Chekhov is very weak after his visit. Please be brief."

I was confronted with a very sad sight when I came into the hospital room. He lay in bed, very weak and pale. He said,

"So you came. Thank you. I don't have enough air to breathe because blood keeps on coming to my throat. I would like to go back to Melikhovo as soon as possible."

I asked Chekhov to help one of my friends, who was an amateur writer, by recommending him to the publisher Suvorin. Chekhov agreed to help me and said,

"Give me your friend's story. I would like to read it."

In a few days, Chekhov returned the short story and wrote a letter of recommendation to Suvorin.

He added a note that said,

"If your friend truly wants to write, he should write and let nothing get into his way. He should submit to newspapers and magazines without caring whether they accept him or not. One good short story a year will not make him a writer, any more than hammering one nail into a piece of wood each year will make him a carpenter. It is like learning how to ride a bicycle for the first time in your life; you have to fall down a couple of times first."

When I was leaving the hospital, Chekhov was in a very sad and depressed state. He was probably disappointed by the sad news about his health.

Chekhov was a leader among writers. He helped every young aspiring artist who came to him for help. He wrote letters of recommendation, spoke to publishers and editors, and he was always happy when one of his protégées was published. When he recommended someone, he always said,

"He is a very kind and good person."

I remember one episode between Chekhov and an editor. Chekhov was earning between 500 and 1000 rubles per short story, and he needed money. One day, I was present as Chekhov was speaking with the editor of a newly established literary journal. The editor said,

"Dear Anton Pavlovich, our journal is on the verge of bankruptcy, and we don't have enough money."

"I am also on the verge of bankruptcy, I am dying, and I don't have enough money," Chekhov replied.

"For God's sake, please give us one of your short stories; it will save our journal," implored the editor.

Anton Pavlovich thought for a while before answering,

"Hmmm, I have just completed a story, but I've already promised it to someone else. However, you can take this story," and he offered a manuscript from his desk.

"Oh, oh, thank you! My dear Anton Pavlovich, thank you so much," the editor exclaimed happily.

"Do not mention it. I am happy to help you."

"And what are your conditions?"

"I do not insist on anything. Just pay me whatever you can. If you don't have enough money at the present, it can wait."

"Can I pay you 250 rubles?" the editor asked.

"That's more than enough."

"Then, here you are. I can pay you the money on the spot," said the editor in a tone of true gratitude and left the room.

I asked Chekhov,

"What happened to you, my friend? You are counting every penny, and you need money. As a rule, you get paid one thousand for a story, and here they paid you only 250."

Chekhov replied,

"Let it go. You know, his financial affairs are not the best; I wanted to help him."

Vladimir Nemirovich-Danchenko. *"From the Past"*

Three portraits of Chekhov stand lined up on my desk. These three photographs are from the three periods in the writer's life.

Period one: Chekhov as "a promising author." Sometimes they are brief pieces published in humor magazines, and these he signs "A. Chekhonte." How many of these short pieces did he write? Many years later, after he had sold all of his works to a publisher and was selecting those worth publishing, he said, "I wrote about a thousand short stories in my youth."

They were all wonderfully witty and amusing anecdotes.

Eventually, Chekhov begins to write lengthier, more serious short stories. He likes being in society, but prefers listening to speaking. The public starts to refer to him in the terms of a talented writer, but no one has yet dubbed him a living classic.

The second period: Chekhov is accepted as "one of the most talented writers of our times." His compilation of short stories, *In the Dusk*, receives a very prestigious literary prize. He writes less, but is received with warmth in any editor's office. People discuss almost every new work written by him. Tolstoy comments, saying,

"He is a very good writer."

A respected writer from the older generation, D. Grigorovich, makes a very bold statement, saying,

"You can put Chekhov's works on the same shelf as those of Gogol. That is as far as I can go myself."

The third portrait: Chekhov at the Moscow Art Theater. These days, he writes much less. In the two or three pieces he produces each year, he has very strict expectations of the quality of his writing. A monumental new feature in his work is that, despite being a realistic writer, he lets his characters make general philosophical statements about life, using wise thoughts and maxims included in his works.

That said, the most important change of this time is that Chekhov becomes a dramaturge, a playwright, and begins to spend more and more time in the theater. His popularity grows daily, and for many readers he soon becomes one of the most popular writers in the country. Only one writer exists whose name is more eminent: Leo Tolstoy.

The more popular he becomes, the closer Chekhov draws to his demise. Readers accept every new work of his with gratitude: they realize that Chekhov dedicates his last efforts to writing them.

These are the three portraits made during the last thirty years of his life. In 1904, Chekhov dies at the age of forty-four.

CHAPTER TWO

Chekhov in Moscow: 1879–1892

Introduction

Leo Tolstoy told me one day, "Chekhov is a strange writer. He throws his words at you, as if at random; yet, every detail is either necessary or beautiful. And what an intellect!"
— A. Goldenweiser. "Around Tolstoy"

I am neither a liberal, nor a conservative; neither a reformer, nor a monk; and I am not indifferent to life.... My holy of holies are the human being, health, intellect, talent, inspiration, and, of course, love and freedom — by that I mean freedom from any malicious force or lie — no matter how the last two are expressed.
— Chekhov. "Letters." His letter to A. Pleshcheev, October 4, 1888

Come to Moscow, and pay me a visit! I love Moscow madly. Those who get used to this city, would not ever leave. I am a Moscovite forever!
— A. Chekhov. "Letters." His letter to S. Kramarev, May 8, 1881

Moscow occupied all his thoughts, and it was truly the promised land for him.
— Sergei Elpatievsky. "Anton Pavlovich Chekhov"

No one knows an occasion in Chekhov's life when he refused to help. Chekhov was not only a kind man, but a true Christian, who did good to others.
— Peter Sergeenko. "About Chekhov"

Anton Pavlovich published his first short story, "A Letter to an Educated Neighbour," in *The Dragonfly Magazine*. I remember his impatience, as he was expecting the response of the editor I. Vasilevsky-Bukva. And the response was published in the classified section; it was as follows:
"Not bad at all, we bless you in your future work."
— Mikhail Chekhov. "Around Chekhov"

25

I received the author's royalties and a copy of your magazine. Thank you
for both. Working in your magazine, *Fragments*, is an interesting experience for me. Many writers, as well as myself, find its bearing and messages captivating.

—Anton Chekhov. "Letters." His letter to N. Leikin,
January 12, 1883

Now I live in the town of New Jerusalem. I have a doctor's diploma in
my pocket, and therefore a feel that I live a "grand" life.... The weather
is wonderful. A lot of free space and no dachniks. I have my mushrooms, my fishing and a village hospital.... Every night, I walk in the
neighborhood, accompanied by men, women and children, all nicely
dressed.

—Anton Chekhov, "Letters." His letter to N. Leikin,
June 25, 1884

*[D. Grigorovich, a famous novelist of the old generation, writes a lengthy
letter to Chekhov, praising his talent—P.S.]*
You possess real talent that places you far above the other literary artists
of our time. It is your calling to write in the future several highly artistic
works.

—A. Chekhov. "Letters." A letter from D. Grigorovich
to A. Chekhov, March 25, 1886

[Chekhov's reply:]
My dear bearer of good news,
  Your letter struck me like lightning. I became very emotional upon
opening it; in fact, I nearly cried. I am impressed by it.... I understand
now that if I have a gift, I should honor it, which I have not always done
in the past.... There is a so-called "literary circle" in Moscow. All kinds
of mediocre writers get together in a restaurant and talk a lot. They
will laugh me in the face if I read your letter to them.... For the first five
years, I only wrote small pieces for newspapers and I became accus-
tomed to this being the only outlet for my work. Secondly, I am a doctor,
and I have been too busy with my profession. I am only 26 years old.
Maybe I will have time to do something; however, the time goes by
quickly.

—A. Chekhov. "Letters." His letter to D. Grigorovich,
March 28, 1886

What about the Prize? *[The most prestigious literary award at the time, the
Pushkin Literary Prize from the Russian Academy of Sciences—P.S.]* Well
... it makes me feel happy. I feel as if I graduated from high school, from
university, and now from one more institution. Yesterday and today, I
did not work at all. I felt like a bridegroom before his wedding. I was
pacing my room and thinking about it.

—A. Chekhov. "Letters." His letter to D. Grigorovich,
October 9, 1888

Zakhar Pichugin. "From My Meetings with A.P. Chekhov"

I don't remember the exact month when this happened, but I remember very well that it happened somewhere in 1882–83. I was living with my friend, a painter, and we'd rented a house in Volkhonka Street. I heard some voices at the door, and I saw Nikolai Pavlovich Chekhov, who was a fellow student at the Moscow Art College. He told me,

"We've been looking for you everywhere. Meet my brother, Anton."

From the moment we met, Anton Pavlovich made a great impression on me. He was a student of the Faculty of Medicine. He was interested in the life of the painters, and he made some very intelligent remarks about the portraits and some other artistic works. You would be completely charmed by Anton, after talking to him for a few minutes.

Sometime later, I visited the Chekhov family. As I came in, I greeted the father of Anton Pavlovich, and heard in reply the words which he whispered in a mysterious tone,

Anton Chekhov, middle of 1901.

"Hush, please don't make noise, Anton is working!"

"Yes, dear, our Anton is working," Evgenia Yakovlevna the mother added, making a gesture indicating to the door of his room. I went further. Maria Pavlovna, his sister, told me in a subdued voice,

"Anton is working now."

In the next room, in a low voice, Nikolai Pavlovich told me,

"Hello, my dear friend. You know, Anton is working now," he whispered, trying not to be loud. Everyone was afraid to break the silence, and you could see that the members of the family had a great deal of respect for the creative process of the young writer.

The next day, as I was passing the Chekhov house, I saw a sign on the door that made me want to stop for a visit.

"Doctor A.P. Chekhov."

Without a moment's hesitation, I went in to congratulate Anton Pavlovich on his graduation from the University.

"I saw a nice sign on the entrance door. Why did you write 'Doctor'?" I asked Anton.

"What do you think it means? If I were to write 'family physician' or 'medical office,' then my patients would not understand, and they would not come. I want to start a practice."

He dedicated himself to literature, but he never refused to see anyone who came to ask him for medical assistance. I saw his abilities as a doctor for myself. The first time I saw him, he brought another doctor with him, a specialist who gave me a very wise piece of advice. Chekhov never took any money for his medical services.

I knew, for example, that he cured the family of my landlord from a serious infectious disease. Once, when my friend, the painter Levitan, was sick, Anton Pavlovich instantly stopped the work he was doing and made a house call.

It is difficult for me to remember all of these cases because there were so many of them. He never took any money, and he would not accept anything in return.

One day, I saw a pack of playing cards on his desk. I asked him,

"Why do you need cards?"

Chekhov replied,

"Sometimes, I play solitaire, and I also use them when I am traveling."

I asked him another question,

"And how about the guinea pigs?"

Anton Pavlovich glanced at a cage containing a couple of guinea pigs at the back.

"They are not for entertainment, but strictly for my medical practice."

He did not tell me how exactly he used them. Maybe he was joking as usual.

Everything I am telling you relates to Chekhov's life on Stretenka Street. Later, I met Anton Pavlovich when he was living on Sadovaya Street, and he told me that they'd moved to a two-story house, and invited me to visit him there.

Konstantin Korovin. "My Meetings with Chekhov"

There is a small hotel in Moscow on the corner of Sadovaya and Diakovskaya Street. It is called the Eastern, although no one has any idea why. It was at this completely inconspicuous place that I met Chekhov in 1883.

Anton Pavlovich reclined on a sofa. He was wearing a grey jacket, similar in fashion to what other students wore at the time. There were also several young men present whom I did not know. They were in a heated debate, complete with raised voices, beer and sausages.

Anton Pavlovich sat near the students, but he was not partaking in the conversation. He had an amiable, open face with laughing eyes. When someone spoke to him, he would look quite carefully into the face of the speaker, then look down and smile with his unique, humble smile.

The students' mannerisms were different from those of Anton Pavlovich, to say the least. They constantly disagreed and argued with all around them. One of them, addressing Chekhov, said,

"If you don't have a point of view, or an attitude, then you cannot really call yourself a writer, you know."

"Yes, I suppose I do lack an attitude," replied Anton Pavlovich mildly.

"Then how can you write a short story, without an attitude, without an idea or message?"

"I have neither ideas, nor messages," said Chekhov.

And so the "argument" wore on. Finally, the student tried one last time.

"When you become a doctor, you will be ashamed of all this work you wrote without ideas, and without argument."

"You are absolutely right about this," said Chekhov, laughing, before adding, "It's such a wonderful day. Let's go out to the Sokolniki Park. The flowers are all in full bloom, and it really is a beautiful day."

And so we went to the Moscow Central Park of Sokolniki. In an hour, we were walking across a very nice park. The students were still angry at Levitan. They asked him,

"So, why don't you put any ideas in your work?"

Levitan replied,

"Why do I need ideas if I want to describe the pine trees in the sunshine and the coming of spring?"

"Look, the pines are nothing. You can build houses with pine lumber, and you can use it in the fireplace. Don't you know that all of nature should belong to the people? Do you understand this?"

The students were getting more and more excited. I was disgusted with their "ideas." Levitan continued,

"It is spring, and the birds are singing. When I look at a pine tree, I do not think of it as firewood. And you are real crocodiles," said Levitan.

"Let me argue with you," several students said in very excited voices.

Anton Pavlovich added,

"Let me also disagree with you. My dear Levitan, we have to explain something to them."

I was walking with Levitan and Chekhov, and the students were walking in a big group in front of us.

"What is that over there? Something is flying in the air. Look, I think it's a falcon." *[The park was named "Sokolniki" after "sokol," "falcon" in Russian—P.S.]* Anton Pavlovich was joking: what we all saw was a crow flying past.

We came to the end of the forest. There was a small road next to the railway, and numerous tables were set up in the open air and covered with tablecloths. Many people were sitting at the tables having picnics and drinking tea. We sat at one of the tables. It was the regular spring picnic at Sokolniki Park.

Several waiters came to serve us instantly. We had bread, buns, salmon and sausages on our table in a minute.

"Dear ladies and gentlemen, let me tell you something..." the students continued with their ideas.

Anton Pavlovich sat quietly and wrote something in his small notebook.

"You know," he said when it was time to go home. "You know that there is some sadness in the spring. Life in nature goes on, but somehow, there is sadness in nature."

When we said good-bye to the students and to Levitan, Chekhov told me,

"You know these students will grow up and become wonderful people and wonderful doctors. And I am jealous of them because they have so many new ideas in their heads."

Grigory Rossolimo. "Memories of Chekhov"

During 1879, many young men from the remote parts of Russia were admitted to Moscow University. Two hundred and fifty students were accepted that year: among them were four students from Odessa like myself, and three from Taganrog, another city in the south of Russia. Chekhov was among them.

I singled out the future writer from the crowd at once, and I remembered him. We did not have any formal reasons to become friends at the beginning, because it was a very crowded university course. Yet, I noticed his interest in writing from the start. Nevertheless, he remained a dedicated student, carefully attending every lecture. As we slipped into the routine of student life, I saw him regularly in the study rooms, libraries and labs. He passed his exams very diligently, advancing from one year to the next.

Chekhov was a good university student. In spite of his creative writing, which distracted him from his studies during his first years at the university, he made a good progress in the medical studies; and diligently attended all lectures, clinics and labs.

After his graduation from medical school, he did not quit medicine, but worked as a country doctor. He treated his patients with great care and softness; he was a doctor, but first and foremost, he was human.

Upon graduation, Chekhov was unable to continue his postgraduate medical studies, but he still read professional journals from time to time. He dreamed of becoming a university teacher, and he told me about this one day; I liked his idea. I told him that in order to teach at the university, he would need to achieve the degree of Doctor of Medicine.

"How can I get an advanced degree? Maybe they could give me one for my book, *Sakhalin Island*?" he asked me one day.

"I think you are right. This should be easy," I told him.

As soon as he gave me his consent, I met with the dean of the Faculty of Medicine, Professor F. Klein. The meeting was a complete disaster. The dean's eyes widened, he looked at me over his glasses, and without saying a word, he turned his back on me. I reported my failure to Chekhov, who laughed heartily. On that day, he stopped dreaming of becoming an academic....

For a well-educated and sensitive doctor who could analyze other people's lives so well, Chekhov treated his own disease, pulmonary tuberculosis, in a very unserious, lighthearted way. In a letter dated September 30, 1900, when his lungs had recently become much worse, he wrote,

"My health is all right overall. It looks like just a small flu and a bit of a cough, but only a very slight cough."

A few weeks before his death, he wrote to me, at the age of 44, on June 17, 1904, upon his arrival at Badenweiler, a spa in Germany:

"My health is completely recovering. I have a fever, and I am out of breath all the time, but this is probably only because I am a lazy man. I have lost a lot of weight. Basically that is it, as far as my health is concerned."

He spoke frequently of his fever and breathlessness, and I understood from his handwriting that he was not well. Yet, he resisted coming to terms with the ending of his life, which was obvious to everyone who knew him. At the time, he was still planning a lengthy sea voyage from Germany back to Yalta.

Ivan Leontiev-Shcheglov. "Chekhov"

We met in December 1887, in the main lobby of the Moscow Hotel in St. Petersburg. I even remember the exact place where we met: at the last table on the right, next to the window. We already knew each other fairly well from reading each other's publications, but I had decided to meet Chekhov in person, as it was his first time in St. Petersburg. He had only recently become well known after the publication of his short stories.

Chekhov was not in his room, so after leaving him a note, I went down to the reception desk, and then to the restaurant in the hotel lobby. I ordered a cup of tea, and had just opened a newspaper, when I heard a soft voice addressing me,

"Are you Mr. Shcheglov? If I am not mistaken?"

I put the newspaper down. In front of me stood a tall young man dressed in a rather casual way, with a kind and open face. I replied,

"And you Mr. Chekhov? If I am not mistaken?"

At that moment we both laughed.

A quarter of an hour later, we were talking as if we had been best friends for ten years. We said good-bye to each other at the main entrance to the hotel, and jokingly called each other in French, "dear Jean" and "dear Antoine."

For many years, this tender relationship of wonderful friendship remained completely unchanged, despite our different literary positions and different twists in life. I cannot tell you how it happened.

This was the wonderful secret that Chekhov took with him to the grave — how to charm people from your very first encounter.

It was not only me who noticed this — he spread his hospitality to everyone. For example, Chekhov also charmed Pleshcheev instantly.

I would like to say a few words about the failure of the first night of *The Seagull*, a play by Chekhov, and the effect that this event had on the author.

This terrible performance of *The Seagull* happened in 1896. In the early spring of the next year, that is less than half a year later, Chekhov was admitted to the Moscow Ostroumov Hospital with the very clear symptoms of tuberculosis.

In 1897, when I was visiting Moscow, I received a postcard from Chekhov dated April 5, with an invitation to visit him,

"Dear Jean,

I would be happy to see you. You can come to me any time, except the interval between 1 to 3 P.M. when there is a time to feed the sick animals here. I will tell the reception desk to open the door for you, and to admit you immediately. I am feeling better, and I can walk.

Yours,

A. Chekhov, Ostroumov Hospital, Room 14."

I was not very happy to see Chekhov there. Our meeting was sad. There were two other sick patients in the same room so we could not talk freely. The room, however, was nicely lit, with lots of air and tall ceilings. Most of our Russian writers can only afford such huge rooms when they fall ill.

Chekhov was lying on his back, with both hands under his head, thinking about something. Next to his bed, there was a terrible tin vessel covered with a white towel where Chekhov coughed and spit blood from time to time. On the other side of the bed, there was a small table with a bunch of letters, someone's thick manuscript and a bouquet made up of fresh flowers.

As soon as he saw me, he stood up from bed, gave me a typically Chekhovian smile, and invited me to sit.

I sat on the chair next to him, and asked,

"So, Antoine, how do you feel?"

He replied,

"Dear Jean, I feel terrible. I am officially enrolled into the team of invalids. The doctors give me consolation that I could live long if I follow the rules, that is, 'do not drink, do not smoke,' and other things. Not a good future, I have to admit."

His sad face became even sadder. In order to change the conversation, I nodded at the manuscript on his side table, and asked, "What is that?"

Chekhov replied, "It's a manuscript by a young aspiring author who asked me to take a look at it. He probably thinks that it is so sweet and pleasant to be a Russian writer. Yet, he is not the only one." Chekhov sighed deeply, and indicated at the big pile of letters on his table.

I thought to myself,

"What kind of people are they? They do not give this man a chance to relax even when he is in the hospital."

Then I asked,

"And what is this? Probably, flowers from a nice-looking young Muscovite female, your admirer?"

Chekhov answered,

"You did not guess correctly. This is from a male admirer. A very rich man, he is actually a millionaire." Chekhov smiled with a bitter smile. "He gave me these flowers and paid me many compliments. Yet if you ask him to loan you a few rubles, he would most likely refuse. As if I don't know those kinds of people — all those admirers." We both sighed.

Chekhov continued,

"And do you know who paid me a visit yesterday? Who was sitting on the very chair where you are now sitting?"

"I have absolutely no idea," I said.

"It was Leo Tolstoy."

"So what did you discuss with him?"

Chekhov frowned a little bit, and said in a vague manner, "He spoke a little bit, but I am not allowed to discuss it. However, with all the respect I have for Leo, I do not agree with him on many things. Yes, many things," he repeated, and then started coughing, probably from great excitement.

It was obvious that Chekhov was pleased by the fact that Leo Tolstoy visited him, but it was also plainly obvious that Chekhov did not accept literary criticism and views as expressed by Tolstoy.

In order not to overtire him, I did not stay much longer. I stood and told Chekhov good-bye. He saw me to the door, and invited me to come and visit him in Melikhovo.

My regular conversations with Chekhov gave me the utmost intellectual satisfaction imaginable. The issues we discussed were viewed from his fresh, rather unusual angle, and that mixture of life and humor can hardly be described in the few words that I put to paper now. We spoke of literature, art, opinions of common acquaintances, and even the most common, everyday things. No matter what the topic was, it was a satisfying conversation.

The first period of Chekhov's literary life, starting in 1896, could easily be called the happiest. It included receiving the very prestigious Pushkin Literary Prize; that is, the national prize in literature. It was also then that he became friends with Grigorovich, Garshin, Tolstoy and Korolenko. Those happy years slipped past so rapidly, melting away like a dream.

Peter Zelenin. "About A.P. Chekhov and His Family"

I met the Chekhov family in the 1880s at the Eastern Hotel, on Sadovaya Street, in Moscow. At the end of my college years I stayed there, where several university students and artists, including the famous painters Levitan and Nesterov used to rent rooms. We all lived in rooms located along a lengthy center hallway.

Naturally, we got to know each other's names, became acquaintances and friends. Illych, the superintendent of the building, had been arranging for us to be served strange veal steaks streaked gray and green in color, and our rooms at times were frigid on very cold days. Then we banded together and spoke to him as one unit, he was forced to listen to us and improve our living conditions.

I first got to know Chekhov's brothers, especially Nikolai the painter. Through him, I got to know Anton Pavlovich and his sister Maria Pavlovna. Later, I met Alexander Pavlovich Chekhov, when he also moved to the Eastern Hotel.

I would like to share my brief memories of these people.

Nikolai was a very talented painter, but it seemed to me he was too laid back and lazy. Later, I found out that he was sick with tuberculosis, and I understood that I made a mistake in making a quick judgment about him. Nikolai was a wonderful friend and a very good brother. He adored his brother Anton, and called him "a great writer" even at that time, when we were still students.

Anton appeared to be a much more sensitive and quiet man. He only talked when we asked him questions about medicine. Soon, he graduated from the Medical Department of the Moscow University. He loved to study sciences. He worked very hard to get his doctor's certificate.

After he graduated, though, he was not a very popular family doctor. Anton was a good doctor, I know this for sure, because one day he treated my own brother. When I tried to pay him, he refused very bluntly. When I said I felt very uncomfortable if he didn't take payment for his work, he decided to accept the money. He put the bills very quickly in his pocket and departed.

I felt that my money had almost "burned" his hands, he had been so adamant about not accepting it.

Maria Pavlovna also visited the Eastern Hotel. She was a very nice and humble young woman. She took courses to become a teacher. She was very feminine, with an inner spiritual beauty that shone in her face.

Alexander, the next Chekhov brother that I met, came to Moscow after the closing of the Taganrog local customs office. The Chekhovs did not drink much alcohol as a rule, but Alexander started drinking after he lost his job. He used to swear around his girlfriend. Each time he did, she would tell him,

"Alexander, stop it! You are not considering me a lady if you speak around me like this." Yet, she did not stop him, as he would become even more talkative. However, he still was a very friendly and kind person overall.

All members of the Chekhov family shared a very special feature. They would all give you their last bite of food, or share their last penny with anyone in need. Alexander Pavlovich was the most generous man. At the same time, the Chekhovs always made ends meet, as they constantly supported one another.

* * *

I cannot complete my memories about Anton Pavlovich if I don't mention one episode.

It occurred during a visit to a public house in Moscow, after we decided to interview the women who worked there. We were accompanied by a doctor friend of Chekhov who just graduated from the university. We decided to find out directly from the white slave women how they ended up in their situation. We did not plan to entertain ourselves at their expense; rather, we went there due to pure curiosity.

We wanted to get to know the life of those who are suffering, to determine a reason for this, and if possible to find ways to stop their suffering and to help these poor women.

The public houses in Moscow were located in the Stretenka district in the Sobolev Street at the time. We went to the first public house to your right, at the beginning of the street. It was very cheap, and you had to pay only one ruble for service. It was a so-called "college students" house, because their regular customers were the students. *[Chekhov depicted the experiences of college students visiting a public house in the Sobolev Street in his short story "The Fit."— P.S.]*

There were six females, and three of us. We split them in equal parts, and every one of us received two girls. We had to work very carefully because we were told that those ladies did not like to share their "pleasant past" with the clients, and we knew that they unceremoniously kicked out such prying people. We had to treat them to alcohol to get them comfortable enough to speak.

The favorite drinks of those ladies were the port wines and sweet liquors. We put all our savings together, and bought several bottles of wine. We spoke to them from 1 A.M. until 4 A.M.

Then we grew too weary, and had to leave. We went to a local restaurant, and shared the results of our interviews there. It turned out that we had the same answers as a result of our interviews.

Nikolai Teleshov. "A.P. Chekhov"

I had numerous conversations with Chekhov and I met him on many occasions, but when I remember all those events, I recollect two meetings more clearly than all the others.

Anton Chekhov with his family, left to right: mother Evgeniya Chekhova, sister Maria Chekhova, and wife Olga Knipper. Yalta, July 1901.

First, I remember him as a young man full of life and blossom.

And the second image, as a desperately sick and dying man going abroad, never to return alive.

I was young then, about 20 years old. And he was young too, just at the beginning of his writing career. It was the fall of 1887, and his first collection *In the Dusk* had just been published under his real name Chekhov, rather than under the pen name, Antosha Chekhonte.

He had only just begun, and literary critics were silent. They paid no attention to him — Mikhailovsky mentioned him in passing, and Skabichevsky wrote that Chekhov would become an alcoholic and die somewhere in the streets.

Later, sometime in the 1890s, the writer A. Kuprin noted that Chekhov had mentioned my name in passing:

"Remind the writer Teleshov — he will remember that great wedding celebration."

Really, we had a wonderful celebration. It was a huge wedding in a banquet hall, with over a hundred people, mostly young men and women. We danced almost without interruption all night, and then we feasted until the dawn.

I was a newcomer who had just started his life as a literary artist. I did not know anyone in the literary world, and could not recognize a single writer — I knew them only from their works. And then, in the midst of the noise and the crowd, Mr. Belousov brought me to a tall young man with an open face and a fair beard and very clear and smiling eyes. He introduced him:

"This is Mr. Chekhov."

I knew Chekhov from his short stories, which I had read only recently. I knew that the respected and well-known writer D. Grigorovich — the patriarch of the older generation of writers — had come to Chekhov in person and predicted a great future for a young man, calling him a talent far above the writers of his generation.

Grigorovich's remark, as well as my own impression of reading his short stories, made this meeting very exciting for me. I wanted to talk to him about literature and books, but Chekhov suddenly asked me an unexpected question,

"Do you play cards?"

"No, I don't."

"Here, Mr. Giliarovsky came with me. He would like to play cards, but he needs a partner. Do you know Mr. Giliarovsky?"

Mr. Giliarovsky joined us and we got acquainted. He was dressed in a tuxedo, and somehow, he was doing several things at once — he greeted someone in the crowd with a wave, he recited some poems to Chekhov, and he stretched his hand to me. It seemed that he was thinking about something else when we were introduced.

After a minute of talking, the music started playing again, and the ladies invited me to dance.

"Go and dance, otherwise the ladies will be mad at you," Anton Pavlovich told me.

I thought that this was the end of my interview, but at the end of the night, after the ice cream and champagne, Chekhov came to me by himself, and said,

"The dawn is here, and the party is over. They want us to leave. So, would you like to take Giliarovsky with us, and go to one of the pubs next door? They open early for the cab drivers."

We agreed. There were four of us. Chekhov's younger brother Mikhail joined us — he was a university student at the time. We took a cab and went to the nearest pub.

Somewhere not too far off, in a tiny little street, we saw a pub window that was lit. It was a frosty morning and it was still dark outside. The pub was very dirty and cheap. It had opened early in the morning — Chekhov was right — for the night cabbies. Chekhov said,

"This pub is good enough for us. When we have achieved greatness, then we will sit and talk in good restaurants, but for the time being — according to our earnings — this is a wonderful place to be."

Someone once described Chekhov and mentioned that he combined two things in his face — the expression of a very intelligent man, combined with that of a village bumpkin. He had smiling eyes. I have never seen such eyes, except for Chekhov — his eyes were really smiling.

We all were dressed in tuxedoes, and the pub owner took us for the caterers from the wedding, just off the night shift. Chekhov was tickled by this. We sat at a table that was covered with a gray tablecloth, still wet from yesterday's beer. The lemon tea smelled like onions....

Chekhov told us that he had lots of plots in his head, and that even the walls of this pub could be a starting point for one of his short stories.

Vladimir Korolenko. *"Anton Pavlovich Chekhov"*

I first met Anton Chekhov at the end of 1886. The exact date escapes my memory, but by this time he had already managed to publish three collections of short stories.

When I first made their acquaintance, the Chekhovs lived on Sadovaya Street, in a slightly small, cozy brick house. A rather tall young man stood before me when I came in. He had a broad, open face with regular features, and a very peculiar expression. Later, my wife remarked on it, and I completely agree with her observation: Chekhov's face was a mixture of the undoubtedly intellectual and the expression of a simple-minded farmer.

The simplicity of movement and articulation were as obvious in his writing as his mannerisms. All in all, Chekhov left me with a very charming first impression.

Once he asked me,

"Would you like to know how I write my short stories? Here, observe." He glanced at my writing desk and picked up the first object that he saw. It was an ashtray. Placing it on the desk right in front of me, he said,

"If you wish, by tomorrow I will write a short story. Its title will be *An Ashtray.*"

His eyes shone with joy. It seemed that the ashtray had already created images, ideas, and a chain of adventures in his mind. All of these would be put on paper, and then spiced with his usual Chekhovian literary effect.

He was always brimming with ideas for new literary projects, all in great detail.

Once, he told me of his plan to start a new journal.

"It will have exactly 25 contributing authors. All of them are young, aspiring literary artists!"

On another occasion, he came to me, lifting his wonderful, shining eyes, and said,

"Listen, Korolenko! I want to come to your city, to Nizhny, and visit you someday."

"I would be happy to see you there," I answered, "were you to keep your promise to come."

"Of course. I will definitely come to visit you," he replied. "We shall write a great drama together, you and I. With four acts. I propose we write it in two weeks." I just laughed at his joke. His ability to charm a person from the very beginning was just one of Chekhov's many secrets....

In the first hours of my first meeting with him, Chekhov showed me letters written to him by Grigorovich. I remember one was from abroad; Grigorovich wrote about the numbing boredom that steeped every aspect of his life at the spa, about his illness, and the feeling of approaching death. After showing me the letter, Chekhov commented, almost as an afterthought: "Here is what it's all come to, you see, the fame, the far-flung career, the colossal royalties from the sales of his books."

His comment seemed odd to me, if only because it had been made by a young man who, at the time, was simply the aspiring author of a handful of comical short stories. Later, I would remember those prophetic words. By then, though, they would be about himself. Chekhov would die at a resort in Germany not twenty years later.

Sergei Sobolevsky. "A Portrait"

I only saw Anton Pavlovich once. I was invited to a party one day that Chekhov was also invited to. At that time, I was the professor of classical languages at the Moscow University.

Chekhov found out from the master of the house that I was teaching Latin and Greek there. Anton Pavlovich approached me, looking embarrassed. I can still remember his very nice smile.

Chekhov asked me,

"Sergei Ivanovich, could you please give me a few of characteristic Latin proverbs and sayings?"

"Definitely," I replied, since it was not difficult for me to assist him with his request.

At the time, Chekhov was already a famous writer, so I was very pleased by his request.

We went to a quiet room, and, without any hesitation, I gave him a dozen or so of my favorite Latin proverbs. Chekhov wrote them down, as well as my commentaries about them. I remembered that memorable evening for a long time afterwards.

I was very pleased when some of the proverbs that I gave to him appeared in the next forthcoming short stories by Chekhov. He used those Latin proverbs correctly, nicely inserting and fitting them in his narration.

Aleksander Lazarev-Gruzinsky. "A.P. Chekhov"

One of the best and most vivid memories of my younger years is my first meeting with Anton Chekhov.

Chekhov used to visit the editorial offices of humor magazines where I would also receive payments for my stories. That is where I first chanced to meet him, and I was eventually invited to his home. This was around the time when his popularity had begun to rise. I spent the whole evening with him, and left with the impression that we had known each other for years.

That day, we spoke for a long time before I noticed that it was getting dark. Every attempt I made to get up and leave was overcome by Chekhov, who told me,

"Please wait! Sit down, let's talk! Neither of us is going to work tonight." *[It was New Year's Eve — P.S.]*

I replied each time,

"All right, then let us talk!"

At the time, Chekhov lived on Sadovaya Street in a little house of a very peculiar design. It was made to look like a miniature castle. I remember well the semicircular windows facing the street looked just like the windows of a medieval tower.

Chekhov indicated the aquarium, the piano, and the furniture around him, and told me,

"It's good to be a literary artist. Literature has given me all that you see here."

When I stared, startled, at all the things given to him by "Literature," Chekhov laughed and told me that he had rented the piano, and the rest of the furniture was rented as well. Later, Chekhov wrote in a letter to a friend,

"Life is grand! Do you remember the piano, and the furniture in my room? Now, do you remember the furniture of Mr. Utkin, our magazine editor? I believe we have all the pieces now." Mr. Utkin had been the editor of *The Alarm Clock Magazine*, a witty and comical periodical that had fallen into bankruptcy. When he left, he paid his authors with the furniture from his office in lieu of the money he owed them.

Chekhov was one of the most friendly and outgoing people I have ever had the pleasure of meeting in my life. Upon hearing of a person who was having problems or needed help, he would ask at once,

"How can I help you?" His desk was always overflowing with stories written by aspiring young writers. He edited all of them, and sent them out to different editorial houses for publication. Chekhov gave advice to every fledgling author. As soon as he saw even a hint of the writer's gift, he encouraged them to be published, and told them,

"You will be a famous author one day. You should publish your work; it will give you a good income!" He had a habit of repeating this all the time, asking us to write more, to write constantly. In one of his letters to me, Chekhov wrote,

"You should build your sentences with care, make them succulent. If you write a short story over five or six days you can constantly work on its structure. Every phrase, before it has been put to paper, should have the chance to simmer and gain form and flavor in your mind."

One day, during a train journey, he showed me his pocket notebook.

"Get yourself a journal like this," he suggested. It was there that Chekhov put dozens of plots, maxims and jokes.

Chekhov loved talent most of all in any person. Chekhov would instantly single a person with just a little bit of talent out in a crowd.

Here are two cases that I remember.

One day, Chekhov and I were talking with two people — a young and aspiring literary artist, and an old journalist, who did not have enough good manners.

The old writer asked the young man,

"So you tell me that you work at the Leikin's Publishing House?"

"Yes, I do," answered the young novelist humbly.

"And I quit my job. I sent the man to hell. I don't need him," said the old man.

Chekhov made a sour face at these words. For a few minutes, they spoke about other irrelevant things. Then, the old writer repeated his question,

"Are you still presently writing at Leikin's periodical?"

"Yes, I do, pretty much so. I work there," the young novelist said in a very confused way.

"And I have sent him to hell. I just quit the job."

Being a delicate, tender and a very quiet man, Chekhov could stop a person who did not have good manners.

When the old man told us for the third time that he quit his job at Leikin's, Chekhov, who was busy smoking his cigarette, turned to him and said in a quiet voice,

"Listen, this young man is a very talented man. He often writes good literature. And for you, literary work can bring fifteen cents per month. So you made a good decision to quit your job."

The conversation about Mr. Leikin and his magazine never resumed.

A little later, the same literary artist, who was going on a long river trip along the Volga River, made a remark while addressing Chekhov's brother,

"Yes, I have spent a lot of money on this trip. And do you have money?"

At this moment, Chekhov, who was listening to this not very tactful remark, intervened in the conversation and said,

"Listen, brother, you have talent. You can just sit at the desk, write a couple of pieces and you would have more than enough money for the trip."

Chekhov had several talented artists amongst those he called his friends — architect Shatter, painter Levitan, as well as actors Svobodin and Davidov, and writers Potapenko and Maxim Gorky. These were Chekhov's best friends.

One day, Chekhov showed me the cover of the *Life Magazine* where cartoonist Mr. Chemnodanov made a collage of many faces of writers. Chekhov said,

"Look at this crowd — so many talented people among them!"

If a person was talented, that was enough to attract Chekhov's attention.

In his letter to Suvorin, Chekhov mentioned that he never lied to him. I also never lied to Chekhov. One day, Chekhov asked me about my future works, including the forthcoming publications and plays to be performed. Chekhov said,

"Listen, my friend, please tell me about your new works. I trust you completely."

I would like to reminisce about one of the funny cases that happened to Chekhov. When we started out with our friendly relationships, we discussed his early short stories. Chekhov did not like some of them, and was hesitant as to whether they should be included in his new collection of short stories.

I told him, "There is only one short story of yours which I do not like. If I were you, I would not include this short story in the publication."

"What story is that?" Chekhov was interested.

"'About the Dangers of Tobacco.'"

It seemed to me that Chekhov looked at me in a strange way, as if he was lost in thought, and then he said, "No, I do not agree with you. I think that this is a good short story."

I repeated, "Nevertheless, I would not include this short story in the new collection."

It seemed to me that Chekhov loved his weaker pieces with the same love that parents show their love for their weak children, However, much later I read in Chekhov's correspondence, in his letter to Bilibin dated April 12, 1886, about this short story that I did not like. Chekhov wrote,

"I have a lot of work. I do not have time to have a proper dinner. Recently, I finished a short story, 'About the Dangers of Tobacco,' which I dedicated to actor Sokolov. I had only two hours to write this short story, and I completely blew it. So instead of throwing it into the garbage, or sending it to the devil, I sent it to *St. Petersburg Newspaper*. I had a good idea, but it was a terrible result."

The letter was written one year before we had a conversation about this short story.

Later, Chekhov omitted this piece from his collection of short stories.

In 1892, Chekhov moved from Moscow to Melikhovo, and I am sorry to say that I seldom saw him after that.

Semyon Podiachev. *"My Life"*

Anton Pavlovich was living in Moscow. I visited a friend of mine, the artist Klein, who had decided to start a literary journal together with another friend of his.

"It's such a good idea," Klein told me.

"I wonder why I have never thought to do this myself," I said.

"We will definitely invite Leo Tolstoy to be a contributor. We will write him a letter, and I am sure he would be happy to participate in this journal."

"He lives far away from here," said one of my friends, "Do you want to simply mail him a letter? It will get lost in the mail."

We realized we had to send someone. They looked at me and said,

"We will send you to deliver the letter." I was frightened.

"Wait a minute," I said. "I don't feel comfortable going. And what shall I tell him? I will die from fear as soon as I see him."

"Just go there and deliver the letter," they said. "There is no one else to send there except for you."

"And then," Klein wondered aloud, "whom should we send to Anton Chekhov? We will send him a letter by courier."

"Where does Chekhov live?" asked the future publisher of the magazine.

"He lives on Sadovaya-Kudrinskaya Street, in a red brick house. You can ask around, and the local people will tell you. He lives with his brother, they say, and his brother is a painter."

"Then how about you go there, and ask him to write a short story for the magazine, about 100 lines?" my friends asked me.

"All right," I agreed. "I will go to Chekhov."

Anton Pavlovich lived on the street across from the huge "Widow's House." I found his house without any problems, but I don't remember exactly how I got inside the house and how I found Chekhov's rooms. I remember, though, standing inside a room where someone sat next to the window drawing, and I later learned that this was Anton Pavlovich's brother. The writer was not at home, and they told me that he would come later. After a short wait, someone said, "Here he comes."

A thin, tall man with a fine, dark beard ascended the stairs. He seemed to me a very joyful and happy young man.

"A pleasure to meet you. How do you do?" I said.

"The pleasure's all mine," he said. Then he added, "Please, take a seat."

I sat down. He sat in front of me, smiled at me, and said, "So, how can I help you?" I told him in a few words the reason for my visit.

"I have heard about this new journal," Chekhov said, smiling and looking me straight in the eye. "I know about it, but I cannot promise you anything. I may give something to the journal to be published, but I am very busy at the moment. Is it true that the editor's house is on Solyanaya Street?"

"Yes," I replied.

"Then I will let you know," he said. "Would you like a drink of vodka?"

"No, thank you."

"You don't drink at all, do you?"

"I do drink, but not today."

"Then, pardon my curiosity, do you write from time to time?"

I did not answer his question, and said that it was time for me to go. He shook my hand as we parted, looked into my eyes in a friendly way, as though he wanted to tell me something.

I quickly said "goodbye" and left.

Natalia Gubareva. "Memories of A.P. Chekhov"

Zvenigorodsky Region, Babkino village.

We lived about 20 miles from the country town of Zvenigorod, a remote part of the Moscow district. My brother-in-law, Alexey Sergeevich Kiselev, had bought the estate for my sister. The doctors had prescribed for her to live in the fresh air that could be found in a village. I remember that he had mentioned the name Chekhov when speaking about a family living not too far from his estate. The Chekhov family was renting a spacious summer cottage at the back of our property.

I visited my sister quite often in 1887. One summer day, my sister, my father and I sat on the deck talking about life. We heard footsteps. My father turned his head and asked, "Anton Pavlovich, is that you?"

"Yes, it is me. I am planning to dig some worms for fishing." As we heard the voice, we saw someone quickly ducking under our balcony. About five minutes later, there was a noise in the backyard. It was the second of the Chekhov brothers, who also wanted some worms for fishing. All four of the brothers came to us to dig up worms before disappearing elsewhere, one after the other. My father smiled and said, "It was probably another practical joke by Anton Pavlovich."

My sister told me that the Chekhov family was going to hold a ball in honor of my father's birthday, and I promised to attend. They served dinner at five o'clock in Babkino. All of the people wishing to talk to us could come and visit then. Around one they would have lunch, and between one and five there was rest or nap time. At five, they would have dinner.

On that night, many people came to our five o'clock dinner. At some point, my father told me that if we were to accept any more guests, they could only be the Chekhov family.

My father and I sat on a comfortable sofa talking to the local doctor, Mr. Arkhangelsky. It was getting dark outside, so the lights in the corridor were turned on when we heard a noisy group of people coming. I did not have time to be surprised before I was confronted by a group of people dressed up in exotic costumes. Four black African servants held a huge black box by its four corners, and a Turkish sultan in a turban was seated on the top of this box. They moved rapidly towards me. The Turkish man pulled out his long knife and attempted to cut off my head. I jumped up as fast as I could, screamed and climbed onto the nearest table that sounded like it would crack under my weight. My father could barely catch me as I was moving so fast. The African men who had costumes appeared embarrassed as well, but the Turkish sultan came closer to me and said in a nice voice,

"Let me introduce myself, I am a painter; my name is Levitan."

The African servants took off their masks and introduced themselves as well — they were the four Chekhov brothers, with Anton Pavlovich among them. I felt very foolish and a little silly about the whole incident.

Next, our children's French tutor sat at the piano and began to softly play music in the background. Chekhov was making such funny jokes, we could not stop laughing. Everyone was laughing except for him. Anton Pavlovich was making one joke after another, without interval, and we continued to laugh and laugh!

We dressed my father and my brother-in-law in the costumes of high school students, and made them dance. They had to dance with their arms sticking to their sides in a funny way because the costumes were too small for both of them. This was so comical that we all laughed heartily.

Chekhov applauded, and then my sister began to play the piano. They turned down the lights a little bit, as she was playing the Moonlight Sonata by Beethoven in the moonlight. Anton Pavlovich stepped out on the porch, and sat on the lowest step. I wanted to join him there, but my father said, "Anton Pavlovich prefers to sit alone."

That sonata made a great impression on me.

Aleksander Pomerantsev. "Memories of A.P. Chekhov"

I can recall Chekhov just as clearly as though he were standing beside me right now: a very graceful, proud, and tender man. He had large, luminous eyes, pink cheeks, and he spoke in a very soft baritone.

He spoke rapidly, with sincerity and emotion. His laughter was always accompanied by a friendly smile that revealed something very naïve and childish, almost feminine, in his face.

In the fall of 1885, V. Giliarovsky, a reporter for the *Russian News* at the time, asked me to show him the homeless shelters in Moscow's Khitrov Market. He told me that he would bring an unknown, aspiring short story writer by the name of Anton Chekhonte with him.

The entire night was spent with Giliarovsky and Anton Pavlovich visiting the dark and disgusting shelters in the core of Moscow. We spent our time surrounded by bums and homeless people, simply listening to their stories. Chekhov kept silence most of the time. He did not ask any questions, instead preferring to sit there and listen.

Later, I found out that he lived on Kudrinskaya Street, that he loved music, and that he had a habit of meeting with young writers and giving them the following advice:

"Your writing should be concise and to the point. Try publishing your short stories in lots of little newspapers and magazines. This is the fastest way to earn royalties. Keep your writing simple, as if you are just talking to a good friend. Use pleasant phrases, and make becoming comparisons. The most important part of my success is that I write short stories of eight pages or less. Longer stories will not please the editors, and they will throw your manuscript in the wastepaper basket. If 'King Herod' [his nickname for editors] should discard your story, do not be discouraged, just send it somewhere else. Literature is a battle, and you have to constantly fight for new territory. The requirements of contemporary literature are very high: try competing with Maupassant, or with him." At that moment, Chekhov would direct a nod at the portrait of Leo Tolstoy hanging on his wall.

Chekhov was very joyful during this period. He liked to go to restaurants and drink wine, and he was always joking.

I met Chekhov again at the Opera, about three years later, in 1889. He had changed a lot over those years; he coughed perpetually, and he was silent and grave most of the time. His eyes were eclipsed by spectacles. His gaze was tired, and he seemed preoccupied by something very sad. His overall appearance seemed to me more than a little gloomy. He told me,

"I feel as if I have already lived for three hundred years; I am bored with this dull and trivial life." That winter, Anton Pavlovich spent two weeks in the Central Hotel in Moscow. Many writers met there, where Chekhov could always be found talking and making jokes.

Chekhov asked me, "Do you know of a cottage for sale somewhere in the south? Maybe in the Poltava Region, for example? I would like to purchase some land. Literature is a terrible thing; I may have a wad of bills in my pocket, but at the same time, I have a lot of debts."

I was an observer of several funny scenes at the hotel which proved to me that Anton Pavlovich was not indifferent to the fair sex. At one point there was a woman's voice coming from the hall outside of his room:

"Anton Pavlovich, can I drop in for a minute?"

"No! You should not come in! We should not see each other anymore!"

"You are cruel, Anton Pavlovich, I just want to see you for a moment."

"No, you cannot enter."

The door shut again with a click, and you could hear sobs in the corridor for a very long time.

"How would you like it? Would you care to listen to these monologues every morning? I am tired of this, I would like to start practicing medicine again. First, I will go to several lectures of Professor Ostroumov. *[He was one of the best doctors in Moscow at the time — P.S.]* Then I will start my private practice."

A month later, Chekhov returned to the same hotel in Moscow, this time with a bleeding hemorrhage in his mouth.

Professor A. Ostroumov put Anton Pavlovich in his clinic, and he had to spend some very long weeks there. His tuberculosis made him feel desperate and upset.

In fact, his illness grew steadily worse. In spite of the tuberculosis in his chest, Anton Pavlovich worked hard, and he wrote a lot. He had a lot of inspiration, and upon his death, he left many works that opened completely new vistas in Russian art.

Today, we have Chekhov Street, the Chekhov Library, several Chekhov Museums in Moscow and Taganrog, the Chekhov Literary Society, and so on. We can say that the memory of Anton Pavlovich Chekhov is still alive. Readers of good books and theatergoers still get excited when they hear this name.

Ilya Repin. *"My Meetings with Chekhov"*

I did not make illustrations of his works, and I do not have any drawings of my favorite, unforgettable writer and my friend.

I was not lucky enough to meet Chekhov very often. I would say that we seldom saw each other. Most of all, though, I remember when we met for the first time. He visited me at my studio at the Kalinkin Bridge, in Moscow. He was a very positive man, sober and healthy, with rational judgments.

He reminded me of Bazarov from the novel by Turgenev.

One day, I was sitting at my studio. He came to see me and spoke of his experiences as a village doctor. He depicted several detailed stories about his autopsies, most of which happened in the outdoors. Spectators used to come from all the neighboring houses and streets, and made a crowd around Chekhov while he set out his medical instruments on the table. The dead body would be lying on a big table in the middle of the street. People were so involved with watching this rather unpleasant business that he felt almost like he had to perform at a drama theater. Chekhov did not notice the people were moving closer and closer. The smell was really bad, even though it all happened in the open air.

Suddenly, as he was changing the position of the dead body filled with gas, the lips of the dead man made the noise, "Burrrr," as the air was going out of the lungs.

People reacted as though they thought the dead man was coming back to life! The boys around the table ran off pushing and stumbling, terrified.

One day, at a meeting of the Literary Society, I made a sketch of his face, and gave it to someone as a gift. I always used to do such things.

I remember this very well: that his eyes had a refined and clear analysis, and this defined the overall expression of his face. He covered himself, shielded himself with cold irony, as of a knight in medieval armor. He was a huge, undefeatable giant, both in his body and in his spirit.

CHAPTER THREE

The Melikhovo Cottage in the 1890s

Introduction

If I am a doctor, then I need my hospital and my patients; if I am a literary artist, then I have to live among my own people, but not in downtown Moscow, on the Dmitrovka Street. I need a little bit of social and political life — I need real life, and not the life enclosed in four walls, without nature, without country, without health and good appetite — this is not real life, not the life it should be.
— Anton Chekhov, "Letters." His letter to A. Suvorin,
October 20, 1891

You will like the Melikhovo estate. Everything is miniature around here: a tiny alley, a pond the size of a fish tank, tiny park and tiny trees. But after you pace along the alley a couple of times, and look more carefully at everything, the claustrophobic feeling that everything is too small disappears. All of a sudden, we have lots of space.
— Anton Chekhov. "Letters." His letter to A. Suvorin,
April 6, 1892

I owe the happiest days of my life to literature.
— Chekhov. "Letters." His letter to A. Suvorin,
December 21, 1895

Chekhov combined huge talent, sharp intellect, bright soul and limitless kindness.
— A. Amphiteatrov. "Chekhov."

Doctors have diagnosed the start of tuberculosis in my lungs and have ordered me to change my way of life. I can agree with the former, but as for the latter, I cannot understand it or accept it at all. They told me to remove myself permanently to the country.... Melikhovo is a healthy place, it is located on the watershed divide, on top of the hill. We have decided that I will live in Melikhovo for now.
— Anton Chekhov. "Letters." His letter to A. Suvorin,
April 1, 1897

Chekhov's study, where he worked for the last five years of his life. Yalta, 1901.

They say that every cloud has a silver lining. Leo Nikolaevich *[Leo Tolstoy — P.S.]* visited me at the hospital; we had a fascinating conversation, which was made all the more interesting for me because I spent most of the time listening. We spoke about eternity.

— A. Chekhov. "Letters." His letter to M. Menshikov,
April 16, 1897

My sister put an ad in the newspaper that we are selling our Melikhovo estate. After the death of our father, we don't want to live there.

— Anton Chekhov. "Letters." His letter to M. Menshikov,
June 4, 1898

My father died after a long illness.... I will probably stay in Yalta for the winter.

— Anton Chekhov. "Letters." His letter to A. Suvorin,
October 17, 1898

Tatiana Shchepkina-Kupernik. "Young Years"

Chekhov loved his Melikhovo estate. He looked completely different there. His best years were most likely connected with Melikhovo. After his difficult childhood, poverty, three-ruble-per-story author's royalties, and cheap apartments, he suddenly felt that he was finally the owner of his own house, he was not going to move out, and he was not in a hurry.

A year after they bought the estate *[Melikhovo — P.S.]*, it changed so much that you would not recognize the property. All the Chekhov family worked hard to improve it. Someone worked in the garden, another in the orchard, and someone else was planting trees and flowers. All the Chekhovs worked hard.

Anton Chekhov was an avid gardener, and he said, in the same manner as Peter Tchaikovsky, that he would not be able to write any more if he did not work every day in his garden.

Jury Avdeev. "Chekhov in Melikhovo"

"Finally, we have bought an estate," Chekhov wrote to his friends.

The Chekhov family had been looking for a country property since 1889. Buying a home at the time wasn't imperative, so Chekhov went to visit his friends in the Suma region of Ukraine. Then, Chekhov's brother Nikolai suddenly died from tuberculosis and their plans changed.

A few years later, in February of 1892, Chekhov visited Melikhovo and instantly decided to buy a property there. He brought new pets on the same day of his first visit there — and put them in the local pond. There is an old Russian tradition that people — before moving into a new house — put a cat or a rooster there, to "warm up" the house. The first inhabitants of the Chekhov estate were 150 perch.

The family moved soon after, in March. Chekhov wrote that he saw lots of migrating birds coming back from the south.

Yet the spring of 1892 was a cold and long one. The summer did not come for a long time. It was warm during the day, as the snow from the roofs melted and the water dripped down; during the nights, it became cold and the roads were icy again. The birds woke up very early in the morning, and the Chekhovs rose with the birds. They had a lot of work to do, both in the vegetable garden and in the orchard in the back yard.

During the first spring, Chekhov planted many cherry and apple trees, as well as lilac and rose bushes.

On one of the first days after his arrival, local peasants came to visit him. They greeted Chekhov with the words, "Good morning, dear sir! Good morning, landlord!"

He replied to them, "Good morning! But I am not a landlord. I am a doctor. And I will take care of you as your doctor."

These were the first words with which Chekhov greeted the local population.

In 1899, the Chekhovs planned to sell his Melikhovo estate and move elsewhere. Chekhov told his friends that after the period of his "living among peasants," life in Melikhovo was finished for him because it did not give him "new impressions."

Chekhov was mistaken in his judgment. It was only one year later that he remembered about Melikhovo and wrote *In the Ravine*. It was a great success, and had great book reviews in all the literary journals. I. Shchukin asked Chekhov,

"Tell me, Anton Pavlovich, what particular village were you describing, in your novella? How did you know about this life, inside out? Is it true that the life of peasants in Russia is so terrible?"

Chekhov said that he remembered life in the central part of Russia, as he knew it, and that all this could happen in real life. Children could start drinking vodka from the age of eight, and live a life of sexual dissipation. He remembered a little boy who had infected every family in the village. He said that he remembered this case, but "did not think it artistic to describe it."

I told Chekhov that one of the most touching moments in the story was when a girl named Lika carried a little coffin with a baby inside late at night.

"You know," replied Anton Pavlovich, "this is not a single event. People in villages often dropped their infants into a boiling pot, where they boiled to death. Many village doctors spoke about such cases. However, I decided not to write about such cases ever again."

Mr. V. Kurkin, who was a village doctor and Chekhov's close friend, remembered,

"Anton Pavlovich combined his work as a village doctor with the work of a literary artist. Later, when he wrote two novellas, *Peasants* and *In the Ravine*, people from the villages were able to recognize the places and events from which Chekhov took all these impressions."

Mikhail Chekhov. "Around Chekhov"

Melikhovo was situated on a big highway. When people found out that Chekhov, a famous writer, bought a property there, many people wanted to visit him. As a result, Anton Pavlovich accepted many visitors — doctors, social workers, and local authorities.

He built several schools, and participated in building a local highway.

Anton Pavlovich loved Lika Mizinova, who had many common interests with his friend, Potapenko. She used to sing, play the violin, and joke around. It was a great time — they had fun together. As it happens, Potapenko and Mizinova came to Melikhovo together. Lika would sit at the grand piano, and play music by Braga, and Potapenko would play violin, and their duo sounded very nice....

Chekhov was paying visits to other villages, accepting patients, and fighting an epidemic of cholera. He wrote to his friends, "Now I work in zemstvo *[a community center — P.S.]*, and at this point in time, please do not call me 'a literary artist.'" But he could not stop writing, of course.

Alexey Yakovlev. "A.P. Chekhov"

It was a beautiful and sunny Easter Tuesday in April of 1887.

Several of my friends and I, students at the Moscow University School of Medicine, decided to pay a visit to the country residence of Anton Pavlovich Chekhov. We bought railway tickets to Lopasnya Railway Station. Rumor had it that Chekhov was ill, and had been admitted to the Central Hospital. I had gone there earlier, only to learn that he had left for his Lopasnya estate.

At the time, not much was known about him, and we, the first-year students, imagined him to be a lonely village doctor who wrote short stories after work. Our train arrived at Lopasnya in the late afternoon. When we came to Chekhov's property, we discovered that Anton Pavlovich lived in a dacha; not by himself as we had previously thought, but with his large family.

A dark figure appeared on the porch. Someone said, "Welcome to our house."

We entered the dining-room. It was packed with people, including the writer's father, mother, sister, several brothers, and several guests. We were offered chairs, and one lady sat close to us. She had serene eyes, and resembled Anton Pavlovich. It was his sister Maria. She told us that after sunset, Anton usually retired to his bedroom, as it had been recommended by his doctors that he go to sleep early.

"However, for you he can make an exception," she said.

We heard footsteps, the door opened and a tall man dressed in a black coat and a hat came in. As soon as he saw me, he came closer, offering his big hand for a handshake, and he spoke to me as if we had known each other for a long time,

"Gentlemen, if you do not mind, let us all go to the garden for a short walk."

We went along the tree-lined alley leading into the orchard. At a short distance to the right of the house, you could see the patch of fog rising from a small pond, and behind the pond, you could see the neighboring village. In the distance were ravines, several farmers' fields, and a little forest. It could have been a typical landscape by Levitan. One of us commented on the striking similarity, and Anton Pavlovich said,

"Yes, yes, this is true. And do you know Levitan personally? He has a powerful talent."

We asked him another question: "Anton Pavlovich, have you read the recent open letter by Leo Tolstoy to the Liberals? And what do you think of students' societies and their social life?"

Chekhov replied, "All these student's protests are not very creative — you students just waste your time and effort without any purpose. Truly intelligent people do not have enough time and power for such things. They spend their energy on work. You should work hard, since we as a society have endless work to do. We have to fight poverty, and fight illiteracy."

We began talking about literary work. My friend was an aspiring writer, and spoke about the difficulties young writers face in trying to establish themselves. Chekhov smiled broadly, as an older brother would smile at his younger brother. He said,

"You should try different editorial houses. Also, try to go to different societies and organizations, and write reports about their work and meetings. I started like that. It is important to make literary work a habit, and to have the proper technique. Gradually, you will meet people from this profession, and will establish connections. It would also help to start a students' newspaper. You could even pay them two cents per line, but profit does not really matter. You could organize something like this, and people will be involved in it."

"Anton Pavlovich, can we ask you another question? Is there a real man behind your 'Story of an Unknown Man'?"

Chekhov smiled and said, "I do not remember who the real man behind the protagonist of this short story was. I think that I made my protagonist from a collection of features of different people."

I asked him, "Anton Pavlovich, have you ever met with Tolstoy?"

"Of course I have. Some time earlier, when I was in the hospital, he paid me a visit. Even before that, I had visited him in his Yasnaya Polyana estate."

Anton Pavlovich told us about his first visit to the Tolstoy estate. He was accompanied there by a friend. As soon as he was introduced to Tolstoy, they were invited to swim together in the local pond, and their first conversation was in the water.

We sat with Chekhov on the bench at the end of the lane. The sun was shining brightly, and its rays lit the garden. Two dogs, Brome and Quinine, played in the dust next to us.

Someone called us in for tea, and we went back to the dacha. This time, there were only us students accompanied by Anton Pavlovich and his sister Maria.

"Anton Pavlovich, how do you write? Do you rewrite different copies, like Tolstoy does, many times over?"

He smiled in reply, "As a rule, I wrote only one draft, and then I rewrite the final version with minor changes. I think each of my short stories through very carefully, for a long time. I imagine every word, and go over all the small details time and time again in my head."

The time had come for us to leave, as we had to catch the return train back to Moscow.

We gathered our bags, and were about to go to the neighboring village to find horses, but Anton Pavlovich convinced us to take his own driver. He said,

"My driver will bring you to our neighbor, Mr. S. He will give you another good horse which can take you to the Lopasnya Railway Station."

While the horses were being made ready, Anton Pavlovich invited us to his study. It was a small, narrow room, furnished in a very simple fashion, and very tidy. The desk stood away from the walls, in the middle of the room. Through the windows, we could see the little pond. On the wall hung an illustration for one of Edgar Poe's works. In it, you could see some ruins, and a moonlit forest.

Anton Pavlovich invited us to come closer to a little book closet. He took out some of his books, and asked us to pick out two that we liked. My friends selected *The Gloomy People*, and I picked up *Ward Number Six*.

Anton Pavlovich put on his eyeglasses, and sat at his desk.

His face became very serious — he had that same expression that you see in his portraits. He asked our names, and wrote, with his accurate and tidy handwriting, "April 17, 1897. Melikhovo. Chekhov."

The horses were ready, and we had to go. Anton Pavlovich stepped out on the porch to see us off. We asked him, "Anton Pavlovich, will you come to see us in Moscow?"

"And where do you live?"

We gave him our addresses, which he put down in his notebook and said, "Thank you. I will visit you one day."

We were welcomed by the friendly landlord. He gave us a good horse with a cart, and it brought us to the railway station. I never saw Chekhov again.

Ivan Belousov. "Chekhov as a Fisherman"

Chekhov was not your typical fisherman.

As a rule, a regular fisherman likes to catch as many fish as possible. Chekhov was different. He simply liked to sit in the sun, on the bank of a river or a pond with his fishing rod — relaxing, dreaming and pondering his literary works, perhaps. He was very happy if he happened to catch a little perch.

Chekhov showed me how to cook fish on a frying pan. He said, "You know, if you cover the fish in egg yolk, put some bread crumbs around it and fry it until there is a nice crispy crust ... now that is a wonderful meal."

In 1888 Chekhov rented a summer cottage near Sumy in the Kharkov region. He invited poet A. Pleshcheev to visit him, and wrote to him,

"I rented a cottage on the Psel River. It is not too far from Poltava, in the Sumy region. The river is rather deep and wide, and is very good for fishing."

The river was the most important thing that attracted Anton Pavlovich. He decided to entice his friend with the temptations of the river and good fishing.

In February of 1892, Chekhov bought his Melikhovo Cottage in the Serpukhov District. When he described his new property in a letter to his friend A. Kiselev dated March 7, 1892, he described it as such: "About 15 steps from my house is a small pond, about 15 meters long by 5 meters wide, which I filled with twenty perch, several carp and other fish. You can basically go fishing from my window! Three kilometers from my cottage, there is a big river; it is very wide and teeming with fish."

Mikhail, Anton's brother, wrote the following in his diary:

> Over the first year of our stay in Melikhovo, our property has changed beyond recognition. We put a small house at the front, with a beautiful flowerbed and a rose garden behind the house, and Anton Pavlovich organized the digging of a pond. He checked the progress of this work on a daily basis.
>
> With great passion, he himself put in the trees around the pond, and put lots of carp and perch in the pond. We brought the fish in a glass jar from Moscow. Later on, this pond looked more like a fish farm more than a regular pond. I do not know any kind of fish except for pike that Anton did not put into his pond. This pond was his favorite creation. He loved to sit on a small raft attached to the bank of the pond and look with joy during the sunset hours when small bunches of fish would surface and then quickly disappeared in its depth.

When Chekhov traveled, he first of all was interested in bodies of water, such as rivers, ponds or lakes — that is, any place where he could go fishing. For example, when he was visiting Vukol Lavrov, the publisher of *The Russian*

Thought Magazine, in his Makeevka cottage near Staraya Russia, we often saw him on the banks of the Moscow River with a fishing rod.

Later, in 1903, a year before his death, Chekhov, with his wife Olga and friend Konstantin Stanislavsky, were visiting a mutual friend who lived close to Naro-Fominsk, the suburbs of Moscow. Chekhov was rather sick, but he could not stop pursuing his favorite hobby, fishing.

Here is what S. Mamontov wrote in his memories:

> During the hot noon hours, when Anton's health could not be damaged by wet weather, and when not a single self-respectful fish could be caught on a hook, we could be found sitting on the banks of the Nara River, with fishing rods in our hands. We were right in the middle of the heat, looking at the quiet surface of the river, covered by the water lilies, listening to the grasshoppers' songs in the tall grass, and the quiet whisper of tall trees on the hill behind us. All these surroundings could not support our lively conversations, and therefore we sat in silence, briefly interrupted by short remarks.

Until his death, Chekhov did not quit his favorite hobby, instead paid special attention to it. He told me repeatedly, "I think that some of the best creations of the Russian literature were thought over and were created during time spent fishing."

Ilya Braz. "New About Chekhov"

[A well-known painter and Member of the Academy of Sciences, Ilya Braz gave a collection of Chekhov letters and memories to the Tretiakov Gallery. These documents deal with the period of 1889–98 and were addressed to Mr. Braz, who painted the Chekhov portrait for the Tretiakov Gallery.—P.S.]

During the summer of 1897, Chekhov felt better and moved from Moscow to his Melikhovo estate, and invited Mr. Braz to paint his portrait. The painter stayed at the estate for over a month, and painted a nice portrait. Mr. Tretiakov, the owner of the gallery, was very happy with it, yet the portrait has been stolen from the artist's studio.

A second portrait of Chekhov was painted in the spring of 1898 in Nice, France. It is interesting to follow the memories of Mr. Braz during the time he painted the first portrait in Melikhovo. Mr. Braz remembers:

> Chekhov, during his stay in Melikhovo, had a favorite hobby. It was fishing. It was his real passion. The first day I arrived, Chekhov invited me to go fishing. We went to the pond.
> I asked Chekhov, "Where should we start fishing? There is no pond here."

Chekhov smiled in reply, "What kind of fisherman are you? For a real fisherman, it does not matter, if there is a big pond or a small hole in the ground. It does not matter if there is big fish or small fish. Fishing is more than that!"

So we started fishing in the tiny pond on Chekhov's property. As soon as Chekhov would catch a fish, he would release it back into the water and continue fishing with passion.

It was very joyful to stay with the Chekhovs in Melikhovo. Chekhov was fond of making practical jokes.

A. Kazanin, E. Vakulov. "Encounters with Chekhov"

In 1892, Chekhov visited the Belaya village located fairly near to his estate of Melikhovo.

Peter Volchenkov, a peasant from this village, was 8 years old and in the first grade of the village school that year. He remembers his first meeting with Chekhov with these words:

> Our lesson started. Someone knocked at the door. Our teacher, Mr. Arkhangelsky, opened the door and into the classroom walked two men. One of them was the chief of the local school board, Mr. Egorov. The second person was completely unknown to us. I remember that he shook his head, and greeted us in a very friendly way. They discussed something with the teacher and then left. The teacher told us later that a man from the city promised to start free lunches at our school.
>
> A week later, a woman from our village named Nadezhda Dubravina treated our students with the first lunch. This lasted for several years. Many years later, I saw the portrait of Chekhov, and I finally understood that he was the man who treated us with free lunches when I was a school student.

Grigory Rossolimo. "Memories of Chekhov"

I had several meetings with Anton Pavlovich while he was alive.

They were all quite short and circumstantial. I remember I met him at the Art Theatre in Moscow, during a performance of one of his plays. I also remember meeting him at his apartment at Malaya Dmitrovka Street, where he was accompanied by a young and very elegant lady. She sat on the sofa, and Chekhov was pacing back and forth in front of her, telling her something. He was dressed in a very handsome way.

Aside from the handful of times I met him, I remember him from my letters. I have a wealth of factual material about Chekhov from our conversations and letters. All of it could accurately describe his personality. I could speak about anything — from his relations with his friends, to his profession, to his illness, to the actors who performed his plays.

I would like to say a few brief words here, based on my memories. He had a very warm and friendly attitude to his friends. He was very nice to the people who knew him from the university. Once you'd met Chekhov a few times, he became closer and closer to you. He loved his friends, and people responded with the same affection for him. I remember one of his friends was Nikolai Ivanovich Korobov, who died recently, and who genuinely loved Chekhov to the end of his days.

Chekhov did not love all of his university schoolmates in the same way, but he was rather close with those who came from his home town. For example, many years after we graduated from the university, one of our schoolmates, Mr. Danilov, had a breakdown. Anton Pavlovich did not know him personally, but when he found out that his family lacked all means of support, helped us to organize financial assistance for his family.

I remember another case. When we visited the town of Serpukhov, we found out about Dr. Vitte, who was paralyzed. I received a request from Anton Pavlovich about the state of health of our former university friend.

I should also say that for many years, every time Chekhov met his university schoolmates, I saw great attention and affection to them on his part.

As I said earlier, Chekhov was a good student, and in spite of the distractions supplied by his by writing, he studied very diligently. He attended all the lectures and labs and he made visits to clinics.

After he graduated from medical school, he did not abandon his practice, but worked as a village doctor in the towns of Voskresensk and Zvenigorod *[both towns are distant suburbs of Moscow — P.S.]*. About seven or eight years later, he organized the cholera epidemic medical station in the Moscow region. During his work in Voskresensk, he found the prototype for his short story "Surgery." People say that he worked as a doctor with lots of love and great diligence.

In Zvenigorod, he planted a long double row of saplings in front of the gates, which by now have grown into big trees.

Chekhov had never said "no" in his medical practice. Whenever he had time and opportunity, he treated medical patients. We even treated the same patients at times, after he sent his patients to me from Melikhovo, and later from Crimea. These were people with nervous illnesses whom he sent to me as a specialist for a medical consultation. He liked to give medical advice to other people, and he followed the latest news from the medical journals. He was very careful and gentle with his patients. He was a writer, a doctor, and a wonderful human being at the same time. I was especially impressed by this feature of Chekhov.

Nina Drozdova. "Memories of Chekhov"

I met Chekhov for the first time in 1895.

I first met his sister Maria Pavlovna when she was taking courses at the Srtroganov Art College. I had just moved to Moscow from a far-off little town in the Kursk region. I was very shy, in part due to the fact that I did not yet know anyone in that big city. Maria Pavlovna invited me to have tea together after class, but I felt too awkward and did not go with her that time.

Another day, Maria Pavlovna took me with her almost by force for a cup of tea, telling me that there would be none at home. On the way she told me, "Would you like to meet my family? My brother is a famous writer, Chekhov. Have you read any of my brother's work?"

I was very embarrassed at the thought of meeting my favorite author. His works had made such a great impression on me, especially his short story "Ward Number Six," that I refused to go!

Sometime later, I learned that her brother did not live in Moscow, but at on the Melikhovo Estate in the country. I decided to take her invitation to meet her family with not a few reservations.

It was the beginning of November, on a rainy, cold day.

After two hours by train, we got off at the small railway station Lopasnya, in the Kursk region. We had to travel for about 16 kilometers by horse and carriage on a bad road before we finally arrived. A little girl servant met us at the porch.

* * *

Anton Pavlovich Chekhov greeted me with a reproach, "It took you so long to visit us. We have been waiting for almost a year!"

As soon as I laid eyes on Chekhov, all my fears disappeared. He had a very warm, friendly and tender expression. He was a very simple yet approachable person. He was dressed in a gray velvet suit with a black bow tie, looking both sophisticated and simple at the same time. I then met all members of the family — including his father and mother.

I was homesick for my own family, and here in Melikhovo, everything reminded me of my own home, making me heartsick even more.

A good dinner waited for us in the dining room. The mushroom soup was delicious, made from fresh picked mushrooms by Pavel Egorovich, Chekhov's father.

After dinner, Anton Pavlovich shared several letters written to him by Leo Tolstoy, and handed them to me to read. I was very excited; this first visit seemed like a dream to me.

Later, my visits to Melikhovo became more and more frequent. Every

Saturday, after our classes finished, Maria and I headed to Melikhovo. After our weekend in the country, we had to get up at 5 A.M. Monday morning to catch the train back to Moscow, for we had to be back at college for our first class at 9 A.M.

Everyone in Melikhovo worked hard. Chekhov worked a lot during the wintertime. He awoke very early, and had his visiting hours before morning tea. He was a doctor to the locals in the neighboring villages. After tea, he created new works with words, while Maria and I would be drawing and painting, using children as our models. In Melikhovo no one had a single moment to spare.

From time to time, Anton Pavlovich used to visit our "home studio," as he called it — Maria's room. He used to come in, and sit on the corner sofa very quietly, and observe us while we worked. Maria would be drawing, and the family's two favorite dogs, Bromine and Quinine, would lie by the fireplace, keeping warm.

Chekhov used to jot down thoughts periodically in the small pocket notebook he always carried with him. He would be so quiet; we never minded working in his presence. After observing us for a while, Anton would head back to his study. At 8 P.M. we had dinner together. Anton Pavlovich would then return to his study, often working past midnight. No one would bother him at home, so he could work at his own pace at ease.

Anton Pavlovich loved to be outside. He always liked to observe the bird migration each spring and fall. He used to take a break while working, see a robin fly by, smile and invite us to come and take a look at the bird. He was happy looking at the clouds, the trees and birds. He was happy living so close to nature, and he was more inspired to create as a result.

Anton Pavlovich had a very small study with two windows that overlooked the garden. The study was filled with a writing desk, several chairs, an ancient-looking book closet covered with glass, a little medicine box, and a collection of classical books on a shelf. Chekhov used to pass me books to read — works by Lermontov, Turgenev and Flaubert. Once when he saw a volume of his short stories in my hands, he gave me Turgenev, and said, "You better read this."

One day, he asked me a question: "Why don't you write? One day, you will have blisters on your fingers, and you will become a writer. I will help you, if you wish. You should not wait for inspiration, but instead write every day. In about six years, you would be a good writer."

Nothing stopped our trips to Melikhovo; not rain, snow or bad weather. We were never too afraid to travel as we knew the warmth, happiness and peace that awaited us at our destination. Sometimes, we used to bring

Chekhov's mail back from the train station. He received a lot of correspondence — newspapers, magazines and many letters from all over the world. I understood the thrill of opening a new magazine, and of discovering something between its pages.

We especially enjoyed the arrival of his mail in the otherwise dreary winter nights. The pile of letters used to sit on the dinner table next to Anton Pavlovich, building the suspense of what they might contain inside! Sometimes he would pass me a small envelope and tell me, "This is for you," as my mother had written me.

In addition to being a writer, Anton Pavlovich was a local activist at the Serpukhov district city hall, where he held his reception hours as a doctor. As a result, he was very aware of the life of the local people.

He was always bringing culture into people's lives. With his own money, he built three village schools in the district of Serpukhov. He was continually asking his friends and acquaintances for money for local charities, especially for building the village schools. One day I brought him about thirty rubles which I collected from my friends and Chekhov accepted them gratefully.

Every morning as a rule, exactly at 6 o'clock, the villagers would bring their illnesses and medical problems to Chekhov, who carefully listened to them all. We all knew he cared deeply for people. He gave both medical assistance and moral support when needed. He never refused simple folks, and tried to help all he encountered the best he could.

All who knew him genuinely loved and respected him. Chekhov could relate to and was interested in everyone he met, and that drew people to him.

Mikhail Plotov. "A Big Heart"

I met Anton Pavlovich Chekhov in September of 1892.

At the time, I taught in the village of Shchegliatievo, which was about 7 kilometers from Melikhovo. I was feeling unwell, so my friend Nikolai, a senior student of the Moscow University Medical School, took me to the local medical office to ask Anton Pavlovich's opinion of my health.

When we arrived, Chekhov, who himself had just arrived from Melikhovo, was about to start admitting his patients. He was a tall and slender man, and had an open, cordial face with regular features, and a small, fair beard. His eyes radiated wisdom and warmth. Altogether, he appeared very friendly and welcoming.

Upon entering, Anton Pavlovich told me, "Please, take a seat. Reception hours are about to begin."

Several old female peasants filtered into his room one by one, and he greeted them in a warm and careful tone. After his patients left, he told me,

"Please come to my Melikhovo estate tomorrow morning, and we will have more time to talk there."

Driving up to Melikhovo the next day, I expected that he would ask me to remove my shirt, listen to my heartbeat, busily note some observations, and write me a prescription. I was mistaken. He asked me about my age, about how I spent my free time, and then about my symptoms. Upon some consideration, he told me that there was nothing seriously wrong with my health, and suggested taking long walks and eating some fresh dairy products.

Anton Chekhov on the balcony of his house. Yalta, August 1901.

I got into the habit of visiting Chekhov once or twice a month in the summers between 1892 and 1898, that is, until Anton Pavlovich left for Crimea, to the cottage he had built there.

He gave me books to read, and I enjoyed listening to him speak of literature. I could not help admiring him, and being impressed by the great force of imagery that he expressed during our conversations. It was typical for a listener to be impressed by his thoughts and his speech, as well as his works. His casual conversations were as light, beautiful and free as his writing. He had a gift for telling many things in a few words.

One of the most appealing features of Anton Pavlovich was his kindness. People from all walks of life were among his friends — of course, they also included literary artists, editors, critics, and painters. However, he had many friends among other sorts of people, that is, village teachers, nurses, university students, local farmers, and any other type of profession you can imagine. He treated all people in the same way, and was an extremely outgoing person who tried to help people in whatever way he could.

Here is one brief story to illustrate this. In 1892, I mentioned in passing that I liked hunting, but did not have a decent rifle. Soon after, he presented me with a very expensive hunting rifle of the best quality.

Tatiana Shchepkina-Kupernik. "Young Years"

Maria Pavlovna, Anton Chekhov's sister, took painting lessons and taught at Rzhevsky High School. At first glance, she seemed to be reserved, and wanting to keep some distance. However, that was simply my first impression.

Very quickly, I began to appreciate her Chekhovian humor and good disposition, and we became friends. Through her, I became acquainted with her brother, Anton Chekhov. The three of us would meet quite often, and have a good time together.

I recollect Maria Chekhova's bedroom vividly: it had a narrow bed, a desk, and a portrait of her brother on the wall. Her brother was the focus for her being, in her room, in her life, and in her heart.

I also remember the room belonging to Anton Pavlovich, with its bright, lofty windows, and the writing desk overflowing with papers. This multitude of sheets scattered on his desk included pages from recent stories, covered with his elaborate handwriting, as well as lists, blueprints and accounts of hospitals and schools, the building of which he sponsored.

The walls were covered with paintings by Levitan and his brother Nikolai, who was also a talented painter. I was constantly surprised at the Chekhovs, whose previous residence had been in a small, provincial town in complete poverty, at how this family could develop sophisticated tastes and furnish their home with such grace. There was not a single piece of furniture out of place. Their noble, harmonious inner life manifested itself both in their actual home, and in their family life itself. The same could be said of their Melikhovo estate, where the Chekhovs later moved from Moscow.

Chekhov wrote about Melikhovo, "Everything is miniature around here — a tiny alley, a pond the size of a fish tank, tiny trees. But after you pace along the alley a couple of times, and look more carefully at everything, the claustrophobic feeling that everything is too small disappears. All of a sudden, we have lots of space."

I feel exactly the same after reading his short stories. You read a page or two, think about it, and then the feeling of a small literary space disappears and you see the great, broad image of all sides of Russian life and society.

Chekhov told me one day that I would force him to marry me.

He also told me that we could not be married, because he was a male writer, and I was a female writer, and that would be the cause of constant quarrels in our family.

He was constantly teasing me, but all of it was in a very friendly way, and he always made me laugh. I knew that Anton Pavlovich only teased people whom he liked. The only person he teased more than me was Lika Misinova.

Upon his fireplace, he put a portrait of me in formal dress and wrote, "Lizet Shchepkina-Kupernik!"

He was following the example of Mr. Urusov, a journalist and theater critic, who loved the French writer Gustave Flaubert so much that when people asked him for an autograph one day, he gave him a photo and signed it, "Lizet Flaubert!"

He gave me nicknames: "The Great Lady-Writer of the Russian Land," or "The Well-Established Novelist."

He also called me "Tatiana E.," a combination of my first name and the middle name of a famous journalist whom I had never known personally. The man was a very short, small and humble person, but Chekhov threatened to forcefully marry him with me, and change my name.

One of his favorite practical jokes was pretending to be the director of the Imperial Theater, and once a day, a butler would report to him, "Dear Sir, the ladies have arrived with the scripts for their plays."

He replied in the same tone of voice as if the butler had said, "The peasant women have brought us some mushrooms."

Then, a group of ladies would come in. Chekhov would tell me, "Come in, my dear writer."

I was supposed to say, "My name is Tatiana E."

Chekhov would ask me, "And who is she, this Tatiana E? Oh, I remember! Then, because you are my old friend, I will accept your play for production."

One day, Anton Pavlovich began writing a one-act play with me. It was about a female writer. The monologue at the beginning started with the words,

"I am a female writer. This is true — just look at my hands. These are the hands of an honest worker. Look, I have an ink spot here — on my finger. There once was a writer in my life. He constantly dreamt of a cottage in the countryside."

Then some dogs would bark, followed by some silence and then, the sound of harmonica in the distance. The writer in the play could be Anton Chekhov.

I never finished my part of the play. The little notebook containing it, along with Chekhov's handwritten monologue, disappeared. At the time, I did not have any regrets, but now, I believe that every piece of paper he wrote on should be put into a collection of his manuscripts.

However, at the time he was just a friend who liked making jokes.

One day, we were going home after a lengthy walk in the country. Suddenly, it began to rain, and we were forced to wait it out in an empty barn. Chekhov was drying his wet umbrella and told me the following:

"I would like to write a musical comedy. Listen to this. Two people are waiting for the rain to end in an empty barn. They are drying their clothes and umbrellas, and making jokes. Then, they confess their love for each other. The rain stops, and suddenly, he dies from a heart attack!"

I said, "You are joking, of course. What kind of musical comedy is this?!"

Chekhov replied, "But does it not happen in real life? We are laughing, making jokes and then — boom! Suddenly, the end."

Of course, he never put this particular plot on paper.

One of his jokes was the following. At the Melikhovo estate, there were several doves of a rare coffee color, with white spots on their wings. There was also a cat of the same color. Anton Pavlovich told me once that these doves were the result of crossing the cat with a regular wild dove that lived in his forests.

After dinner, Anton Pavlovich used to play with his dogs. He had two dogs. One was a brown female, by the name of Quinine Markovna, whom he also called "the suffering lady" because she was always sick. He took her to the hospital on a regular basis. Then, there was another dog, Bromine Isaacovich, who — as Chekhov told us — had eyes similar to Levitan's. What he said was true; that dog had unusually sad and dark eyes.

Once, Chekhov played with them with a small sable fur that I had been wearing around my shoulders. The dogs began to bark unceasingly, and Chekhov laughed at them. Not knowing the cause of the commotion, I was quickly tired of this. I was surprised and puzzled when, a few minutes later, the dogs began leaping and barking at a cigar box that stood on the fireplace. Later, it turned out that Anton Pavlovich had quietly placed my stolen sable into the box.

Sometimes the jokes changed into serious conversation. Anton Pavlovich gave me advice — in a very delicate manner — on how to improve my writing. He spoke about one of my novels:

"Everything is very pretty and artistic. However, you should not say, 'This was a very touching moment.' You should express events in such a way that the readers would feel that that was a touching moment. In general, you have to love your characters, without openly stating this to others."

Anton Pavlovich also chided me for using the set and worn-out idioms, and suggested that I find fresh words when writing descriptions.

I greatly appreciated his literary criticism of my works. Never in my life have I met a writer as friendly and supportive of his younger colleagues as Chekhov. He was always asking editors to support some new writers, he was always helping someone publish their works, and he was renowned for supported new talents.

I recollect that he was the one who helped the young Gorky in the beginning of his career. Chekhov never felt professional jealousy towards others.

I visited the Chekhovs often, but mostly during the fall when there were no other visitors and all of them were at home. They always welcomed me warmly.

I remember Chekhov would always get emotional whenever he listened to music. After listening to the Moonlight Sonata by Beethoven, he told me, "That was extremely beautiful."

Chekhov also liked compositions by Tchaikovsky and some songs by Glinka. He went on to describe music in works like "The Black Monk." It is hard to discern what was more important in Chekhov, a kind human being or a great artist. He possessed a bright, well-rounded personality, put together in perfect harmony.

Pavel Egorovich Chekhov. "Diary"

[Pavel Egorovich Chekhov was born in the Voronezh region, to a serf family. Shortly after his birth, his father managed to save enough money to buy his freedom. Pavel Egorovich wrote his diary for a long time. Despite never receiving any formal education, he was a talented man; he had a good musical ear, he liked to read books, and he enjoyed intelligent conversations. During his life in Melikhovo, he wrote diary entries on a nearly daily basis. The elder Chekhov's diary entries, although not detailed or descriptive, were to the point; he took note of who was visiting Melikhovo at the time, the weather, what the family members had done that day. This diary continued for almost 20 years.— P.S.]

April of 1892.
Sunday, April 12. The last of the snow is melting.
April 15. Anton has gone to Moscow. The ice on the pond has melted.
April 17. The two hired laborers have started plowing the land. We spent the day working in the orchard.
April 18. Our cow has joined the village cow herd. It is warm today: 15 degrees.

April 19. We bought a new plow. It is 15 degrees, and a nice, sunny day. Anton and Ivan have just returned.

April 20. Today is a very warm day; it was 18 degrees.

April 21. E. Konovitser visited us.

April 22. A. Suvorin *[Chekhov's publisher- P.S.]* came to visit us. The tree buds have opened and the leaves have sprung from the bare branches. We bought barley — seeds for the new crops.

April 23. We bought small potatoes — seeds for a new harvest.

April 24. A small frost.

Jury Avdeev. "To the Memory of Maria Chekhova"

When we were creating the Chekhov Museum in Melikhovo, his sister, Maria Chekhova, was an active and energetic contributor.

As we met with her, she told us many memories of the Chekhov family.

She said, "I was very surprised at how I managed to do so many things with Anton Chekhov. I managed charity projects of building new schools, worked around the house, assisted Anton with his literary work, helping him with his vast correspondence, helping teachers from neighboring schools, and buying building materials. Do you know that we built the local Melikhovo School with money raised by our family?"

"Could you tell us more about your life in Melikhovo?"

Maria Pavlovna remembers,

All of us tried to do our best. We did not live a life of luxury, and the whole family had to work hard. We woke up at six in the morning and worked all day long. We had a vegetable garden where we grew our vegetables, and Chekhov called this place "the South of France." We also grew flowers. Anton Pavlovich grew amazingly beautiful roses under the windows of his study.

He used to tell me, "No matter what kinds of roses I plant, only white roses grow here. Why does this happen?"

"My dear Antony," I answered him, "this happens because you have such a pure and loving heart."

We had a small picket fence in front of the entrance to our cottage. The village girls used to walk back and forth along this fence, singing country folk songs. Anton Pavlovich, in one of his short stories, "Peasants," describes the village of Melikhovo and the songs the peasant girls used to sing.

"Look here," Maria Pavlovna gestures. "This landscape on the wall was painted by the famous painter Braz at the time he was working on a portrait of Anton Pavlovich.

"Do you see the small forest in the distance? We called this place 'a rectangular.' There were a lot of mushrooms there. Early in the morning, our mother used to go there to pick them, and Anton used to talk with her."

Maria Pavlovna can recollect a lot of little details about life in Melikhovo.

"I remember the last night in Melikhovo, just before we left," she remembers. "We were sitting on the front porch of this little cottage, with Anton Pavlovich. It was a wonderful summer evening, and there was music in the air around us. We had an excellent time remembering music from Tchaikovsky's *Evgeny Onegin*. We had to say goodbye to this beautiful place, to our cottage, our yard, and our garden."

Alexander Roskin. "Young Chekhov"

In the early spring of 1890, Chekhov wrote, "In the next few weeks, migrating birds will return from the south. Yet the forthcoming spring seems alien to me, since I am going away very soon."

Chekhov was leaving for Sakhalin. He made this decision unexpectedly for everyone, including his close friends. At the time, Sakhalin was a high-security prison, on an island in eastern Siberia [*close to Japan*—*P.S.*] where the most dangerous prisoners were sent.

The Trans-Siberian Highway was not yet built at the time, and the prisoners, with heavy shackles on their feet, had to walk for months, sometimes even for years, to get there. The prison was a hard forced labor facility, and people rarely returned if sent there. Some died from hard work; others from infectious diseases; some were punished for attempting to escape and died from the resulting flogging.

Chekhov had a very long way to go, about eleven thousand kilometers, mostly on horseback. His health was not very good, and he often coughed up blood; but even this could not stop him.

Chekhov began by doing his research. He studied books on geology, geography, the history of prisons, etc. Spring came, the ice on the roofs melted, and Chekhov decided it was time to go.

One of his friends gave him a bottle of good brandy at the Moscow Railway Station, and asked him to open it at the shore of the Pacific Ocean, at the other end of the country. Chekhov promised to do this; however, it was not an easy task to get to the ocean.

The roads were terrible, and very often the horse carts got into deep mud or into rivers and creeks. When Chekhov was crossing River Tom, he almost drowned. After Krasnoyarsk, the skin on his face was burnt by the sun and the wind, and covered with peeling patches.

Chekhov spent three months on Sakhalin Island. He alone made the complete census of the island's population. He went to every house, every prison cell, every hut, and personally spoke to every person on the island. Sakhalin had ten thousand people, and Chekhov filled out ten thousand census cards in his handwriting.

Sakhalin turned out to truly be hell on earth, a real inferno. The prison officers did a lot of horrendous things there — sometimes they committed worse crimes than the prisoners they had to guard and supervise.

Chekhov returned to mainland Russia by ocean boat, around India and through the Suez Canal. He crossed the Indian Ocean, the Red Sea, and visited Hong Kong and Singapore. He took a railway across the Island of Sri Lanka. While he swam in the ocean, he met with a shark that almost took his life. In the Chinese Sea, the boat got caught in a huge storm, and Chekhov put a loaded gun into his pocket, to commit suicide in case the boat would start sinking. However, he managed to survive.

In eight months, Chekhov returned to Moscow. He remembered with joy the tropical beauties on the island of Sri Lanka, and he remembered with horror the terrible life in Siberian prisons.

Sakhalin gave him a lot of impressions for his future work. He said that in Sakhalin, he saw everything you could imagine.

Alexey Suvorin and Anton Chekhov. "Works. Letters"

[Anton Chekhov was an astonishingly active lover, as we can see from the letters below. Here are a few tantalizing snippets, from the letters to his publisher A. Suvorin, who was Chekhov's close friend. Several of these letters below were written from Siberia and Sri Lanka, during Chekhov's trip to Sakhalin Island. After almost 100 years in the archives, these intimate Chekhov letters were published by the Voskresenie Publishers in Moscow in 2009. — P.S.]

I have seen many dissipated women and sinned on many occasions, and therefore, I do not believe Zola....

It is not so easy to find a place in the city where you can properly "use" a woman. I have not once seen a single apartment — in the homes of decent families, of course — with furniture that would permit you to take and "use" a fully dressed woman, so that the family members would not notice it. All this terminology — while standing or while sitting — is a complete nonsense. Women who are "used on every sofa," so to speak, are suffering from nymphomania. I curse all sofas for this deficiency....

An affair with a woman from a respectable family is going to take far too much of your time.... First, you need to do this at night. In the hotel

room, your lady will fall into a fit of terror, trembling and exclaiming: "Oh my God, what am I doing? Oh, no, no." Then it will take you another hour to undress her and to talk her through it, and on the way back home, she will look at you as though you have raped her, and mumble all the way home, "No, never, I will never forgive myself for this."
— Anton Chekhov. "Works. Letters." His letter to A. Suvorin,
November 24/25, 1888

A Japanese woman has a clean room and she wastes no time. She does not dim the lights; the experience is more like riding a thoroughbred at a dressage school ... she laughs and jokes all the way through, using the sound "ts" in her speech.
— Anton Chekhov. "Works. Letters." His letter to A. Suvorin,
June 27, 1890

Then I came to Ceylon, a place that looked like paradise. I traveled for almost 100 versts [about 65 miles] across this paradise, until I was sick of palm trees and bronze women.
When I have a child one day, I will tell him with pride, "Do you know, you son of a bitch, that I made love to a dark-eyed Hindu woman? And do you know where? It was in a cocoa forest, in the moonlight."
— Anton Chekhov. "Works. Letters." His letter to A. Suvorin,
December 9, 1890

[In the summer and fall of 1890, Chekhov visits Sakhalin, an island and a prison in the Eastern Siberia. He talks to people, and collects materials for his future stories, and takes the census of the Sakhalin population.— P.S.]

I stayed at the Northern Sakhalin for exactly two months.... I don't know what will happen from it, but I have done a lot. It will be enough for three dissertations. Every day, I got up at 5 am, and went to bed late, and I was so stressed out, that many things have not been completed.... I made a census of the Sakhalion population. I filled out over 10,000 census cards. There is not a single prisoner or a settler on Sakhalin with whom I did not talk.
— Anton Chekhov. "Works. Letters." His letter to A. Suvorin.
September 11, 1890

Mikhail Chekhov. "Around Chekhov"

When Chekhov was completing his book *Sakhalin Island*, he was working very hard each morning. Chekhov wrote to A. Suvorin then,

"On Mondays, Tuesdays and Wednesdays, I am writing my book *Sakhalin Island*. On all other days except Sundays and Saturdays, I am working on my novel, and on other days, I write my short stories."

Every morning, Anton Pavlovich used to wake up early at 4 A.M.

He did not work at his writing desk as you might expect, but at the windowsill, looking at the park. He would be either writing his novel *The Duel* or organizing his materials for the book *Sakhalin Island*, which really was a huge undertaking. He would write without any interruptions until 11 in the morning.

After that, he would head into the forest, to either pick up some mushrooms or to go fishing in the local pond. He would fish with his rod or net.

Around one in the afternoon was lunch time. At around three, Anton would resume his work, and did not cease writing again until evening. It was then that he would debate and converse with his guests and neighbors. Biology Professor K. Wagner was among them, and they would discuss the rights of the strongest, the natural selection of species, etc. All these ideas were described in the philosophizing made by the protagonist of *The Duel*, Chekhov's newest short novel.

During these conversations, Anton Pavlovich repeatedly stated that a person's willpower could always overcome negative things in our lives, such as bad circumstances, negative character flaws or inherited illnesses.

A. Chaikin. "Anton Chekhov: My Traveling Companion"

I asked my traveling companion if he had read the short novel *Steppe* that I have just finished reading in a magazine. He replied that he had not only read it, he had written it! I cried out,

"Please, let me interrupt you. How could you have written it if it was written by the famous Chekhov?"

At that moment I opened the magazine and gestured to the author's name with my finger.

"I am Chekhov, and I am on my way to visit Sakhalin Island," my traveling companion replied.

I must have had a rather freaky and amazed expression on my face, because the man took off his coat, and pulled out his business card from his pocket that said, "Doctor A. Chekhov."

He then turned it over, and wrote, "April 27, 1890. Perm. A.P. Chekhov." He wrote this on the back before handing it to me! I was completely shocked by this meeting, and as we approached a railway station, I took Anton Pavlovich by the arm. Chekhov politely freed his arm and said that otherwise people might think that I was a railway conductor and I had just caught a passenger who did not pay for his ticket!

Anatoly Koni. "Selected Works"

Chekhov's trip to Sakhalin attracted the attention of the Ministry of the Interior, and the Department of Prisons. Several experts, after Chekhov's trip and his report, visited the prisons he described, and made sure that all that Chekhov wrote was true.

Two experts — Mr. Kudrin and Mr. Solomon — visited Sakhalin shortly after his trip, and their detailed reports approved the results obtained by Chekhov.

A few years later, after my meeting with Chekhov, I met the actress Komissarzhevskaya. We spoke about the theater, and about the new plays. She recommended for me to go to the opening night of Chekhov's new play *The Seagull*, which had started a new trend in theater.

I went to the theater to see the play, and greatly enjoyed the performance. I did not even expect the effect it produced on me. Yet, I noticed that the image of the seagull did not attract the attention of the public. People looked at the scene with dull and bored expressions. However, for me, it was an amazing play. Later, the play became more and more popular.

When I met with Chekhov in Yalta, he gave me a wonderful reception. He was dressed in a warm, dark coat, but he smiled at me and told me, "Today is a wonderful spring day here in Yalta."

Later he told me about his life. He coughed a lot in Yalta, and doctors advised him to go drink horse milk, a popular folk remedy. He wrote to me that the doctors found out that the disease was spreading down his lungs, and that he needed to have treatments at the spa.

He wrote to me, "I got embarrassed and I got married, and went to the south to drink horse milk. Now I feel much better. I gained eight pounds. I don't know if this is due to me drinking milk every day, or me getting married. My cough has almost stopped. Olga sends her regards."

However, this improvement in his health did not last for a long time. As his fame grew, his health deteriorated. He became weaker and weaker, and then he died. He died in a remote place, in Badenweiler, Germany, at the moment when he dreamt of going back to Russia with all his heart.

When I read most of his numerous works, I think that he was a very special and unusual person. From his early years, he went his own way, and he never followed or imitated anyone. He followed the advice of Pushkin:

"Go along a free highway, where your intellect points you in the right direction."

All his life, he preached spiritual freedom, freedom of ideas, freedom from stereotypes, finding new ways and new forms of expression.

Mikhail Chekhov. "A.P. Chekhov and Mongooses"

The special A-train arrived at the Tula Railway station five minutes ahead of schedule. Mother and I came to the railway platform, but could not find Anton. When I went inside the railway station building, I located him sitting on a bench in the corner talking to a navy officer. Anton introduced us to the officer, and then we found our railway car and boarded the train. Anton showed us his vast amount of luggage, as he was bringing many things. Once settled, we met another traveling companion, a wide-faced man named Irakly. He was a missionary priest from Siberia. All the way from Tula to Moscow we drank wine and played with the exotic animals we were bringing back with us.

We arrived in Moscow late at night. We had a rented house on Malaya Dmitrovka Street at the time. Anton bought two mongooses, but it turned out that it was a mongoose and a palm cat. We let the mongoose off the leash and released the palm cat out of its cage, to let the animals stretch after their long trip.

At once, the palm cat ran beneath the bookcase, where it stayed most of the time, very seldom leaving. The mongoose believed itself the master of the house. It was an interesting animal. Yet, it was continuously attacking all our visitors. Anton Pavlovich was very embarrassed, and we all waited for the summer, so we could put the mongoose into the cottage. The palm cat never grew used to living around people.

Alexandra Khotiaintseva. "Meetings with Chekhov"

Chekhov loved flowers very much. In Melikhovo, he had an exquisite rose garden, and he was very proud of it. Whenever ladies from the neighboring estates paid him a visit, he personally selected and cut a rose bouquet for them.

However, he cut only "ripe flowers"; only those that had to be cut according to gardening rules. The ladies, on their way home, were always surprised to see their roses dropping petals as soon as they left Chekhov's estate. One particular lady was especially disappointed by this, and he gave her the nickname, "Adelaida," after a heroine from one of his short stories.

"She looks exactly like my Adelaida," he said.

Next to the roses, there was a vegetable garden full of "red vegetables," that is, tomatoes, and "blue vegetables," that is, eggplants.

One day, I decided to draw Chekhov's summer cottage. A small red flag fluttered on the top of the roof, and this little signal for local farmers meant that the owner of the house was at home. They could come over to ask his advice, if they wished to do so.

This time, the master of the house paced along the alley behind my back, back and forth, and spoke to me as I drew. Chekhov was accompanied by his constant escorts, two little dogs called Bromine and Quinine. The dogs also had nicknames given to them by Chekhov, "Fast Train" and "Red Cow."

While I drew, my shoe was hanging off the tips of my toes, because I was so engrossed in what I was doing. After I had finished my drawing, and attempted to get up, I could not stand properly on my feet: Anton Pavlovich had put an onion into one of my shoes.

It was hard to imagine Chekhov even slightly ill, since he simply overflowed with energy.

He said to me once, "Levitan and I both failed to value the beauty of life when we were young and healthy. But now, when we are both sick, we truly appreciate the charm of it all."

During my time in Melikhovo, Anton Pavlovich was selecting short stories for his *Complete Works*. His brother was selecting those published in magazines from a huge stack in front of him and read us a short story.

Chekhov used to burst out in laughter, "Is that really my story? I don't remember it at all. But it is really so funny!"

He used to make practical jokes and tell discreet anecdotes all the time. Anton Pavlovich often picked on me by saying, "It is the privilege of wise people to say stupid things."

CHAPTER FOUR

Writers and Friends

Introduction

When I met Chekhov, I saw the most beautiful and refined human face
that I ever saw in my life.
— Alexander Kuprin. "Chekhov. In Memoriam"

Leo Tolstoy loved Chekhov as a father loves his son, and you could see
in Tolstoy the creator who was proud of his creation. Tolstoy said that
as a master of artistry and style, no one can reach the top level of
Chekhov's skills. And the future historians of literature would have to
say that the Russian language was created by Pushkin, Turgenev and
Chekhov.
— Maxim Gorky. "A.P. Chekhov"

In the five years when Anton Chekhov lived with us in Yalta, our life was
filled with many interesting events. Many nice people visited us there.

Writers, scientists, artists, and politicians surrounded the writer, many
of which liked to visit us especially in spring. We had a lot of things to
listen to and to talk about. Maxim Gorky, Leo Tolstoy, Korolenko, and
Kuprin were here. Gorky was the most frequent visitor.
— Maria Chekhova. "My Memories"

Chekhov as an artist cannot be even compared with the old, traditional
Russian writers, such as Turgenev, Dostoevsky or me. Chekhov has his
own artistic form. And there is another feature that tells us that Chekhov
is a real artist — you can read and reread his works many times.
— Leo Tolstoy. "Complete Works. Diary. Letters"

When there is such a man as Tolstoy in literature, then it is easy and
pleasant to be a writer; even if you realize that you yourself have not
accomplished, and do not accomplish anything, it is not frightening,
because Tolstoy works for us all. His work is the justification of the hopes
people place in literature.
— Anton Chekhov. "Works. Letters." His letter to
M. Menshikov, January 28, 1901

I do not write these days, or write very little because of my illness. Please
feel free to include any of my earlier published stories in a charity col-

78

lection, in the support of the Jewish families who suffered from the pogrom in Kishinev. It gives me great and sincere pleasure to give you my permission.

— Anton Chekhov. "Works. Letters." His letter to
S. Rabinovich (Sholom-Aleikhem), June 19, 1903

In 1900, we started a new literary circle in Moscow. We called it "Literary Wednesdays." Most of the promising young writers of that time were constant members of this circle: Gorky, Leonid Andreev, Veresaev, Bunin, Skitalets and Kuprin. Chekhov lived in Yalta, but he was always interested in our circle, and regularly asked me to write him the latest news about it.

— N. Teleshov. "A.P. Chekhov"

Maxim Gorky. "A.P. Chekhov"

Chekhov spoke of Tolstoy with a very special feeling, with a tender smile in his eyes. His voice was low, almost a whisper, as if to indicate that this was something significant, needing carefully selected words. At the time, he mentioned that Tolstoy lacked a secretary who could record all Tolstoy's great ideas and witty thoughts.

"You should become his secretary one day," Chekhov said to Sulerzhitsky. "Tolstoy loves you and speaks very kindly of you."

One day, Tolstoy especially admired one of Chekhov's short stories. He said,

"This is like a fine lace, the embroidery of words. You know, in the old days, there was a type of lace made only by young maidens, who wove all their dreams of happiness into its design."

Tolstoy spoke with tears in his eyes, and with great emotion in his voice.

Chekhov had a fever that day. He sat next to us, his face covered with red spots, his head bent to one side; he was wiping his glasses. He was quiet for a long time, and then he muttered, embarrassed, "This story was published with quite a few typos in it."

One day, I saw Chekhov sitting in his garden, trying to catch a ray of sunlight in his hat, and then put his hat, illuminated, on his head. He liked practical jokes; he was a funny man.

We could go on speaking of Chekhov, but you must be careful to clearly record all the details and that is what I cannot do. Whenever I recall that wonderful man, I feel filled with energy, and my life is colored with deep meaning. He was the axis of the world that revolved around him, that's for certain.

A. Melkova. "Tatyana Tolstaya and Chekhov"

Tatyana Tolstaya, the daughter of Leo Tolstoy, met with Chekhov several times and maintained a correspondence with him. M. Menshikov wrote to Chekhov from the Tolstoy estate, Yasnaya Polyana, on 20 August, 1896:

"Tatyana loves you very much, and feels somehow sad without you. She says that you have great talent, but you are too much a materialistic person at the same time."

It has been established that there was a deep admiration between Tatyana Tolstoy and Anton Chekhov.

Tatyana Tolstaya was planning to write a big chapter, "Chekhov," in her book dedicated to the visitors to Yasnaya Polyana. Therefore, she asked Chekhov's sister, Maria Pavlovna Chekhova, for a volume of Chekhov's correspondence with Russian writers. In her letter, Tatyana Tolstaya mentioned,

"I am very grateful to you for this volume of Chekhov's correspondence.

I will read it from beginning to end, in the same way I have read everything that is written by Chekhov and about Chekhov. Our family — and I am not talking about my father — could give him something that he would greatly appreciate."

In her diary dated 19 April 1896, Tatyana Tolstoya wrote:

"My daddy read today from a new story by Chekhov. It was a bit unpleasant for me that his major character was a seventeen-year-old young woman. *Chekhov is a man to whom I could be very much attached in the future* [my italics — P.S.]. There is no one else I have ever met that has impressed me so much, from our first meeting, no one else in my life."

Chekhov in Yalta, mid–1901. Photographer Orlov.

Maxim Gorky. "Leo Tolstoy"

"You, you are a typical Russian man," Tolstoy addressed Chekhov. "Yes, you are a very typical Russian." And, smiling tenderly, he embraced Anton Pavlovich. Chekhov was embarrassed, and started talking in a low subdued voice about the Yalta Tartars and his dacha....

Tolstoy loved Chekhov, and every time he looked at him, it seemed that he caressed Anton Pavlovich with a tender glance. Once, when Anton Pavlovich was walking along an alley in the park, and Tolstoy, who was sick at the time, was sitting in an arm-chair, Tolstoy indicated Chekhov, and told me in a low voice,

"What a wonderful person he is! Very humble and very quiet. And he walks as if he were a young woman. He is a wonderful person!"

Ivan Bunin. "Chekhov"

I got to know Chekhov in Moscow at the end of 1895. I remember a few specifically Chekhovian phrases that he often said to me back then.

"Do you write? Do you write a lot?" he asked me one day.

I told him, "Actually, I don't write all that much."

"That's a pity," he told me in a rather gloomy, sad voice which was not typical of him. "You should not have idle hands, you should always be working."

And then, without any visible connection, he added, "It seems to me that when you write a short story, you have to cut off both the beginning and the end. We writers do most of our lying in those spaces. To make it short, you must write shorter."

Sometimes Chekhov would tell me about Tolstoy:

I admire him greatly. What I admire the most in him is that he despises us all; all writers. Perhaps a more accurate description is that he treats us, other writers, as completely empty space. You could argue that from time to time, he praises Maupassant, or Kuprin, or Semenov, or myself. But why does he praise us? It is simple: it's because he looks at us as if we were children. Our short stories, or even our novels, all are child's play in comparison with his works, and he looks at us in the same way as he would at some obscure Semenov. However, Shakespeare ... For him, the reason is different. Shakespeare irritates him because he does not write in the way that Tolstoy does.

You know, I recently visited Tolstoy in Gaspra. He was bedridden due to illness. Among other things, he spoke about me and my works.

Finally, when I was about to say goodbye he took my hand and said,

"Kiss me goodbye."

While I bent over him and he was kissing me, he whispered in my ear in a still energetic, old man's voice,

"You know, I hate your plays. Shakespeare was a bad writer, and I consider you even worse than him."

Sergei Semenov. "Chekhov Meets Leo Tolstoy"

During the time when Leo Tolstoy was working on his novel *Resurrection*, we anticipated a visit from Chekhov to Tolstoy's estate, Yasnaya Polyana. Everyone expected that Tolstoy would show his new work to Chekhov.

After hearing word of Chekhov's arrival late one evening, plans were made to read the first pages of *Resurrection* aloud for the first time the following day.

That afternoon, Lev Nikolaevich [Tolstoy] felt unwell and retired to his room to rest.

We, a group of five or six people, put ourselves in a cozy corner, and began to read. At first Chekhov, and then Gorbunov, read excerpts from the novel out loud.

Chekhov listened quietly and attentively, remaining silent. After reading for about two hours, we all trooped downstairs to the study to discuss the novel. Tolstoy was curious about what people would think of his new work.

Anton Pavlovich commented in a quiet voice that everything was very well-written. The court scene, he said, was especially realistically depicted. Chekhov had just recently performed jury duty, and had seen with his own eyes that the lawmakers did not truly care about the individual cases. Everyone was caught up in his own interests. Also, he said, it was correct for the merchant to be poisoned, and not killed in any other manner. Anton Pavlovich had recently returned from visiting the Siberian prisons on Sakhalin Island. He said that most of the female prisoners were sent to Siberia for poisoning. However, he did find one factual mistake, when Mrs. Maslova was sentenced to two years of hard labor.

"They do not give such short-term sentences," he said.

Tolstoy accepted this remark and corrected his mistake.

It was late at night when we left Tolstoy's study. The tea was not ready, so we went out for a walk.

Chekhov did not participate actively in the general conversation, but from time to time, he made small remarks. He was probably impressed by the astounding charm of Leo Nikolaevich, and was thinking about him.

At the end of our walk, Chekhov told us that he was very upset by A.

Suvorin. He did not like the way Suvorin expressed his political views in the newspapers, and he wanted to ask Leo Nikolaevich to write to Suvorin and ask him to stop this political audacity. Leo Nikolaevich was probably the only person who could influence Suvorin. Unfortunately, Chekhov did not get the chance to talk to Tolstoy. Instead, Sofia Andreevna, the wife of the writer, and Tatiana Lvovna, his daughter, spent the rest of the evening with us.

I don't know if Chekhov visited Yasnaya Polyana after this. Even though I visited Leo Nikolaevich quite often, I never met Chekhov there. Nonetheless, the members of the Tolstoy family had very good memories. His new works and publications were always read and discussed. Leo Nikolaevich spoke often about Chekhov and always admired his writing ability. He said that Chekhov "could create music with his words," and that one could reread his works again and again, which is not always possible with other acclaimed writers.

Tolstoy greatly admired Chekhov's "On the Cart," "My Little Darling" and the more recent "Wife." He said that these short stories could hardly be compared with works by other authors, and were some of Chekhov's best works.

Leo Nikolaevich also praised some parts of "My Life" by Chekhov. Tolstoy said that Chekhov was good at depicting the protagonist, Viazemsky, and the changes that took place when a man turned from a life of a noble to that of a laborer.

Tolstoy did not like the plays by Anton Pavlovich.

To him, the form of Chekhov's plays was wrong. To set the mood, you use a poem, not the entire play. A play should resolve a question that people cannot solve easily, and the playwright solves it through one of his characters according to his own beliefs. Chekhov, however, did not approach drama in this way.

When the first volume of the *Complete Works* of Chekhov was published by Marx, Leo Nikolaevich read and reread it. He enjoyed the Chekhovian humor, and came to call Chekhov one of the best humor writers.

"Drama" was Tolstoy's favorite story from this collection. He recommended it to others, and sincerely laughed every time he read it.

The last time I saw Anton Pavlovich was in the winter of 1904, the year of his death, on a visit to N. Teleshov in Moscow. It was a wonderful evening; several other writers were also present, namely Andreev, Gorky, Veresaev, Bunin, Serafimovich and Razumovsky.

Mr. Goltsev, the one who has recently died, gave a short speech about the philosopher Nietzsche. Anton Pavlovich looked very sick, and I could not believe that the man I was looking at was the one I had once known.

Anton Pavlovich was painfully thin. It seemed as if he did not have a chest — his suit simply hung off his frame, as if he had hangers for shoulders. In spite of his health, Chekhov appeared friendly, and was constantly joking. He spoke about himself and how he had started his literary career. Everyone listened, enraptured, to his anecdotes, and everyone was laughing, but it was a little sad, because we all understood that he would not live long.

In the spring of 1904, one of my books was published, and I sent it to Anton Pavlovich. I had found out from the newspapers that he was sick, and I felt uncomfortable about bothering Anton Pavlovich. Then, suddenly, I received a letter from him. It was written immediately after he left Moscow to go abroad. He thanked me for the book that I had sent him, and wished me all the best. He promised me to send me an autographed copy of one of his last books as soon as the doctors gave him permission to return home. However, only his body made it home from abroad.

The people of Moscow met him with a huge procession. Chekhov was buried at the Nove-Devichie Cemetery.

Anton Chekhov. "Letters"

Two reporters of the *Odessa News* came to the room of the Northern Hotel where I was staying. When they found out that writer Chekhov had just left, they almost cried from desperation. They had been told by their editor to write an interview with Chekhov.

They asked me if they could publish a totally invented conversation with Chekhov. I told them that it was out of the question, quite impossible. "Could we mention that we heard it from one of Chekhov's friends, namely you?" they asked.

I told them to leave me alone. I even regret that I am telling you now about all this. However, the *Odessa News* published an invented "Interview with Chekhov" on the next day, that is, 9 December, that read,

"Chekhov has just left Odessa. It will take him a few days to arrive in Moscow. It seems to us that he is heading home in order to die. He will be torn to pieces by both inquisitive readers and publishers after his long trip abroad. One of our friends gave him the advice to pretend he cannot speak, or — even better — to cut out his own tongue...." The piece continued as such throughout the fictional interview.

[A letter from A. Shcherbak to Chekhov, December 9, 1891. — P.S.]

Vassily Maklakov. "Memories of Chekhov"

[The interview was recorded and published by V. Ermilov.— P.S.]

When Mr. Maklakov visited Moscow, I interviewed him, and to begin with I asked him a few questions concerning his memories of Chekhov.

Maklakov met with Anton Pavlovich on a regular basis, since he had an estate only ten kilometers from Babkino, where Chekhov used to live. They became neighbors, and soon became friends. Their initial meeting happened earlier, in Moscow. They both had been invited to a big dinner, where Mr. Davydov, a famous literary artist at the time, was a chairman. I remember Chekhov was very friendly, but kept silent most of the time. I remember a very talkative and joyful Mr. Maklakov.

Yet their real friendship started after Chekhov visited Yasnaya Polyana, the estate of Leo Tolstoy.

Maklakov remembers the following:

I recollect how Tolstoy was very interested in Chekhov. Even earlier in Moscow when he was reading works of Chekhov, he had sympathy for the young writer. It was not a professional jealousy, but Tolstoy told me that Chekhov touched the inner, professional springs inside of his own soul. Tolstoy said, however, that there was a lack of deep messages in the early Chekhov stories, and the short story "The Gloomy People" was completely nonsense. Despite this, he greatly admired Chekhov's power as a writer and his descriptions of nature, and loved to read lengthy selections from Chekhov's works to his friends and family members.

When Chekhov came to visit Tolstoy, Tolstoy was filled with excitement. He met Chekhov in a friendly and welcoming way, but being a man of great willpower, he maintained his very strict daily schedule of work in the mornings and socializing in the afternoon.

We had several lengthy conversations during our long walks in the garden. Chekhov was embarrassed. He was charmed by Tolstoy and his personality. He could not get back to his normal state, saying, "I cannot put two words together in a sentence when I am around Tolstoy!"

We came to the entrance of Tolstoy's estate, Yasnaya Polyana. Chekhov looked at the gates, and commented that the entrance to the estate looked very nice. We then had some time for a more serious conversation. We spoke about Chekhov's works. Tolstoy was very pleased with Chekhov's *Sakhalin Island*; however, he was disappointed that Chekhov did not say anything about nature, the local people, or about the great power that you could get from the great Siberia.

Tolstoy asked, "Why did you not depict nature in your latest work?"

Chekhov did not answer. Probably he was too shy and did not know what to say. Chekhov was very humble, and he never showed himself to be an important man. Being humble was a key feature to his character, and he was embarrassed by the great power of Tolstoy.

Chekhov left without saying much. He lived his life without saying much as well; he just inserted casual remarks from time to time, and spoke very little over-all.

Yet, his remarks were always up to the point. Sometimes he could make a brief remark, and everyone around him would burst into laughter. At the same time, he could look serious and a little gloomy. He was very seldom joyful. Yes, he made great jokes, and kept us laughing, but he remained serious. His hobbies were also silent. First and foremost was fishing. He used to lie down, having a nap on the grass of a riverbank, and wait for the fish in complete silence.

The estate of Savva Morozov was about three kilometers from the Malakhov estate. Chekhov went there along with his wife Olga. The first thing he did when he arrived was to take his fishing rod and head for the river. You should have seen him — so childish and happy — when he caught his fish. He cried out, "Hurray, hurray!" He was very happy and joyful as if he had just won a lottery or bet.

Anton Pavlovich was well loved by all, and he loved others equally. He had a wonderful family and a wonderful house.

Alexander Sumbatov-Juzhin. "Three Meetings"

I saw Leo Nikolayevich Tolstoy for the last time when he visited Anton Pavlovich Chekhov in the spring of 1899.

I remember that Tolstoy's new novel, *Resurrection*, had been published in monthly installments in the *Niva Magazine*. I remember how Tolstoy came into Chekhov's small study, where he used to work. Anton Pavlovich had just come from Crimea to Moscow.

They did not have many serious conversations, and just exchanged several remarks. Chekhov asked, among other things, "Did censorship cut out a lot from your latest novel *Resurrection?*"

"No, nothing important," replied Leo Nikolaevich, and began asking Chekhov questions about Crimea.

Chekhov, with his regular way of talking to people, in a half-serious and half-joking way, replied that he had been bored by his life there.

"Why are you looking at me in such a serious and gloomy way?" Lev Nikolaevich suddenly demanded, looking at me.

Chekhov answered with a smile, "Mr. Sumbatov isn't gloomy because of you, but because of me."

"So why does he look so melancholy, anyway?" asked Tolstoy.

"It is because my latest play is not being performed at his theater, the Moscow Maly Theater."

"And why is it not performed there?" Leo Nikolaevich asked me.

I was one of the actors of the theater, and I wanted to explain in detail why we did not end up performing the new play, *Uncle Vanya*, despite all the actors' efforts, and the desires of the theater director, Telyakovsky.

Chekhov suddenly interrupted me and said, "A new theater is being born. A young, but very charming theater. And so I gave my new play to them. Therefore, please do not be angry at me."

Then, Chekhov smiled at me, with the very characteristic wrinkle between his eyebrows.

Leo Nikolaevich looked at me and smiled as well.

[Chekhov gave his play to the newly formed Moscow Art Theater, directed by his friend K. Stanislavsky. Chekhov's future wife Olga Knipper was one of the leading actresses of this new theater — P.S.]

Ivan Belousov. "About A.P. Chekhov"

Anton Pavlovich sat in front of a fireplace, as if looking at the flames. From time to time, he tore a piece of bark from the birch log in front of him, and threw it in the fireplace, obviously thinking intently about something.

His room maid called him from outside. He left for some time. Finally, he returned, and when we asked him for the reason of his delay, he reluctantly replied, "I had a medical patient waiting for me."

I was surprised. "So late? Was it a friend?"

Chekhov replied, "Not at all. I saw her for the first time in my life. She needed a medical prescription for a medicine that can be poisonous. They can only dispense it from a pharmacy with a prescription."

"You did not write it, did you?"

Anton Pavlovich did not answer anything. He sat at the fireplace, and threw in some more firewood. Then, after a long silence, he said quietly,

"Maybe this is better for her. I looked into her eyes, and understood that she had made a decision. There is a big river not far from here, and the Stone Bridge. If she jumps, she would be in great pain before she died. With the poison, she would be better off."

He was silent. We grew silent as well. Then, to change the subject, we began a conversation about literature.

Fyodor Fidler. "Mister Golikov"

Chekhov told Fidler his story about how he met the poet Polonsky.

The poet asked Mr. R. Golike, the managing editor at Suvorin's publishing house, to introduce him to Chekhov.

When Chekhov and Golike arrived at Polonsky's home, Golike handed his business card to the butler. As they entered, Golike did not personally introduce Chekhov, as he felt it was redundant.

Golike and Polonsky began a lively conversation during which Polonsky completely ignored Chekhov and spoke only to Golike. Chekhov was embarrassed by this, and finally Golike mentioned to Polonsky that Chekhov was the other man present in the room.

Polonsky was completely stunned by this remark. He jumped to his feet from his chair, faced Chekhov and said, "So, are you really Chekhov? I have been thinking all this time that you were Golike!" [This is a funny-sounding name since "golyi" means "naked" in Russian — P.S.]

Chekhov remembered that his friends call him "Mr. Golike" for some time after this incident, as a joke.

Evgeny Karpov. "Two Last Meetings with Chekhov"

I remember most clearly my two last meetings with Chekhov.

While living in Moscow in June of 1902, I visited an actress, V. Komissarzhevskaya, who was performing at the Fish-Tank Theater. After a brief conversation, just as I was about to leave, Chekhov came in. I had not seen him for about two years, and was very happy to see him again.

As Chekhov came through the door, we saw that he was completely out of breath. He had climbed the first four flights of the stairs in the hotel. Once he had finished greeting everyone, he was still visibly out of breath, and sat down on a sofa to rest.

Then Chekhov said, "I am quite tired. You stay in a rather tall building, Vera Fedorovna."

He began coughing. I still remember his crooked back, his bent head and his long arms hanging between his knees, as he sat on the sofa. His thin grey face looked exhausted. His wet hair stuck to his forehead. His eyes were focusing on one spot. He looked worn out, and quite ill.

Anton Pavlovich was coughing every time he spoke, covering his mouth with his handkerchief.

"Why are you staying in Moscow at this time of year, Anton Pavlovich? It is pretty hot around here in summer," I inquired.

Chekhov replied, "I cannot leave Moscow. My wife was ill, and now I have important business to complete. I was planning to leave the city all the time, but then I have had delay after delay day after day."

I asked him again, "Are you headed to Crimea, to your place?"

He replied, "Yes, probably I will go to Crimea. I want to go abroad, but

I can't because I have things to do here. Yet, it is so boring to stay in Crimea all the time."

Vera Komissarzhevskaya asked him, "Are you planning to write anything for the theater these days?"

Anton Pavlovich smiled back in a rather confused way, "Yes, I am writing right now, yet I am not writing what I would like to. It is a kind of boring to me. I should not write when I am like this. I would like to write a different kind of play, something optimistic and strong."...

Chekhov used to speak a great deal about the theater. He spoke of actors like Svobodin and Komissarzhevskaya, about his new play *The Seagull,* of V. Davydov in his play *Ivanov,* and about how his plays were staged by the Moscow Art Theater. He referred many times to the characters in his plays and how the actors were performing them. Chekhov said,

"Look at the play *Cherry Orchard,* for example. Is it my *Cherry Orchard?* Are they my characters? Except for two or three actors, they are not my characters at all. I am writing about our life. This can be a very grey and not very exciting life, but it is not a boring life. These actors make it a bore. Now I know I am not a boring author, after all, I have written several volumes of humorous short stories in the past; and now the literary critics make me out to be a writer who is constantly whining or complaining about life."

Anton Pavlovich spoke with great interest about Gorky, Andreev, and Kuprin and new trends in literature. He criticized the newest trend, the decadent writers, telling me that they were just imitating the foreign trends and tendencies in literature. Chekhov said,

"Symbolic and decadent writing should not exist in our Russian literature. It has neither a past nor a future. It will be forgotten shortly after it has been written. Yet, such realistic writers as Kuprin, Gorky and Andreev will remain in our literature, as people will read their works for a long time."

Our second meeting happened in the spring of 1904. One day as I was walking along the Yalta waterfront, I suddenly encountered Anton Pavlovich. He looked much better this time. The hot southern sun, the blue sky, and the soft Crimean air were a good influence on Chekhov. It seemed to me that he looked much younger. He was sunburned, and he had gained some weight. His eyes appeared full of energy. I could not believe my eyes when I saw him.

"You look good, in fact wonderful," I said as I shook his hand in greeting.

"It so happens, I feel better these days. And you — you came here for a vacation after a busy season?" said Chekhov.

"No, I came here to work. I am writing a new play," I said.

"It is not pleasant to work here. You should come to Crimea to drink good wine, to eat grapes, and enjoy life. You should enjoy the sea and nature," Chekhov told me with a playful smile.

"Have you been here for a long time?" I asked him.

"Yes, but I am planning to leave at the beginning of May," he said.

"Why are you heading away from this nice weather?" I asked Chekhov.

"I have to go to Moscow. My wife is there. Then, we will go abroad. I have no choice. The doctors are insisting on this. Besides, I would like to go abroad once again. Yes, I am leaving on May 1."

[Chekhov left for Germany, where he died in a few months.—P.S.]

Evgeny Yasinsky. "The Novel of My Life"

Chekhov stayed at the Loskutnaya Hotel, where I used to stay when in Moscow.

My room was exactly in front of his room. I had not seen him for a few years, but the color of his face, his overall complexion, was slightly darker now. Chekhov did not joke all the time as he used to. He now made selective intelligent jokes only from time to time, with what some refer to as "refined humor" which many could not understand at all.

Chekhov told me one day,

"You know what? I have been thinking about this. All of our short story writers should not submit their work to any journals or magazines. They should be able to be completely independent. Otherwise, the publisher can boast that he was discovered, trained and took care of them. Then many of us would die from tuberculosis and exhaustion at an early age, and healthy publishers would live until the ripe age of a hundred."...

One very cold night, writer Potapenko and Chekhov took me to a restaurant to celebrate a special occasion. When we arrived at the restaurant, we shared a bottle of warm port wine. After two glasses of wine, Chekhov's face turned red, but he remained sober.

Chekhov made wonderful remarks about our fellow diners that night. He said that some were tradesmen, some were bankers, and the rest were black market dealers. He told me that if he had not been a writer, he would have become a doctor specializing in psychiatry.

Vladimir Giliarovsky. "Optimistic People"

Me and journalist Chaplin visited Chekhov when he was in Melikhovo. I think it was the best time in the Chekhov's life: for his health was relatively good, he was in good spirits, he was filled with life, and enjoying nature.

He kept busy with his literary work; and taking care of his new estate, his garden and his pond. When he was not writing, he was always working the soil, moving trees or flowers around his backyard, or working as a doctor.

He would start receiving his visitors for the day by treating a crowd of local peasants who came to see "their doctor," as they used to say. He also had a lot of other visitors as well. Too many visitors, to be honest, especially beautiful ladies.

Afterwards we, his closest companions, would move with Anton Pavlovich to his bathhouse at the end of his property. It was a nice little house with several rooms, nicely furnished, with several sofas and beds.

We would have a wonderful time there: good wine, tea, and lots of reading and literary conversations from night till morning.

Ignaty Potapenko. "Interview"

Chekhov was always a calm person, with an even temper, and often a little reserved in his friendship with others. It seemed as if he was wearing iron armor; as if he was trying to protect his inner world from the peering eyes of others.

It was not the deliberate secrecy of one who wants to look or seem mysterious. No, it was something of quite a different nature. I believe I have found an explanation for this aspect of Chekhov's character. It seems to me that every second of his life was dedicated to the creation of literature. Every moment, from the moment he awoke to the moment he fell asleep, was devoted to creating literary works, working without ceasing.

Perhaps this work was at times subconscious, but he nonetheless felt the processes going on inside of him. This was the deeply personal process of creation. To always be a man of privacy was a rule he followed more than anyone else. He never wrote his stories in someone else's presence.

The process of creation for Chekhov could not tolerate the intrusion of others into his inner world, not even his friends. I could even say that — if we were to speak completely truthfully and honestly — that Chekhov did not have any friends at all. Many people considered themselves to be Chekhov's friends, especially after his death. I am sure they confided their deepest secrets to him with sincerity. However, he never revealed his secret life to anyone else at all.

When Chekhov traveled to another city, he did so swiftly and suddenly, without giving any warning to anyone, and just listening to his inner voice.

For example, during one of his stays in Moscow, we would plan to see a drama at the theatre. People would invite him, and he would promise to go. No matter what he had promised, if he got the desire to leave, he would leave without any notice.

Very often, he was simply tired of this busy, noisy and hectic Moscow life, and he would return to his quiet study in Melikhovo. Or perhaps he had gotten some new ideas connected with his literary work, and he would leave to work. Sometimes, he left because he wanted to get away from something or someone he did not like. I should tell you that people had a habit of bothering him with trifling worries when he stayed at the Grande Moscow Hotel.

People were often knocking at his door, and they were often people that he had never met in his life, who had no right to demand his time.

Some people believe that a writer belongs to the public. These people have a habit of coming to a writer unexpectedly and spending the entire day or evening together, talking about themselves, asking "clever" questions, or even sitting there in silence, making the writer entertain them. Sometimes the best thing in such cases is to say "goodbye," but Chekhov was too polite to do this. He was a stickler for having good manners all the time. No matter what.

People knew that when in Moscow, Chekhov stayed at the Grande Hotel, in Room 5. Later, they even called this room "The Chekhov Room." People knew this, and they often knocked at the door and visited him without any reason. It was even more difficult for Chekhov to say "no" to his friends than to the many strangers who visited him. If such a "friend" had nothing to do for the evening, he could come to Chekhov, and Chekhov didn't have the ability of hurting another person, and so had to spend his evening with his "friend."

For example, I know a novelist who considered himself "a good friend of Chekhov" whom Chekhov had described to me as someone "whose loud laughter made him unbearable."

Once, on a short business visit to Moscow, Chekhov told me in the first day that he was going back to Melikhovo at once.

"Why are you leaving?" I asked Chekhov.

"I just met Mr. N. He came to me in the street, as I was getting out of my cab. He embraced me, greeted me, and asked me if I was going to stay at this hotel. He promised to come and spend the evening with me. He asked me to say 'hello' to you. So please, meet him, greet him, and entertain him for me, since I have to leave."

I told Chekhov that we could find some other solution, for example, we could tell him we're busy, or go somewhere else, and write a note to Mr. N.

with our apologies. However, Chekhov did not change his mind. He told me,

"He will find me anyways at some other place, and will start laughing at me. He is a humoristic writer, and he likes to laugh at me, and this is his misfortune."

That day, he left for his estate in the country. I knew that Chekhov had urgent business at the *Russian Thought Magazine*. Five days later, Chekhov had to return to Moscow again to settle his business.

Also, Chekhov had a fear of making speeches, especially speeches of gratitude at different celebrations, when people congratulated and praised him for his work. He tried to avoid such situations at all costs.

Ivan Novikov. "Two Meetings with Chekhov"

I met Chekhov only twice, and we never spoke of literature. Yet, those meetings helped me to understand him as a writer. At the time, I had just begun to publish my own works, but I did not mention this in our conversation. Chekhov, like most writers, tended to avoid the topics of writing and literature, but he spoke a lot about everyday life.

I met him when I was going to Southern Moldova on a charity mission, and I visited to ask him a few questions about this.

We spoke about his favorite city, Moscow. Although it was January, it was warm in Yalta. Everyone was in summer clothes, with little roses blossoming all over, amidst many other flowers. It was obvious that he was missing the real frost and cold of mid-winter, and missing Moscow.

From the window of his study we could see that it was getting dark outside, but we sat and talked, and we did not stop to turn on the lights.

He spoke of his life as a student in Moscow. His manner of speaking

Chekhov in Yalta, 1902. Photographer Paleolog.

was much like his writing: in short phrases, thinking a little, and pausing from time to time in his speech. His voice was quiet and careful, but nonetheless, he spoke very clearly. In his gestures, likewise, his motions were scarce and small, sometimes hardly noticeable, and yet definite.

I noticed that Chekhov was very attentive and careful to others, even those whom he met only briefly or on occasion. This was not literary interest; he was interested in people as human beings.

During my second meeting with Chekhov I noticed this interest again. It went beyond the professional curiosity of a writer; it was a sincere and friendly interest in other people's lives, filled with compassion and warmth. I happened to meet him at one of the art exhibitions in Moscow. I noticed him in the gallery, but did not dare to approach him since we had met only casually once before, some time ago. He looked at me for a second, recognized me, and came over to me first.

"Look at this painting," he said. "I want you to see this one. This is really good."

I don't remember the name of the painter, but I remember what was on the canvas: a dark evening, some factory buildings in the background, a young worker with a little child held very carefully in his hands, with an awkward tenderness. I believe Chekhov aroused similar emotions as I got to know him through his work. His brilliance as a writer and his profound understanding of human nature were not immediately obvious, and yet his compassion, his tenderness, and his pity for other people were; he always wanted to help.

Alexander Serebrov-Tikhonov. "About Chekhov"

"Please, be my guest," Mr. Morozov said as he hopped out of the vehicle.

A tall, thin man climbed out and stood next to him. He held a dark suitcase, and wore a wrinkled bow tie. His face was long and narrow; his gray beard appeared to be covered with dust from a long trip. He took a few steps to the side, away from us, and coughed for a long time. He then unhooked a small flask from a strap on his shoulder and, in a perplexed manner, spat inside the flask. He silently stretched out his hand to me for a handshake, adjusting his eyeglasses. Looking down the hill towards a river winding through the valley in the distance, he said in a low voice,

"There should be pike in that river. Let's see if we can go fishing."

This man was Chekhov.

We discovered during his stay at the dacha that we had many common interests. We sat under a steep hill next to the dark river, passionately fishing. We caught lots of perch and sometimes a few pike. He was right: the river was a good spot for fish.

"What a wonderful sport, fishing!" Chekhov told me once while baiting his hook. "It is a sort of quiet insanity. You are happy with life, you are happy with yourself, and you are not a danger to anyone. And the most marvelous thing is that life is good!"

He took off his coat and glasses as he lay down on the grass in the sunshine. He was a wonderful fisherman: he always caught more fish than we did, although we sat next to each other.

We also had a small dog trailing us. As soon as we caught a fish, it would instantly bark at the river. Chekhov gave the fish to the dog, and it devoured the fish raw. Still alive, the perch would slap the dog's face with its tail as it struggled to gulp it down.

Chekhov said with disgust, "Look, this dog behaves exactly like our literary critics. I can say that for sure."

Alexander Goldenweiser. "Around Tolstoy"

Gaspra, Crimea, September 12, 1901.

Anton Chekhov was here yesterday. He does not look well; he appears old and he coughs perpetually. He speaks in short sentences, but they are always to the point. He gave us the account of his life with his mother during the winter months in Yalta. Tolstoy was very glad to see him.

Gaspra, Crimea, September 16.

Life flows on here, quietly and slowly. After dinner today, Obolensky and I took turns reading several of Chekhov's short stories out loud. Tolstoy greatly enjoyed reading Chekhov. The other day, I read him "The Tedious Story." Tolstoy was very happy with Chekhov's writing and his understanding of life. He especially praised the quality of writing and the original ideas in two novellas by Chekhov, *The Bet* and *The Steppe*.

January 2, 1902

Tolstoy made a remark:

"I love Chekhov very much as a person, and I love his writing, but I could not force myself to read his play *Three Sisters*.

"What is it all about? Generally speaking, contemporary writers talk of feeling drama. Drama, instead of simply telling us a person's life, should place a person in such a situation, should create such a knot — that when it is untied, the whole essence of a man becomes visible. I used to criticize Shakespeare. Yet every character is alive in his works, and it is clear to the audience why a character behaves the way that he or she does. During the time of Shakespeare, there were boxes on the scene with the letters, 'a house,' or 'a garden,' because all of the action on scene focused on the substance of the drama.

"Now, with contemporary moderns writers like Chekhov, it is exactly the opposite."

Leo Tolstoy. "Diary" (from Complete Works*)*

September 7, 1895.
Several visitors came to see me during the day. I had just finished the first chapters of my new novel, *The Resurrection*. I read it to Mme. Alsufieva, Taneev and Chekhov. I was disappointed with my writing. I am very upset with this novel, and I want to either stop writing it, or rewrite it completely.

During the last couple of days, I have been walking though the forest, selecting trees that I could give as a gift to neighboring peasants and farmers.

I think about death more and more often, think of how it can take me away.

November 29, 1901. Gaspra.
For almost two months, I have not read anything. I have been feeling unwell. However, now I am slightly better. I'm still troubled some by rheumatic pain and weakness.

I am glad that Gorky and Chekhov visited me. I have been thinking about important things, and here is what I have to write down.

Number One. I mix up people's names these days, my daughters, my sons, and some of the visitors, because in my memory I do not remember the face, but mainly the spiritual essence of a person. I think about every person as a separate being, but some of them are very similar to me. However, I understand myself.

Number Two. On the subject of literature. I've been talking to people about Chekhov, and I understood that he has taken literary forms to a new level. He developed a completely new form in literature. This is Chekhov's great merit.

Vladimir Simov. "From Memories of Chekhov"

He was one of the patrons of the Russian Opera Company at the Bolshoy Theater.

We have all heard accounts of Chekhov among his friends in Moscow, or in Melikhovo, or in Yalta; we all know of his literary acquaintances from their memories. However, there was another, smaller, group of people that Chekhov often visited, and spent time with. This part of his biography has never been written before.

In order to imagine this part of his life, you have to take your imagination to Moscow in the 1880s.

The situation with our Opera was very disheartening. There was too much bureaucracy at the Bolshoy Theater, the performances were weak at best, and the Opera Company was poorly managed. Then, all of a sudden, the Private Russian Opera Company had been created, and the Bolshoy improved greatly. Many famous visual and literary artists were invited to make set designs, among them people such as Vasnetsov, Polenov, Vrubel, Korovin, and Serov.

We all enjoyed the visits of Anton Chekhov. He always brought joyful moments to our company. He joked constantly every time he spoke, like breathing. He was a very refined person full of humor, very sensitive to true beauty. We all felt great sympathy towards Chekhov. He was amiable and well liked by everyone. As soon as he entered, he would go to and warmly greet his brother. Then he would walk around and behind the scene, climb the ladders at the back, and offer his opinions, making very acute and sharp remarks about the set design despite not being a professional artist.

For some brief minutes, he always read us a few of his new humorous and witty short stories. We all listened to his deep voice, rich in overtones, and were almost dying from laughter. The narrator himself smiled slightly with the corners of his mouth, and looked in a friendly way at his listeners and friends. Anton Pavlovich used a lot of pauses; he imitated different voices, gestures, and his stories were so hilarious that we laughed without pause until our stomachs cramped with the pain of laughing so much.

Mr. Levitan, the most emotional among us, would fall on the floor on his back, laughing loudly, and waving his arms in the air. Obviously, the great artistic talent and the high quality of Chekhov's writing added to this scene. Shortly after this in 1892, Chekhov bought his new estate in Melikhovo. There he spent his summers and winters, year after year. He had dreamt about life in the country for a long time, and so for several years he lived out his dream in Melikhovo until his illness forced him to move south to Crimea.

Mikhail Nesterov. "The Old Days"

It is always pleasant and a little bit sad to speak about Levitan. Not only a wonderful artist, he was also a great friend of mine, and was a real man. My friendship with him started many years ago, when we were students of the Moscow College of Visual Art.

He was a young Jewish teenager, very handsome, similar in appearance to the young Italian men from ancient paintings of Napoli or the old squares of Florence. All spoke about him as a "great talent."

Levitan was among the charity students, and people told fantastic stories about him. They said that, although he had great talent, he was poor as a pauper, and that he sometimes did not have a place to sleep the night.

At one of the students' exhibitions, Peter Tretiakov bought a small oil painting by Levitan, "A Road in the Forest," where our common friend Nikolai Pavlovich Chekhov *[Anton Chekhov's brother — P.S.]* had added a woman's figure. It was a regular practice at the time, where several painters could work on the same painting. Such was the case with Levitan and Nikolai Chekhov.

The time of need passed, and the art lovers in Moscow bought works by Levitan more and more often. One image stands out from that time. It was late at night in the middle of winter. I remember a small hotel room, with three windows facing the street. There was a dim lamp and several unfinished paintings in the room, next to the walls. The sick man lay moaning from pain in the otherwise silent night. Several friends, mostly other painters, took turns standing watch at the bed of the sick painter Levitan. They spent the whole night with him.

In the early hours of the morning, a tall, young doctor came by. His name was Anton Pavlovich Chekhov.

Levitan eventually got better, and in the spring went to Crimea. The beauty of the southern nature, the Black Sea, and the blooming flowers simply enchanted him.

Leonid Sulerzhitsky and Vasily Kachalov. "Interview"

We had a stage worker N. who pretended that he was a leading actor of the Moscow Art Theater. He also pretended that he was a great novelist.

One day, he asked me to give his manuscript to Chekhov for his opinion. I could not reject him, and so passed on the manuscript to Chekhov. A few days later, Chekhov returned the manuscript to me and said,

"That novel by N.! Please, tell him that he should never write anything ever again."

Chekhov thought for a little while, and then asked me, "Please tell me, is this N. a woman, by any chance?"

"Why are you asking me this, Anton Pavlovich?"

"Women are hard working, and they can achieve something with lots of work."

"No, he is not a woman," I replied,

"Then, please tell him never ever to write anything else in the future."

I was too polite to tell this to N., and so I told him that this novel did not fit the profile of the *Russian Thought Magazine.*

Then Mr. N. told me, "So what? Then I will send it to the *World Life.* They will publish it there."

Anton Pavlovich was right — when I read that lengthy manuscript by N., I was ashamed that I had passed it to Anton Pavlovich to read — it was complete nonsense.

Mikhail Chlenov. "A.P. Chekhov and Culture"

From the first year at the university, Chekhov displayed strong literary interest and attraction towards literature. His brothers, Alexander and Nikolai, who had come to Moscow before him, supported him in this. Alexander submitted some of his jokes to the humor magazines, and Nikolai was a student at the School of Art, and was illustrating literary works.

Chekhov wrote in his autobiography, "I started publishing my short stories when I was in my first year of the university, and my literary work became my permanent profession in the early 1880s."

During the last three years of his student life, Chekhov wrote a lot, and supported his low-income family with his literary work. Chekhov wrote a great deal at the time. For example, his brother Ivan Pavlovich told me that Chekhov had to send one short story every Monday just to St. Petersburg, plus some other work. In spite of all this, Chekhov did not quit medical school, and attended all lectures and clinics....

People write a lot about Chekhov. However, in their memories people neglect to mention the most important feature of this great artist: his deep, inner grace.

He did not come by his genius through upbringing, or education, but by his own rich character. This inner culture of Chekhov's was amazing, especially keeping in mind that he was born into a poor farmer's family.

"It was difficult for me to move up the social ladder," Chekhov told me several times. "Just imagine, by my origin I was a peasant by birth, and my grandfather was a serf. Look at Levitan — he has such a great history and a powerful, ancient culture in his family, and it is much easier for him than for me."

In spite of this, I have rarely seen a person who could so respect science and education, and believe in the happy future of the mankind. He wrote to me in one of his letters,

"I don't belong to those literary artists who hate science. Personally, I genuinely love science."

As we know, he was simultaneously both a writer and a doctor. He was grateful to medicine, and was interested in medical science to the last days of his life. He very diligently subscribed to all medical journals, and followed all recent discoveries in medicine. Even when he lived in Yalta, he dreamt of coming to Moscow and, with a group of friends, founding an institute of postgraduate studies for medical practitioners. Not only medicine and the sciences, but also all other facets of human culture interested him — that is, theater, visual art, agriculture, transportation, and any other field of technology. For example, he was fascinated in reading about huge ocean liners at one point.

I met Chekhov for the first time in 1897, when he left *The New Time* magazine, and began working in the most prestigious literary journals. He was a very well known writer at the time.

Between our first meeting and his death only several years later, I recollect him to be a very active social figure, with established views on life — views that he never renounced. At the same time, Chekhov was a very humble man, and did not like to talk about politics. Yet everyone knows the infamous story of when he denounced his position as a member of the Academy of Sciences after they expelled Maxim Gorky from its membership. Have you heard of many people who have done a similar heroic deed?

Nikolai Panov. "About Chekhov's Portrait"

"Please come tomorrow. I'll spend the day thinking over my future work, and you can paint my portrait," Anton Pavlovich told me.

It was a hot and suffocating day. The windows were all flung open, but there wasn't even the hint of a breeze, not even the slightest wind coming in from outside.

Chekhov sat at his writing desk, immersed in his thoughts.

I gazed at his tired, mournful eyes, trying to make a sketch of his head tilting to one side.

His mind was on his work, but his face looked drawn, and his features — it seemed to me — were dissolving into the air. He had a kind of curve in his spine, and his entire posture indicated that he was exhausted. He had lost a lot of weight, and he looked gaunt.

His posture, including his tilted head, his tired face, the tense movements of his thick hands — all this asserted that this was a person listening to his inner voice, to a voice which a strong, healthy man would never hear, due to the process of the illness going on inside of him.

It was very difficult for me to look upon the features of a person so very sick. Yet, at the same time, the experience was invaluable for the entire country.

"Have you found anything worth painting?" he asked me about his portrait.

I looked at his somber face and replied, "No. It does not look anything like what I wanted to depict. You seem too sad and tired in this portrait."

"Then let us leave it as it is. Please, do not change anything. The first impression is always the most truthful."

Alexander Pleshcheev. "Visiting A.P. Chekhov"

I heard the name Chekhov for the first time from Mr. Leikin, who published the small humor magazine *The Fragments* in St. Petersburg.

One day, Leikin came to the editor of a national daily newspaper, the *St. Petersburg News*, boasting in a happy voice,

"I have discovered a new talent, a new Shchedrin. Just read the latest issue of *The Fragments*. Just look at the stories by Chekhov! I recommend him to you!"

Shortly after, the first serious short story by Chekhov appeared in the *St. Petersburg News*.

Dmitry Grigorovich, an old and well-known writer, once asked me, "Have you read the story by Chekhov in the *St. Petersburg News*?"

He mentioned the title of the story, and if I am not mistaken it was "The Hunter."

Grigorovich visited Suvorin [a major publisher — P.S.] and read him "The Hunter." Suvorin at once understood the great artistic talent of the author and demanded the address of the new writer. At the time, the magazine *The New Time*, published by Suvorin, was the most prominent literary magazine in the country. It had a section, "Saturday Short Stories," where they published a new short story every Saturday.

Anton Chekhov started visiting Pleshcheev, getting to know him better after numerous visits to the editorial office. They established a very friendly relationship between them — my father, editor Alexey Pleshcheev, and the young, aspiring writer, Anton Chekhov.

If you read their correspondence, you will find out that it was full of deep, mutual respect. At the end of the 1880s Anton Pavlovich invited my father to visit the summer cottage he had rented at Luka, in the Sumy region of Southern Russia.

"All my circle would otherwise consist of young people and your presence would be greatly appreciated and welcomed," Chekhov wrote to my father.

After Pleshcheev paid him a visit, Chekhov wrote again,

"I tell you this with utmost sincerity: the time I that have spent in your company here was one of the best and most interesting in my life."

The warm relationship between my father and Anton Pavlovich gave me the opportunity to spend some time together with Chekhov. We soon became friends. Our meetings became regular — we met at my father's editorial office, at the theater, etc. Sometime, I visited Moscow, and then I always visited the Chekhov family. We spent numerous evenings at Chekhov's house, or at restaurants, together with friends, actors, writers and journalists.

Anton Pavlovich liked journalists and you see this in many short stories by him where he described the lives of editors and journalists. Chekhov liked actors as well, and actors repaid him with the same love.

Chekhov's popularity grew, but he was completely indifferent to it. He remained the same Chekhov at the beginning of his career, as when his fame grew and he became one of the best writers in the country. He was the same humble man. He could not be different.

However, he would be in a slightly gloomy mood most of the time. I noticed that, even at the most joyful moments, Anton Pavlovich remained a bit melancholy. Maybe it was a consequence of the childhood he had spent in poverty, or the concerns of the illness that he had developed and monitored as a doctor.

I would like to repeat that the young Chekhov, and Chekhov in his middle age — they were the same man. His fame grew, his position in life changed, but his attitude towards his friends did not change at all.

Several years later, in 1901, I visited Chekhov in Yalta. He was laughing to himself, making jokes, and showed me his cottage. The cottage was not situated in Yalta itself, but in the village of Alupka in the suburbs. I should say that all of Alupka is made up of several houses along Alupka Street, which goes up from the town of Yalta. He had a small house on Alupka Street, with a nice view of the mountains above and the blue sea in the distance below.

The garden was young and seemed tiny at the time, but by now it has probably grown and enclosed the house from the sun.

Anton Pavlovich liked Yalta, and was happy there; however, he was tortured by thoughts about his tuberculosis.

He told me that the illness was progressing in his lungs, and the entire time he would pull out a small glass container from his pocket, and spit there, and then looked inside to examine it.

We were sitting in the tiny study of Chekhov; it was an almost empty room. On his desk, you could see several manuscripts, books, and many portraits of people such as Tolstoy, Gorky, Kuprin, Pleshcheev, Polonski, Komissarzhevskaya, and Vasnetsov. Above the fireplace hung a landscape by Levitan. It depicted nature late at night, and from the distance it appeared as a dark green spot on the wall. Chekhov told me that he loved Levitan dearly; there was a sign on the wall, "Do not smoke," to preserve the image.

Most of the time, Chekhov lived by himself. The man who served him lived in a tiny house in the back field.

When I came, I heard the phone ring in the house, which showed that Yalta had a cultural life.

Chekhov met me with a smile. "Can you imagine that I have just received a letter from Belousov? He recently died. He writes a letter and dies, and then I receive it as if from another world!"

Chekhov loved Yalta. He said, "It is a nice, beautiful city. Even in December, you have days as nice as today. But sometimes it is too dull and boring. If you do not have anything to work on, in a few days you will be ready to hang yourself."

At that time, Chekhov was going to go to Moscow, where they planned to stage his play *Three Sisters*. Then he would go to the south of France, to its southern seashore, but he also dreamt of making a trip to Africa.

"I sit for too long a time in one place, and then I want to travel. So far, we have been to Caucasus in Georgia, and I have already been there three times. Sometimes, I take a steamboat to Gurzuf. I like it very much."

Anton Pavlovich used to work early in the morning as a rule, until about 12 o'clock. This was an exception among the writers that I knew — most of our writers worked at night, and often very late.

One day, we decided to go to Gurzuf. It was about three hours by horse cart. We got up early in the morning and hired a cab. The road wound along the seashore, and we admired the beautiful sea vistas. At the time, Gurzuf was one of the most beautiful spas in Crimea, with elegant hotels and restaurants. We spent a wonderful day there.

Alexey Suvorin. "Diary"

1898, April 28.

I had dinner at Ivan Shchukin's house. Several people were present: Chekhov, Tchaikovsky, Dr. Botkin, and Dr. Roberti. The dinner lasted until ten. Ivan Ivanovich treated us in a very hospitable manner, as a true Muscovite.

After dinner, we had a lovely conversation, exchanging our views. Chekhov told me he thought they were all very nice people....

Saturday. Today Chekhov was leaving Moscow and going north, to St. Petersburg. Several people saw him off at a railway station....

After St. Petersburg, Chekhov was going abroad, to Paris. I gave him gifts — a small pillow for his travel and golden cuff links, which I had bought earlier at a jewelry store on Rue de la Pain in Paris.

Lydia Avilova. "A.P. Chekhov in My Life"

"Do you remember the first time we met?" Chekhov asked me. "I must admit, I was deeply interested in you. It was quite serious for me; I truly loved you. I believe there has never been another woman in the world that I loved so much. You were so beautiful, so fresh and attractive, and I loved you so passionately that you never left my thoughts."

He sat on the sofa with his head tilted back on the cushions; I sat in the armchair in front of him. Our knees almost touched. His face was strict, and his eyes looked cold, as he spoke in his deep, wonderful voice:

"I loved you once. Did you know this?"

He took my hand, and then put it back down.

"Oh, you have such cold hands," he sighed.

He quickly stood up and looked at his watch. It was two-thirty in the morning.

"I barely have time to eat, then talk to my publisher Suvorin before I leave. We will never see each other again."

I stood up slowly and took a few steps to the door to see him off.

"We will not see each other again," he repeated.

I lived on the fourth floor, and the stairs were well lit. Standing at my door, I watched him walking down the stairs.

I called his name, "Anton Pavlovich!"

He stopped and lifted his head. Fleetingly, he glanced at me, and then ran quickly down the stairs.

I did not say another word....

One night, I sat in the study of my husband, Mikhail, reading a book. My brother, who had come to visit us from Moscow, was playing on the grand piano in the living room, and my husband was writing something at his desk.

Suddenly, I heard the piano lid slamming, and my brother Alex came into the room. He said,

"I cannot bear to be bored like this. Why did I come to visit you to St. Petersburg — to be bored? Let us go out!"

Mikhail looked to at the clock and said, "Look at the time; it is almost twelve o'clock at night. Everything is closed. You are out of your mind!"

"It is still before midnight; we have time. If we hurry, we can still find something."

My brother grabbed my hand and began pulling on it.

"But where can we go?" I protested.

My brother persisted, saying, "Today Mr. Suvorin is having a masquerade ball. We will be just in time."

"What would we do for costumes? And masks? We have neither!"

"Since you ask, I will find something, for you. This is nothing." With these words, he pulled me to the bedroom. He said, "Get dressed. I will wait for you."

I dressed myself, but as we were going towards the door, my husband said, "I am not going anywhere. And you are both out of your mind!"

My brother jokingly answered, "Be quiet, you office rat."

There was a small store that rented costumes at the corner of Vladimir-skaya Street, but it was closed. Alex knocked at the door loudly.

"What are you doing? The police will come," I implored him.

I was right: in a few minutes, the policeman came. Alex was unperturbed. He whispered something in the officer's ear, and then it was the policeman's turn to knock at the door. The door was immediately opened by the store owner, a woman wearing a nightgown.

The policeman asked her to help us, and even helped me out of the cab and saluted us.

I did not see too many costumes in the dimly lit room. For me, there were only a small, black mask and a matching domino costume. Nonetheless, I was happy to find even these at this time of night.

"Please do not leave me by myself," I told my brother on the way to the masquerade.

The theater was so packed with people that you could only move together in the direction of the crowd.

I found a couple of walnuts in my pocket — since I kept them there for giving my children treats during the day — I put them in my mouth. This way, if I were to meet any of my friends, they would not recognize my voice.

My brother warned me, "Be careful to not swallow the nuts. Oh, look! On your right!"

In the corner stood Chekhov, looking above people's heads.

"I suppose that now I am free to go," my brother said smiling, before disappearing into the crowd.

I came up to Anton Pavlovich and said, "I am so happy to see you."

"But you don't know me, mask," he replied.

I trembled with excitement of meeting him here. He took me by the hand, and we went around the hall. Mr. Nemirovich-Danchenko appeared, and said,

"Hello there, I see you have found yourself a pretty lady for company!"

Chekhov bent to my ear and whispered, "If they call you by name, do not reveal yourself."

I tried to change my voice and replied, "No one knows me in this place."

Mr. Nemirovich came up to us again and said, "So, how are you?"

Chekhov ignored him, and told me quietly, "Let us go to another room and have some champagne."

We pushed throughout the crowd with difficulty, went up the empty stairs, and found ourselves inside the theater hall. Chekhov said, "Here we are, it is nice and quiet here."

I was afraid that Chekhov would call me by my name or somehow reveal my identity.

"Do you know my name?" I asked him. "Can you guess who I am?"

He smiled and said, "My play will be performed soon for the first time."

I said, "I know, the title is *The Seagull*."

"Are you going to come to the first night?"

"Yes, I will."

"Then be careful and pay attention. I will give you a signal from the scene. But pay attention, and do not forget."

He took my hand and pressed it into his.

I asked him, "What are you going to tell me from the scene?"

"A lot."

We took the stairs up to a theater balcony. The box belonged to Mr. Suvorin, the theater director. In it, there was a small table with a bottle and several glasses on it.

"Let us sit and drink some champagne," said Chekhov

"I cannot understand you. How can you tell me anything from the scene? How will I understand that these words relate to me? You don't even know my name."

"You will understand everything. It is stiflingly hot in here. Let us have a drink."

I came closer to the mirror on the wall.

"Would you like to fix your makeup?" he asked.

I was really looking at his reflection in the mirror. He sat with his back to me, and did not look in my direction. I did not take off my mask, though.

We had a drink.

"Do you like the title of my new play, *The Seagull*?" Chekhov asked.

"Yes," I answered.

"*The Seagull*. You know, it makes a very distinct noise when it sings," he said.

"Why were you looking above the people's heads? Are you bored being among them?" I asked him.

He said, "You have guessed wrong. I am never bored with people."

"So what will you tell me from the set? I have some doubts — maybe you will put me in the play as one of your protagonists?"

"No," Chekhov said.

"Besides, you do not know my real identity and my real name," I said smugly.

"Let us go downstairs," Anton Pavlovich suggested.

We first went for a walk around the hall, where Chekhov asked me,

"Tell me about yourself. Tell me about your new *roman*. [*It sounds like a pun, because "roman" in French, as well as in Russian, literally means "romance," but also means "novel."— P.S.*]

I replied to him, "I am not writing a novel at present."

He said,

"I meant the romance of your life. Have you ever truly loved someone?"

I saw the masks and heard the orchestra from a distance. My head was spinning, I was nervous and my heart beat loudly in my chest. I nudged Anton Pavlovich with my shoulder, gazed across the short distance into his eyes, and said,

"I have loved only you, my darling."

CHAPTER FIVE

Chekhov and Theater

Introduction

For me, narrative prose is a legal wife, while drama is a posturing, boisterous, cheeky and wearisome mistress.... I am writing my novel, by and by, and I feel good when I am writing it. I feel as if I am lying down on a pile of freshly cut hay in my garden, having a rest after a nice dinner.

> — A Chekhov. "Letters." His letter to A.N. Pleshcheev,
> January 15, 1889

IVANOV (1887)

I visited the Korsh Theater twice, and both times Mr. Korsh asked me to write a play for his theater. I replied, "Will do, with pleasure."

The actors told me that I could write a good play, because I play on their nerves. I told them, "Thank you."

> — Chekhov. "Letters." His letter to M. Kiseleva,
> September 13, 1887

Chekhov took a thin notebook from the desk, and while gesticulating and changing his voice, read a very lively and amusing little play to us. He read to us as a great actor would.

> — A. Lazarev-Gruzinsky. "A.P. Chekhov"

SEAGULL (1898)

The Seagull is the only contemporary play that interests me as a theater director, and you are the only contemporary dramaturge who is of great interest to our theater.

> — Anton Chekhov. "Letters." From V. Nemirovich-Danchenko
> to Chekhov, May 12, 1898

In spring of 1900, we had a great holiday in our house. We had great celebrations that continued for two weeks. In these days, the Moscow Art Theatre visited us with its complete cast, including its great directors, Stanislavsky and Nemirovich-Danchenko.

> — Maria Chekhova. "From the Distant Past"

THREE SISTERS (1901)

Can you imagine, I wrote a play? ... It was very difficult for me to write it. Three female characters in it, each one a unique personality, and

A. Chekhov, winter 1903-1904.

all of them general's daughters! The action takes place in a provincial town, something like Perm', and the environment is full of artillery officers.
— Anton Chekhov, "Letters." His letter to M. Gorky,
October 16, 1900

After each rehearsal we love your play more and more. We remember you often, and we are struck by your sensitivity and your knowledge of the theater, the kind of theater of which we can only dream.
— Anton Chekhov, "Letters." A letter from K. Stanislavsky
to Chekhov, December 29, 1901

During the final dress rehearsal of *Three Sisters,* I sat in the theater and shed tears. Their acting was excellent.
— Maria Chekhova. *"My Memories."*

Three Sisters is performed wonderfully. This is a triumph. When the actors perform the play, they make it better than I wrote it.
— Anton Chekhov, "Letters." His letter to L. Sredin,
September 24, 1901

CHERRY ORCHARD (1902–1903)
   I did not have such a great summer for a long time. I go fishing every day, five times a day. The fishing here is not bad at all, and it is so great to sit on the river bank that I cannot express it with words....
   I have not started writing the new play yet. I am just thinking it over.
— Anton Chekhov, "Letters." His letter to K. Stanislavsky,
July 18, 1902

I have just finished reading your play. I am completely shaken and cannot recover. I am completely delighted. I think this play is the best you have ever written. I heartily congratulate its brilliant author. I feel and appreciate every word.
— Anton Chekhov, "Letters." K. Stanislavsky's telegram
to Chekhov, October 20, 1903

I received so much praise on January 17, during the first performance of *The Cherry Orchard,* that I cannot come to my senses even now.
— Anton Chekhov, "Letters." His letter to
F.D. Batuiushkov, January 19, 1904

The Moscow Art Theater will take up the best pages in the book that will one day be written about contemporary Russian theater.
— Anton Chekhov. "Letters." His letter to
V. Nemirovich-Danchenko, November 24, 1899

Konstantin Stanislavsky. "Works. My Life in Art"

   The actors of the Moscow Art Theatre performed in the way that Chekhov taught us. This happened because we found a new approach to performing Chekhov. He is a very special, unusual artist, and this new approach to reading his plays was our major contribution to art. We knew that Chekhov spoke to us about Humanity....

This was the spring of our theatre, the greatest and the most joyful period of my life. We came to visit Anton Pavlovich in the Crimea. We decided the following: If Anton Pavlovich couldn't visit us due to his illness, then we could visit him, as we are all in good health. We came to Yalta from Sevastopol. Almost all the literary world was waiting for us there: Bunin, Kuprin, Mamin-Sibiriak, Chrikov, Staniukovich, and Elpatievsky. Maxim Gorky also lived in the Crimea because of the tuberculosis he had.... There were many artists and musicians, in addition to the writers, and amongst them was young Sergei Rakhmaninov. We had daily dinners at Chekhov's house, and we all spoke about literature....

In April, 1901, Chekhov came to Sevastopol, about 100 kilometers from Yalta, to see the performance of his latest play, *Uncle Vanya*, by the Moscow Art Theater. K. Stanilsavsky, the company's artistic director, remembered: "It was an extraordinary success. The author was called to the stage an unlimited number of times, without any restraint. Chekhov was happy with the performance this time.... During the intermission, he came backstage to my room and made only one writer's comment on Astrov's departure: 'He is whistling, you should hear him whistling! Uncle Vanya is crying, and Astrov is whistling!' ... Such a remark could be done only by a great man of the theater!"...

Chekhov sent a small scene once to the theater. It was a real treasure.... on another occasion, he sent a wonderful, brilliant monologue in the fourth act of *Three Sisters,* about two pages long, on what a wife means for a provincial gentleman. Suddenly, we received a note that the whole monologue should be deleted, and replaced only by the words, "A wife is a wife."...

In April 14–23, 1901, the actors of the Moscow Art Theater and a group of young writers, among them Gorky, Bunin, Mamin-Sibiriak and others, visited Chekhov in Yalta, and gave several performances. A noisy group of writers and actors spent most of the time during this week in Chekhov's backyard. In one corner of the backyard there was a literary discussion; the other group of people behaved like young boys and threw stones; in the third group Ivan Bunin *[later, Russian Nobel prize winner in literature — P.S.]* did some impersonations, and next to him, as usual, Chekhov was simply dying from laughter. Parties like this were held in Chekhov's house almost every day.

Vladimir Nemirovich-Danchenko. "From the Past"

Chekhov's artistic ideas and his influence on our theatre were enormous, despite the fact that he only spent five brief years at the theater.

One of our greatest writers worked together with our theater, and we worked so closely, as if we were one collective artist, sharing the same ideas and aspirations. Fate itself pushed us close to each other, to create a new artistic movement, one that cannot be forgotten in the theatre history....

As to the beauty, unity and the maturity of the form, *Three Sisters* is considered now the best among the Chekhov plays. At the time of production, the theater directors already knew how to convey subtle movements of the Chekhov plays.... Finally, all members of the Art Theater were filled with mutual love for Chekhov....

All of the theatrical and literary Moscow public gathered in the theater for the performance *[The Cherry Orchard, on January 17, 1904 — P.S.]*. They wanted to congratulate their favorite writer and dramaturge. After the performance, they called him and invited him to join them. At first he refused, but people came to his apartment and convinced him to come. It was a very touching and sincere celebration.

Alexandra Glama-Mesherskaya. "Memories"

"This is Anton Pavlovich," my friend quietly told me. And then, looking into the dark corner, he whispered in a meaningful voice,

"This is Chekhov himself."

There were many actors in the room, and the sounds of laughter and joyful voices spilled out the door to greet me. Everyone was having a really good time. Someone was playing with children's toys in a dark corner of the room. I did not recognize him, and asked one of my friends.

At this point, I saw a mechanical toy moving across the floor at me, and I noticed Anton Pavlovich walking towards us. The other actors told me later that all of Chekhov's pockets were packed with mechanical toys. Anton Pavlovich explained, apologizing, that he was a doctor, and that earlier that day he had some children among his patients, and that they stuffed his pockets with toys.

"Look at this! I have too many toys," continued Chekhov. "One, two, three."

The toys moved across the floor.

At the rehearsals of his new play, *Ivanov*, he sat in the hall, but he never interrupted the director's work. He never made a single remark on the actors at all. I never saw a more humble author in my life. The actors repaid him with great love and attention. At the time, all of us, including Mr. Korsh, the theater's owner, were thrilled to have this young author.

Anton Pavlovich was not very satisfied with his play, and later on, during its production in St. Petersburg, he made several major changes to the final scenes.

Several days after opening night, I sent him a photo with an inscription. Shortly after, I received a reply from Chekhov. He wrote:

> 15 November, 1888.
> My dear Alexandra Yakovlevna. I apologize for not answering you at once to thank you for your lovely photo. We've had terrible weather, and the doctors would not let me out of the house. So I shall wait for the weather to improve, and in the meantime, I am sending you my photo. If you do not like it, just throw it under your desk. If one might speak about a person's character based on hand-writing, I would say that you are very gentle, noble, and generous. I hope that you are not really angry. I admire you, and I remain entirely devoted to you. Anton Chekhov.

After *Ivanov*, we performed a couple of his one-act plays, *Bear* and *Proposal*.

He was very popular at our theater.

Vsevolod Meyerhold. "Diary"

One of the actors remarked that it would be nice to have the singing of frogs, the clattering of grasshoppers, and the barking of dogs in the background in *The Seagull*.

Anton Pavlovich asked him in an irritated voice, "Why would we need all this?"

The actor answered, "To make it more realistic."

Chekhov smiled and after a short silence replied, "What do you mean by 'realistic'? Theatre is a form of art. Our painter, Kramskoi, has a wonderful painting with striking faces in it. What if you were to cut off one of the painted noses, and replace it with a real, human nose? The nose would be real, but the painting would be spoiled by it."

Alexander Pleshcheev. "The Staging of Ivanov"

I had very good memories of the staging of *Ivanov*, first in Moscow and then in St. Petersburg. *Ivanov* was the first major play by Anton Pavlovich that was staged on the professional stage. Vladimir Ivanovich Davydov, the theater director and leading actor, told me some more details about this.

One day, Chekhov visited the Korsh Theater and went behind the curtains to talk with the theater director Davydov in the dressing room. Chekhov looked kind of embarrassed, as if he wanted to say something, but he did not have enough determination to start talking.

"Anton Pavlovoch, if you have something to say, please just tell me. Am I right?" Davydov asked Chekhov.

"No, I just came to say hello," he heard in reply.

"Please, tell me that I am right." Davydov insisted.

"No, I came with no particular business, just to say hello."

Anton Pavlovich hesitated for awhile, and then, just before Davydov went out to perform his scene, Chekhov pulled out a notebook and put it into Davydov's pocket, and said,

"Please do not look at it now. Read it later. Goodbye, Vladimir Nikolaevich. You can give me your opinion later."

So, later during that day, Davydov wanted to take a look at the manuscript in Chekhov's presence, but Chekhov stayed his hand, and asked him not to. Then Anton Pavlovich left the theatre.

Davydov found the play *Ivanov* in his pocket. He told me, "When I got home, I pulled the manuscript out of my coat pocket, and started to read. After I read ten pages, and was enthralled. The more I read it, the more I liked it. I read the whole night through, as I could not stop reading. In the morning, I instantly rushed up to Chekhov, and blurted out,

"My friend, please, let us stage this play in my theater."

"No, you do not have my permission," Chekhov said.

Davydov spoke to Chekhov for a long time before he convinced him to allow the play to go on stage.

"All right," Chekhov said finally, "the responsibility will be completely on your shoulders in the case of failure."

Davydov told me in a very excited tone, "I was completely charmed by this play *Ivanov*. It was something completely new, something big and unexpected. It was a huge success. On the first night I saw the biggest standing ovation that I can ever remember having seen."

"And who was performing on the first night?" I asked.

"We invited our best actors. Sara was Glama Mesherskaya, Shurochka was Menshinskaya, I was Ivanov and Samoilov was the doctor."

I went to St. Petersburg, where M. Jurkovsky was the theater director. He was looking for a new play for the season and told him, "I have a wonderful play for you."

The next day, Jurkovsky had completely read *Ivanov* and instantly said "yes." He told me that he read it without getting up once from his desk. He sent a telegram to Chekhov, who came to St. Petersburg for its opening. The crowd's reaction was the same — the play was a huge sensation.

"Chekhov visited our rehearsals. A humble man, he was hiding in the last rows of our theaters, but he was there. He was present at all of our rehearsals," Davydov said.

On the opening night, Chekhov was very nervous and excited. Many years later, when I performed, read and reread the plays of Chekhov, I thought that no matter what was happening in the country, the works Chekhov created remain very dear to us and to our culture. We should not forget this.

Fyodor Chervinsky. "Meetings with A.P. Chekhov"

One day, as I visited Chekhov, I met a strange short man with red hair at his place. It was a playwright named N. Ezhov. He brought along a musical comedy he had written and asked for permission to read it out loud to us. It was an extremely long and boring musical comedy. As he read it, it seemed to me that it was somehow covered with dust.

Chekhov listened to it right till the end, mumbled something under his nose, and then spoke about musical comedies in general,

"Look at my play, *Ivanov*. I could break it up into several pieces and produce a dozen musical comedies from my *Ivanov*. Or, alternatively, I could make a dozen short stories out of it. It would be much more profitable for me. I could make about four thousand rubles. And the theater critics would not scold me then."

The short man was listening carefully, with attention, looking at Chekhov's mouth as he spoke. Then he stood up, said words of gratitude, and left. Chekhov said,

"After all this, I would like a shot of vodka."

Nikolai Ezhov. "Humor Writers of the 1880s"

We had a literary artists' gathering. There were quite a few people present. Chekhov decided to have a reading, and asked the actor Lensky to read his short play, *Proposal*.

The play was a success, and we all applauded to the author for a long time. Chekhov stood up and bowed in a comical fashion.

Then, suddenly, Isaac Levitan, who applauded louder than others, said, "Let me read something to you. This will be *Demon* by Lermontov."

"It is a long poem. Are you going to read it all?" asked Chekhov.
"Boo-boo-boo,"
The painter Levitan recited in a dull voice. At one point, he was out of breath. Chekhov instantly started applauding him, and then said in haste,

"After the wonderful reading of the comedy, and the poem by Lermontov, let us now listen to the musicians. Please, gentlemen, begin playing!"

Mr. Ivanenko and Mr. Semashko, two literary artists, stepped out with a flute and a viola, and started playing. That was the end of our party.

Konstantin Varlamov. "Meetings with Varlamov"

My first meeting with Chekhov happened under very interesting circumstances.

I went to the theater and headed directly into my dressing room to begin getting ready for that evening's performance. My dressing room was separated from the neighbor's room by only a thin barrier.

I looked around me and saw a pair of galoshes sticking out from my neighbor's side. I saw letters on them, "A. Ch." Yet, I was not paying close attention at the time. I took off my winter coat, and then stopped. I heard someone playing viola over there. I hung up my coat and went to the other room. A tall man in eyeglasses was standing in that room casually talking to someone, as others were playing their instruments. This man had a wonderful sounding voice.

I could not stop myself from asking a question, as I approached the stranger: "Do you sing often?"

"No, I have never tried to sing," he replied.

"Then you should take lessons. You have such a wonderful speaking voice," I said.

The owner of the voice looked at me in a puzzled way, and said, "Let me introduce myself. My name is Chekhov."

Vladimir Giliarovsky. "Moscow and Moscovites"

Chekhov once told me, "I've just shown my new play to the Korsh Theater. But in response to my proposition, they asked me, 'What kind of a title is this, *Ivanov*? Who in the world would go to a play with such a bland name?'"

Gradov-Sokolov, an actor present during my conversation with Chekhov, remarked,

"Well, I think they're mistaken. First off, the author is a wonderful playwright. Secondly, *Ivanov* is a good title for a play. Everyone with this common-sounding surname *[Ivanov is one of the most popular family names in Russia — P.S.]* will want to know what Chekhov has written about him.

"So even if only people named 'Ivanov' go to see it, tickets will still be completely sold out." Gradov-Sokolov's prediction came true. After the performance ended and people were leaving, all you could hear at the theatre entrance was:

"Taxi for Mr. Ivanov!"

"Mr. Ivanov's vehicle to the entrance!"

"Colonel Ivanov's driver trying to pass! Let him pass!"

Tickets were completely sold out, and the play turned out to be a huge success.

Vladimir Korolenko. "Anton Pavlovich Chekhov"

I will try to recollect what I can about Chekhov. Thinking back to the first time we met in his living room, I see Chekhov's mother, who always sat by his side. I also remember the compassionate smiles of his sister and brother. Theirs was a very friendly, welcoming family.

I look back to an even older memory of him as a young man, charming and talented, with a captivating smile and joyful eyes.

I think those memories are towards the end of the happiest period in his life. The drama in store for the Chekhov family was just about to begin. I remember seeing some very dubious feelings in the expression of Chekhov's face. Until then, he had been the most joyful and happy man I had ever known, always ready to laugh at anything and brimming with ideas for short stories. He had lots of ideas.

Sometimes, he would wake up in the middle of the night and knock on the wall to wake up his sister, Maria, and share a new idea about yet another plot. With time, a noticeable change came over this outward lightheartedness. At the same time, his family recognized that Chekhov was not simply a captivating jokester who could entertain and feed his family; his gift was of a more precious metal, and to care for this treasure was a great responsibility.

On his return from his trip to St. Petersburg, Chekhov began appearing in *The New Times* with more serious short stories. I was unsurprised by the substantial topics being addressed in his stories: these were signs of his future glory and fame.

When I asked his mother about his trip, she heaved a sigh, replying,

"Yes, you're right. I think that Anton doesn't belong to me anymore." As is so often true, his mother had very accurate intuitions about her own children.

We had agreed to meet Chekhov at the editorial office of the magazine *Fragments*. The date and time had been chosen earlier, in the office of the publisher Mr. Leikin. The highlight of our meeting was the following incident. Mr. Leikin had recently told Chekhov about receiving a short story from an obscure author living somewhere in St. Petersburg's suburbs. The editor had been so happy with this story that he had invited its author to his office to discuss regular submissions in the future.

Chekhov wanted to read this manuscript. To his astonishment, it was one of his own early short stories, carefully copied from the published original. It was signed with a completely unknown name. Strangely enough, this was a good sign: a sign of Chekhov's coming fame. The plagiarist had recognized the writer's potential, and wanted to profit from it.

Sometime later, Chekhov told me, "I want to come to Nizhniy Novgorod and write a play together."

I replied, "By all means, visit me, but it will be a better play if you write it on your own."

Chekhov kept his word. He came to Nizhny and, although we didn't get much writing done, he managed to charm everyone he met.

On my next visit to Moscow, I found him writing a drama, this time by himself. When I came to his house, he momentarily stepped out of his study to confirm, "Yes, I am writing a drama." I did not want to bother him and was about to apologize, but he cut me short, saying, "This time I'm writing one called *Ivan Ivanovich Ivanov*."

I objected, "But there are thousands of Ivanovs!"

Chekhov replied, "Yes, and my Ivanov is just an ordinary man, not a hero at all. You know, when you're writing, sometimes you can see two scenes very clearly, but you're still missing some sort of link, a bridge of some kind. There is still an empty place to be filled."

I said, "Since I'm a writer myself I know what you mean, and I've come across it many times. You're saying you will have to fill this gap with logic instead of imagination?"

"That's right." Chekhov agreed.

I continued, "I suppose you must come across this all the time when you write a play. You cannot create a drama without using logical bridges to hold everything together."

During my visit, Chekhov seemed a little upset and tired. Writing and staging his first drama was incredibly hard for him; perhaps it was one of the hardest things he'd ever done. It brought him his first literary turmoils, the excitements and challenges that came hand in hand with being a well-known writer.

Then Chekhov's frame of mind shifted again. I remember many people criticizing *Ivanov*. It lacked his former playful attitude to life, which had been present in all of his previous works. This was an authentic drama, a true reflection of Russian life, and the young writer felt that it was his first real drama. Its creation was not easy for Chekhov, and the process could be a separate investigation for future biographers.

Maria Chitau. "A.P. Chekhov"

By the time *The Seagull* was performed on the stage of the Alexandrinsky Theater, several young dramaturges and writers, including Chekhov, understood the necessity of new forms of theatrical expression. However, the public, the theatergoers themselves, hadn't an inkling about these new forms and ideas, which had yet to appear on stage.

Ivanov was the first memorable play by Chekhov staged at our theater.

The play was wonderfully performed, and it was an immense success. The actors were fantastic, and the audience loved every moment.

However, Chekhov's second play, *The Seagull*, was not so lucky, and its first night turned out to be a disaster, for a number of reasons.

Chekhov was supposed to arrive at the theater and read his new play (with comments) in the dressing rooms. He was late, and the actors milled around, chattering, whispering, and constantly checking the clock. Eventually, Mr. Karpov, the artistic director, came out to speak to us. Chekhov had sent a telegram from Moscow saying he was unable to come to St. Petersburg. We had expected that the author would be present to explain to us how to perform the "new ideas" in his play. Instead, it was Mr. Karpov who presented the play, and then we began rehearsals.

I should also say a few words about the performance itself. Afterwards, many people spoke and wrote about the public's reaction to this play. We had never heard so much booing. For as long as I remember, no other performance in the history of our theater had ever failed so completely.

By the middle of the performance, the actors realized that it would be a complete disaster.

During the second act I went into the dressing rooms. Anton Pavlovich was there, head cocked to one side. A lock of hair had fallen over his forehead, and his glasses were balanced crookedly on the tip of his nose. I sat down without saying a word. A few seconds passed in complete silence. Chekhov quickly stood up, and, without saying a word, left the room. He left the theater and the City of St. Petersburg in a rush, as unexpectedly as he had arrived.

A few days later, during the second performance of the play, there was a magical change. There were numerous cheers of, "Bravo! Author, author!" And yet, we performed it no better the second time around.

Olga Knipper-Chekhova. "About A.P. Chekhov"

I was playing several major roles in Chekhov's plays. It is difficult for an actor or actress to perform Chekhov, because you have to perform not just a role, but to be a real person while onstage. Yet, if you grasp the major message, then you can find something new each time the play is performed.

I remember *Seagull* during the first season of our theater. All the actors were young, except for Stanislavsky and Vishnevsky. Even if the play had a great showing, we did not perform well enough. The love and enthusiasm we felt for the play and the author simply was power-flown into the theater public.

Anton Pavlovich visited one of the rehearsals of *Seagull*. We were all exceptionally excited when we saw our favorite author. He appeared to be just a very simple person, and he did not try to explain to the actors about how to perform while on stage.

We thought that he would reveal the secrets of the *Seagull* any moment, and were in suspense. We would ask him for his direction on how to perform, but the only reply we got was a smile, touch of his beard, adjustment of his eyeglasses, or a glance at the theater set. We never got a straight answer, rather a short joke, and we could not tell if he was serious or not. Later on we understood that these little remarks by the author were actually revealing the inner world of his characters.

It took us some time to understand this strange way of communicating with the author, but when we understood his way, we became excited. We later realized that he was absolutely right and to the point each time.

When we performed *Seagull* for the first time, out theater was not even completely sold out, and it appeared to be a bad day. No one was either talking, or making eye contact. All of us kept silent when not on stage. We did not want to destroy the impression of the first day.

Nemirovich paced up and down the hall the entire first act. During the second act, we could not understand anything. During the third act, there were several protests in the theater hall. Everything seemed new, and hard to explain — such things as complete darkness in the theater; the fact that the actors were sitting with their backs to the public during the play itself.

We were waiting for the last act. When the play was over, there were a few moments of complete silence. Then it seemed that a huge water current had destroyed the dam that was holding it back. We could not understand what was happening — it was complete madness, and a total triumph. Both the theater viewers and the actors were united in one single body. We were standing, embracing each other, and kissing, hugging and cheering. There was a seemingly endless ovation. Some of the public were in tears. We requested that a telegram should be sent immediately to Chekhov in Yalta, informing him that both the play and the playwright were a complete success.

Several forthcoming performances of *Seagull* had to be canceled due to my bad health. I had serious bronchitis with a high running fever. I lost my voice, and for a few days, could only lie in bed and sob.

Chekhov received the telegram of the great success, and then the following news that actress Knipper had to cancel her upcoming performances. He decided that my illness was just a pretext so as to not make him upset by the new failure of the *Seagull*.

However, I felt much better in a few days. Then we were all happy to be back to performing that very successful play again and again.

Three other plays by Chekhov — *Uncle Vanya, Three Sisters* and *Cherry Orchard* — never achieved the same success as *Seagull*, although both the actors and the public were more excited by these plays when they were performed.

Anton Pavlovich could not visit all rehearsals due to his own illness, and came to visit us in Moscow only during the rehearsals for *Cherry Orchard* during the winter of 1903.

Chekhov gave me lots of directions in his letters how to perform the major roles in his plays.

Vera Komissarzhevskaya. "Memories"

When they told Chekhov that actress Komissarzhevskaya would play a major role in his play *The Seagull*, Chekhov replied that he had never heard of her.

It was in 1896 when Anton Pavlovich gave his play *The Seagull* to the theater and asked Madame Savina to perform Nina. However, Madame Savina did not come to the rehearsal, and wrote a letter to Mr. E. Karpov, the theater director, refusing to play Nina. She later wanted the role of Masha, but ultimately decided not to perform in the play at all.

It was only after the first rehearsal that director Karpov invited Komissarzhevkaya to play Nina. After some initial hesitation, the actress agreed.

On the second rehearsal there were even more changes to the cast — this was likely the main reason why the play was poorly performed on its opening night.

Chekhov came to the theater for the fourth rehearsal. He was very upset to find out that Nina was not being performed by Savina, and told Karpov,

"Nina is the most important character. She means everything to me in this play. I don't know what to do."

By the end of the rehearsal, however, Chekhov grew calmer, and said,

"The young actress playing Nina is not bad. Overall, she looks the part. The only thing I don't like is that she is too emotional while she is acting. When I wrote these monologues, I meant them to be performed very simply. However, I can tell that Mrs. Komissarzhevskaya is a talented actress."

The more time Chekhov spent at the rehearsals, the more he liked how it was being acted. He told Karpov,

"Komissarzhevskaya is acting in such a way that it seems like she was present when I wrote the play, as if she was listening to my inner voice. She is a very sensitive, sophisticated and wonderful actress."

During the last dress rehearsal, all the actors performed wonderfully. Chekhov was thrilled. He told Karpov that if the actors performed like that on opening night, everything would be simply wonderful.

Yet the crowd present at the opening night made a bad impression on Chekhov. *Seagull* was performed in the second half that night, after the personal performance of an elderly comic actress, Mrs. Levkeeva. People were expecting comedy, and the actors did not perform well that night. Suddenly, hissing was heard in the theater. People simply could not understand or weren't able to comprehend his play.

Komissarzhevskaya was trembling all over as she asked the theater director Karpov, "Why are they laughing all the time? This is terrible! I am scared to go back on stage. I cannot perform. Why are those idiots laughing?"

The actors tried to calm Chekhov down. At the end of the third act, Chekhov was completely pale, biting his little beard, with a frozen smile on his face. He came into the Karpov's office and said,

"The author completely failed tonight."

Karpov tried to reassure him, but Chekhov shook his head in disagreement, and said, "Thank you." Then he left the room. They said that he left St. Petersburg that same night.

When the actors left the theater, they were crying, distraught over the failure of *Seagull.*

On October 21, 1896, the same play *Seagull* was performed rather successfully at the same theater with the same cast of actors.

Komissarzhevskaya wrote to Chekhov:

> Dear Anton Pavlovich,
>
> You should have been at the theater tonight. You won! *Seagull* is a success — a complete, unanimous, and total success. It was supposed to be a success, and it could not be otherwise. I wanted to see you watch the people in the theater, crying, "Author, author!"
>
> I became a part of the play, as well as many of the other actors. Think about your friends, and do not be afraid of life. I want to shake your hand.

This letter was the beginning of the correspondence that Chekhov and Komissarzhevskaya would have until the author's death in 1904.

Konstantin Stanislavsky. "Works. The Moscow Art Theater"

Our situation was dire, since our theater was running out of funds, out of money. We did not expect any profit from our new production, Chekhov's *Seagull,* but the work was already underway, and we had to do it. We knew that this performance would put at stake the whole existence of our theater, considering our financial shortfalls. That was not all: more weight was added to it.

Just before a very unsuccessful dress rehearsal, Chekhov's sister, Maria Pavlovna, came to visit us. She was worried by the bad news coming from Yalta. She worried about the possibility of another failure in the performance of *The Seagull,* and that the news could seriously damage her brother's health.

She was horrified by what she saw, and said that we should not risk staging this play altogether. We were also afraid, and we did discuss the possibility of canceling the performance. This would effectually amount to closing down the theater. It would not be easy to end so many years of hard work, to quit the job that I had loved for years, and put all the actors out on the street to starve.

The night of the performance came. I do not remember what happened during the first act. The only thing I remember was that many actors were drinking valerian to calm their nerves, and the air reeked of it. I remember sitting in the chair on the stage with my back to the audience, feeling slight, cold shivers along my spine. I inconspicuously clasped my knee with both hands since it trembled with nervous excitement.

The curtain fell in complete silence. The actors approached each other, and formed a close-knit group on the set, awaiting what would happen. Complete silence. A few stagehands stuck their heads out from behind the curtain and listened. Complete silence. Someone began to cry. Mrs. Knipper attempted to suppress her hysterical sobbing. We all moved to exit from the stage.

Suddenly, there was a huge burst of applause. The public began yelling and cheering with great enthusiasm. The curtain was raised. People asked why we weren't facing the public. We simply stood on the scene, looking at each other with terrible expressions on our faces. Someone told us to face the audience and take a bow. Even then, no one understood what was happening. A few of the actors simply sat down on the chairs, right on the set.

It was a huge success, followed by a longwinded celebration on the set and in the hall. Some people ran up onto the stage and started kissing the actors. Someone fell to the ground, screaming joyfully to the point of hysteria. People were embracing each other and dancing with joy.

The evening wore on, yet the applause never stopped. Late that night, the public demanded that a telegram be sent to the author. From that night onwards, we developed a good relationship with Anton Pavlovich. Along with him, we felt almost like one big family.

Vassily Kachalov. "From My Memories"

I remember very well how I met Gorky and Chekhov together in 1903.

Maxim Gorky was a young man and he was present at the first night of *The Cherry Orchard* when Chekhov received a standing ovation during the intermission after the third act.

I remember how Nemirovich said to Chekhov,

"Today is your birthday, and there is a saying that St. Anton brings more sunshine, more warmth and makes the days seem longer. With you, we also have more light, more warmth, and more joy in our theater."

People used to make long speeches that started "My dear sir." When one of the numerous speakers greeted Chekhov another time, "My dear and highly respected...," Chekhov quietly whispered to one of his friends standing close to him, "My dear and respected wardrobe..." It was in the same play, earlier in the first act that Gaev, played by Stanislavsky, had a monologue where he spoke to a wardrobe, which began with the words, "My dear and highly respected wardrobe."

I remember that Anton Pavlovich looked very tired and pale that day. He coughed into his handkerchief, and he could hardly stand on his own two legs during the lengthy ovation, and needed to be supported by two actors at one point.

Some people cried, "Please, Anton Pavlovich, sit down! Sit down, please."

He made a calming gesture to the public.

At the end of the celebration, I went to my dressing room at the back of the scene. I heard the voice of actor Vishnevsky speaking loudly,

"Here is Kachalov's room. Let us bring Anton Pavlovich here."

Chekhov came into my room, supported on both sides by Gorky and Miroliubov. Andreev was walking right behind them, and Vishnevsky was following at the end of the procession.

Gorky said, "I am so tired of this public display of emotions, this endless celebration! They almost killed Anton Pavlovich with their endless speeches. I am both disgusted and disappointed! They could have simply killed him."

I saw that Gorky was very upset when he was telling this.

"You should lie down, and stretch your legs," I told Chekhov.

"I am not going to lie down forever and stretch my legs for good," Chekhov made a joke. "Yet, I would like to sit down."

Gorky interrupted him, "Put up your legs on the sofa, here, next to Kachalov. He is not a smoker. And you Vishnevsky — you make too much noise — so leave. And you, Miroliubov — you also have a loud deep voice — get out of here."

They all left and two of us, Chekhov and me, stayed in the room.

"Really, I agree with you. Do I have your permission to lie down?" asked Chekhov.

A moment later, we heard the really loud voice of Alexey Maksimovich as he was lecturing Miroliubov, the publisher of *Magazine for Everyone*, for yelling at people in Chekhov's presence.

Chekhov said, "Yes, Miroliubov likes to yell at cab drivers, waitresses and even at the police officers; every person has his weaknesses. But we should not yell at him just because he is this sort of person."

We heard noisy steps as Gorky came to the door. He took the last drag from his cigarette, waved his hand to clear the smoke, and finally entered the room.

Chekhov said, "You are such an energetic man, full of so many plans."

Then Chekhov stood up and added, "I am feeling much better now. Let us go and say goodbye to my *Cherry Orchard*. We will see how the actors will be coping by the trees."

Then he stood up and left. That was during the opening night performance of *The Cherry Orchard* at the Moscow Art Theater.

I remember the summer of 1904. Chekhov's funeral. A huge crowd moved from the railway station to the Novo-Devichie Cemetery, stopping briefly in front of the Moscow Art Theater. Many in that crowd were crying. There was music by Chopin. The theatrical workers brought out a huge wreath with flowers. I saw two faces in the crowd — Evegenia Yakovlevna, the mother of Chekhov, and the face of Gorky. They both were standing next to the coffin. They both had red eyes, as if they had been crying for hours, and looked emotionally distraught.

The crowd arrived at the cemetery, paid their respects, and filled up the grave with soil as some began to leave. I stood with the actor Zalushsky, who was next to the grave. Then together we drew closer to Gorky.

"You were crying a lot today, Gorky," I said.

Gorky replied, "I never knew that I could cry from anger. I am very angry. I am angry with all those people, angry at the railway car for fresh oysters in which they brought the body from Germany, and with the huge crowd. You cannot escape from these people."...

When Anton Pavlovich gave advice to an actor, one would sometimes end up completely confounded, whether it was praise or subtle criticism. Once he congratulated me on my performance in his drama *Three Sisters*.

"You perform this role of Tausenbach in a most wonderful way. This is truly wonderful," he said very clearly. I nearly went lightheaded with happiness. After a few moments of silence, Chekhov added in the same positive and assured way,

"And Mr. N. also performs his role in *Gentlemen* very well."

The entire world, for God's sake, knew that Mr. N. was a terrible performer. His performance in another theater was simply an abomination, a failure of the worst kind. To this day, I do not know whether Chekhov liked my performance of this role or not.

When I performed Mr. Vershinin, he said, "This is good, very good. But when you salute the other military officers, you do it as if you are a junior officer, like a sergeant or a lieutenant. You should be more assertive, more representative of your rank." Then he did not say another word. That was all.

Later, when I performed Grigorin in his play *The Seagull*, Chekhov invited me up to his room to discuss my performance. He said,

"You know what? The fishing rods, you know — they should be crooked and not so straight. He cut them from the bush with his pocket knife. And the cigars — they should be of good quality. Maybe they are not even good cigars, but they should be in silver wrapping."

After reflecting some more for a while, he repeated,

"Yes, the most important thing should be the fishing rods." Then he was silent.

Chekhov's House in Yalta photographed between 1908 and 1910.

I went on asking him questions about different parts of the play: how I should perform, and what themes and messages I should develop. He made a grimace and said,

"Hmm, I don't know, really. You should perform it as it's supposed to be done."

This didn't dissuade me from asking more questions. He looked at me carefully, and said,

"All right, watch this. When you are drinking vodka with Maria, this is what you should do. Look at me!"

He stood up, stretched his shoulders, fixed his vest and cleared his throat in a very awkward way.

"You see. You see, this is what I would have done. When you sit for a long time, you always want to stretch your body."

"But how should I play such a difficult and complicated role?" I went on with my queries.

Chekhov grew slightly upset and said,

"I am not going to tell you anything else about it. Everything is written there." I did not speak to him about the role again that night.

Anton Pavlovich was always concerned about my health, and he told me to drink codfish oil and sleep more. He repeatedly asked me to stop smoking. I tried to drink the fish oil, but it was so disgusting that I told him I would never drink it again. As to my smoking, I promised him to quit.

"You are right, quitting is a marvelous idea," he said. Then suddenly he added,

"You know what? It's a pity that you are planning to quit smoking, because I was going to give you a nice cigarette holder."

I saw him upset only once. At the Heritage Theater, after the end of the play, there was a huge crowd of students waiting outside. They had planned to start an ovation, demanding, "Author, author!"

Chekhov was completely outraged by this.

Nikolai Teleshov. "A.P. Chekhov"

Chekhov knew how to love. Texts like "The Lady with the Dog" or "About Love" could only have been composed by one who has experienced real love. He wrote the following:

"If you are in love, when you speak of love, you should elevate your conversation to the highest possible values, higher than simple happiness or unhappiness, or sin, or virtue in its everyday meaning. Love is superior to all of that. Or you should not speak of love at all."

It seems to me that he said this regarding his short stories about love.

One day, Chekhov told me, "It is not true that love dies with the passage of time. No, true love does not go away; it comes back and grows stronger with time's passage. It is only gradually that you understand how close you are to the woman that you love. Love is like a fine old wine: you need to acclimatize to it, to drink it for a long time, in order to understand its beauty."

Chekhov questioned me about the Moscow Art Theater, and about the rehearsals of his play, *Uncle Vanya*.

"How do you like my *Uncle Vanya* on stage?" he asked me one day.

I replied that *Uncle Vanya* was being staged by the Art Theater and that it made a very strong statement. But I had to ask, "I cannot understand one thing: why did you make Uncle Vanya shoot Professor Serebryakov twice in the back? It seems unnatural. Vishnevsky takes aim, standing just two steps away from Luzhsky, and doesn't even scratch him, after shooting almost point-blank."

Chekhov replied, "I thought that there should be a gunshot here. Uncle Vanya should shoot at this point, in order to wake up the audience. By this time, they have been talking and philosophizing for quite a long time, the people in the theater may be tired, or maybe even asleep, so I decided to wake them up with a gunshot."

Chekhov told me that many of his ideas and plot twists came from his visual observations, as well as from overhearing other people's conversations.

He could create new literary works in his head almost instantly. Chekhov told me that he had a huge number of new plots coming to him with his new visual and audio impressions. Whenever he saw or heard anything, he had a new plot for it.

Gorky told me about a very characteristic case. One day, Gorky and Chekhov were walking along the Yalta waterfront talking about the importance of the writer's imagination, when a black cat ran next to them.

Gorky said, "Here, Anton Pavlovich! Look! Can you create a story titled 'A Black Cat'?"

And Chekhov, without hesitating for an instant, told him a story about a black cat. It was as follows:

> In St. Petersburg, on Vasilevsky Island, there is a five-storied yellow apartment building. A dark and narrow staircase smells of cats. At the very top, on the fifth floor, there is a door which is covered with worn-out black vinyl. It leads directly into a kitchen, which is divided by a thin cardboard wall. Behind the wall, a female university student sits at a small desk reading John Stuart Mill's *The Emancipation of Women*.
> On the near side of the wall, another tenant, a laundress, is wringing her clothes out and talking with the old crone who is the landlady to these two ladies. She says,
> "Please do not argue with me, I know things about life! I will tell you the truth. If you want a man to fall in love with you, here is my advice: You have to catch a black cat, and boil him alive in a pot of boiling water, and then you have to take the lower chest bone from the cat and quietly poke the person you want to charm, and he will instantly fall in love with you. He will become so attached to you that you will not know how to get rid of him. You must believe me — I do not imagine things. I know things about life."
> And the very next moment after the ladies in the kitchen have shared this secret, the university student snaps *The Emancipation of Women* closed, and goes out to catch a black cat.

That was the story that Chekhov created on the spot.

Chekhov loved Gorky, just as he loved to discover any talented young writer. He sent many aspiring writers to me, somehow trusting my writer's intuition.

Chekhov's own literary criticism was often unusual in its form, but most of the time it was very much to the point.

Ivan Volkov. *"Meyerhold: A Biography"*

Meyerhold wrote a major article about naturalistic theater and the theater of emotions. He included several very important remarks, little details about the early performance of Chekhov's play, *The Seagull*.

"In the early productions of the play, at the beginning of the first act, you cannot understand where people are going. They simply disappear into the darkness of the stage. Later, in further productions, people come in with wet hats, galoshes and raincoats, and you imagine the heavy rain outside."

This little quote shows us that as early as 1888–89, Meyerhold applied his naturalistic ideas for the performance of Chehkov's plays. At the same time, he also applied similar ideas in his productions of Ibsen's plays.

The theatrical season of 1888–89 ended in February with the performance of *The Seagull*. Then, in the spring of 1889, after the first performances of *The Seagull*, Chekhov became close to Meyerhold, who played Mr. Trigorin in his drama. Chekhov was attracted to Meyerhold because he was a great intellectual.

Vladimir Nemorovich-Danchenko. "From the Past. The Birth of a Theater"

Chekhov wrote his drama *Thee Sisters* during the summer of 1900 in Yalta. Then he rewrote it during the winter of the same year. He used to write one act in two or three days, and take a break for several days or a week. He could rewrite a dialogue or a whole new act each week. During the last years, he developed this particular way of writing his play. He used to say,

"I remember it all, and I write from my memory, scene after scene, act after act, the whole play in this way."

I don't recall that many of Chekhov's biographers mention this. He did not write like Leo Tolstoy, who memorized just the overall plot and the development of events, and then created his works during sessions of writing and rewriting.

Chekhov's creative process was different: he had little sketches of the plot and some key words, and he thought it all through, including all the little details.

I remember that in early 1900, he was in a very good mood. After writing *Three Sisters*, he told us very sincerely that it was meant to be a farce, a comedy, and we did not believe it until the end, until now. The play was written for particular actors, to be performed in the presence of actors and Chekhov himself. However, when the actors asked him for explanations of how to perform some particular scene or episode which seemed unclear, he never gave us any explanations, giving very short answers. For example, when we asked him what the following meant, he never replied. The scene was like this:

MASHA: Tara-ra-ra.
VERSHININ: Tram-tram.
MASHA: Tara-ra-ra.
VERSHININ: Tra-ta-ta.

Chekhov answered by shrugging his shoulders, saying to us, "This is nothing; this is just a joke of mine."

Later, people asked him again what he meant by his joke, but he never gave a definite answer. It was not always easy for an actor to figure out how to perform Chekhov's jokes.

Chekhov showed an inner freedom in his creation of theatrical dramas in a way he had never done in his other works. It really was a new manner of writing, a new way of creating theater.

I would like to briefly remind you of the history of *The Cherry Orchard* as it remains in my memory.

In the spring of 1903, the Moscow Art Theater was discussing the possibility of performing a new drama. We did not yet have a new play for the season, so we asked Anton Pavlovich for a play that he had promised us. We knew that he'd spent the summer in the distant suburbs of Moscow. Rumors about his new play, very short and scattered rumors, came to us, but we knew that he had kept it a secret from the theaters, and only whispered a word or two into somebody's ear.

Of course, I was a close acquaintance of Anton Pavlovich's. I knew his world and I could make a few deductions. When Chekhov came to Moscow, the doctors allowed him to spend the winter there. He missed Yalta very much, but he decided to be present at the rehearsals. We exchanged many letters discussing every detail, and in some letters we even discussed the distribution of roles for his new play. I did not agree with the casting that Chekhov suggested. For example, despite his delicacy and good manners, he did not give the lead role to his wife. *[Actress Olga Knipper — P.S.]* We knew that Knipper should perform Ranevskaya, and I insisted on this. Later on, he started coming to rehearsals, where he became very nervous, and he disagreed with the way we performed his play. He did not like some of the actors, he did not like the directors, and he said that too much of his text had been changed. He got excited to the extent that we had to ask him not to visit rehearsals any more. This was not an easy thing to do.

Obviously, there were mistakes on our part, and on the part of the theater as well. He was right in his casting suggestions. That was true. At the same time, we had different approaches to directing. One was the inner approach, showing the inner psyche of a character; the other was showing the beauty of outer effects. For example, in the second act there was a very particular noise that we could not imitate. The author's remark said that a big pail had fallen down a deep coal mine in the distance. Chekhov went behind the curtains, and said that we should imitate this noise with a human voice. I could not agree with this. In the other act, when mosquitoes were to be in the scene, Chekhov said that it should not be so naturalistic. Also, Chekhov was very worried in general about the future of his new play. One day, he said that he was not happy with the performance, and he told his wife,

"I would like to buy this play for a few thousand, and sell it to someone else."

However, Chekhov went on coming to our rehearsals, and actors came and spoke to him, even if he was silent most of the time.

This lasted until January 17. Then Chekhov's health got weaker, and we decided to make a special celebration for him. Chekhov did not want to come to the theater, but we convinced him to come. I am sure that you have read the good reviews about the success of opening night. It was a great expression of people's love for our writer and playwright, a touching outpouring of emotions, and a huge celebration.

It was an astonishing success. Yes, and that success lasted for at least 25 years. I should tell you the truth, though; although Chekhov's success as playwright was great, the initial success of this particular play was not impressive. I thought that Chekhov had put his best writing into this play. Yet, as is so often true in the history of the theater, this wonderful creation was initially not accepted and understood.

Konstantin Stanislavsky. "The Moscow Art Theater in Yalta"

When the actors came to Yalta to visit Chekhov, we asked him questions about his health. Anton Pavlovich said in an embarrassed way,

"I am feeling wonderful. I am completely healthy."

He did not like it when people asked him about his health, even if they were his friends, and even if at the time he was unwell.

Soon he left the hotel, and we did not have another chance to talk to him. The next day, we performed a dress rehearsal for Anton Pavlovich before opening for the public of Crimea. I saw him very briefly. He came to look at his theater set, and at the hall. It was fairly cold inside the theater, and people kept asking him about his health. He replied in a very short way,

"Listen to me! I am healthy!"

The theater was very cold inside because the building had many holes, and it was not heated. A few kerosene lamps gave off light and a little warmth, but the strong sea wind blew even this small heat away from the building.

On the day of the performance, we were all freezing. With every costume change, the actors would run across the street to a nearby hotel where they could warm up. At 4 P.M., the bell signaled to the public the start of the first performance of *Uncle Vanya*. Chekhov hid in the director's balcony, behind his wife and Nemirovich, but his presence excited us greatly. The first act passed to a rather cold reception. However, at the end of the third act, there was a great ovation. They demanded "Author, author!" numerous times.

The next day, Anton Pavlovich found out that the actor Artyom could not come to rehearsals because he was sick. As soon as Chekhov learned this, he said that he was a doctor, and that he would give medical treatment to his favorite actor. We went to his hotel room. Chekhov took out his small doctor's hammer and his stethoscope.

"I cannot do this without medical instruments," he said in a very concerned way. Chekhov listened and knocked on the patient's chest for a very long time, and then he tried to convince the actor not to take any medicine. He just gave him a mint candy, and said,

"Listen to me! Eat this! This should be enough!"

That was the extent of the prescription, and Artyom was completely healthy on the following day.

Anton Pavlovich enjoyed visiting rehearsals. However, the theater was very cold, so Chekhov only sat inside from time to time. He spent most of the time outside in the sunshine, where many actors went out to get some warm air. Chekhov spoke to them in the following way,

"Look, just listen to me — it is a wonderful thing that you are doing, and your whole theater is a wonderful thing as well."

That was a rather casual, often repeated phrase by Anton Pavlovich at that time.

The Seagull was performed in terrible conditions. The wind blew in from the sea with such force that both curtains had be to held by the stagehands at all times, and they had to make a real effort to keep the curtain from falling into the audience. From time to time, we heard the sirens of steamboats passing by the Yalta harbor. As we performed, we could hear the flapping of the wind in the curtains, and the noise of the rain outside. It was raining.

This caused another issue. At some point in the performance, we needed a lot of light on the scene, and the only way to do it was to turn off the lights in the central city park. We had no other way, and at a certain moment Nemirovich made a sign, and they turned off the lights in the city park. The performance of *The Seagull* in Yalta was a great success. The people gave us a thundering ovation.

Whenever we visited Chekhov, we noticed that he always had his dinner table set for guests, whether for breakfast, or dinner, or tea. The house where he lived was still under construction. There was a very small garden at the back of his property. He took care of the garden himself.

Anton Pavlovich was full of life and had completely changed. It seemed to us that he had been resurrected from the dead. It was as if he was a wooden house that had spent the whole winter with its doors and windows covered by planks, and then, with the coming of spring, someone had opened its doors and windows, letting in lots of light, warmth and joy.

He was continuously going from one place to another, constantly joking and fixing his eyeglasses. He would go out to the porch to show us the latest books and magazines, or smile and make a joke, or go out to his yard and his garden to show us the fruit trees he had planted himself. From time to time, he went to his study to have some rest.

We came and left several times during the day. We finished our breakfast and in a few hours we returned for tea. Maria Pavlovna worked the entire time to set the table and feed us. Olga Leonardovna, currently Chekhov's fiancée and his future wife and the mistress of the house, also helped around.

We had literary discussions in the garden; one group of actors behaved like high school students, and had a competition to see who could throw a stone further. Another group stood around the writer Ivan Bunin, who was doing comical imitations and telling anecdotes; and next to Bunin you could always find Anton Pavlovich, laughing heartily.

No one could make Chekhov laugh as joyfully as Bunin, and put him in such a good mood. Gorky was also charming as always. I often looked at Anton Pavlovich, observing him closely, and noticed that most of the time he seemed very happy, joking and smiling because of our theater's visit to Yalta.

Konstantin Stanislavsky. "A Trip to Crimea"

This was the springtime of our theater, the most beautiful moment in its life. We were going to see Anton Pavlovich Chekhov. We were going to tour Crimea.

People were waiting for us to arrive there, and people were talking and writing theater reviews about us. We were the talk of the town, not only in Moscow, but also in Crimea, in Sevastopol and in Yalta. We decided to make a statement with this trip. We said,

"Anton Pavlovich cannot visit us because he is sick. Therefore, we shall go and see him. If he cannot come to us, we will come to him."

The entire theater was on the move from cold Moscow to warm Crimea that spring, including the actors, their wives, children, tutors and nannies, as well as nurses, theater workers, set designers, costume designers, hairdressers, and several railway cars full of costumes and equipment.

We had to remove our winter coats and put on light dresses and summer clothes on the train ride there. Even if it did not feel warm enough, we knew that we would warm up under the rays of the southern sun. We booked a whole railway car. We would go south for two months. Everyone was joyful and happy, and on the way there we were cracking jokes and making new friends.

Here we are, in white Sevastopol! There are very few cities nicer than this. White sandy beaches, white houses, chalky mountains in the distance, a bright blue sky above and the blue sea with white foamy waves. Little clouds and white seagulls in the sky. But by the end of the day, the clouds covered the sky completely and we had rain mixed with snow for a few hours.

Poor Anton Pavlovich had to come to us from Yalta. We waited for him in vain, and then received a telegram that he was sick, and that he could not come to Sevastopol.

The local theater was only designed for summer performances. It stood on the seashore, and its doors were nailed shut with planks for the winter. When we finally opened the door and entered the theater, it seemed to us that we had reached the North Pole.

Yet, in a few days the weather warmed up. Suddenly, Chekhov turned up in Sevastopol. Every morning, he attended rehearsals at the theater and spoke to us, and during the day we went to the city park for walks.

One day, Anton Pavlovich heard that we were looking for a doctor for one of our leading actors, Artyom, whom he knew well and for whom he had written a part in his play *The Cherry Orchard.*

Chekhov told us, "Listen, I am the doctor of this theater company." He was sincerely proud of being a doctor, and he considered his medical work to be more important than his literary work.

"I am a doctor by trade, and sometimes I do literary work in my free time," he often told us, in a serious manner.

On that day, Chekhov went to see Artyom, and he prescribed valerian drops, the same medicine that Dr. Dorn, one of the characters from his play, jokingly gave to everyone.

That day was the first night of his play, *Uncle Vanya.*

Chekhov sat at the back of the theater. It was a great success. The public cried, "Author, author!" repeatedly, and applauded for a long time.

Chekhov looked happy as well. He saw our complete theater set, with all the actors and all the costumes for the first time. During the intermissions, Chekhov came into my dressing room. He was silent for most of the time, and made only one remark about Astrov:

"He whistles all the time. Uncle Vanya is crying, but Astrov whistles." Later, I tried but could not get any more information about how to perform the play from him.

"How could this be?" I asked myself. "This is a very sad play, so why does one of the major characters whistle?" So in future performances I made an attempt to whistle on the scene. That was it! Astrov whistled because he was cynical, and he did not care about people and about life. However, he loved nature and grew trees.

Among others, we also performed a play by Hauptman. Anton Pavlovich saw that performance and said, "This is a great play, and a great performance. I am not a playwright. Listen, I am a doctor by trade."

At that time, almost every major author came to Crimea to see the performances. Kuprin, Bunin, Mamin-Sibiryak, Chrikov, Stanyukovich, Elpati-evsky. Even Maxim Gorky came to Crimea, because he had to treat his sick lungs at the sanitarium.

Aside from the writers, there were many actors and musicians, among them the young, but already famous Sergei Rakhmaninov.

All these actors and writers used to come to the Chekhov house in the morning for breakfast. It was served by Chekhov's sister, Maria Pavlovna, and his mother, an old woman whom everyone loved. One day, Chekhov's mother decided to go to the theater to see the performance of her son's new play, to all of our great astonishment.

At the breakfasts and dinners in the Chekhov house, we spoke a lot about literature and art. Many writers spoke openly about their secrets. Chekhov tried to convince other writers to write their plays for the Moscow Art Theater. One guest told us that one of Chekhov's short novellas could be performed as a play. We brought out the book, and one of our best actors, Mr. Moskvin, read a piece out loud.

Anton Pavlovich loved this recital so much that, for every day after, he invited this talented actor to read something out loud after dinner. Moskvin became a regular reader of Chekhov's short stories and novellas at our charity concerts.

Eventually our tour of Crimea ended. Both Chekhov and Gorky promised to write a play and give it to our theater to perform. To tell you a secret, this was one of the reasons all along for going all the way to Yalta to perform in front of Chekhov.

Kleopatra Katarygina. "Memories of A.P. Chekhov"

In July of 1889 Chekhov was visiting the city of Odessa, on his way to Yalta.

Between 1883 and 1900 I performed at every summer tour of the Moscow Maly Theater. We performed at Odessa, Kiev, Warsaw, and all over Russia. In the summer of 1889 we were visiting Odessa, where we met Chekhov. We knew that Chekhov's brother Nikolai, the painter, had died recently, and we decided to invite Chekhov so that we could entertain him a little bit. He was a future star and a great literary talent. I had read quite a few of his short stories, which I simply loved. We came to Odessa, and decided to go for a swim in between performances. On a nice sunny day, we went to the city beach. The male actors had their swim and then went up to the upper deck, where they started a conversation. I noticed a young man, rather tall and slim, with a nice-looking face and a small curly goatee. He wore a well-cut gray suit, a very sophisticated tie and a crisp white shirt. He looked very elegant and sophisticated — but oh, my goodness — he also had a huge white hat, and he was holding a bag of sunflower seeds and eating them.

"Who is this?" I asked.

"Don't you know? This is Chekhov!" someone told me.

I saw the future star, the great literary artist — eating sunflower seeds on the beach! I was very disappointed by his bad manners. Lensky, one of our leading actors, cried out,

"Anton Pavlovich, come over here, please! This is Kleopatra, one of our actresses, and she will not believe that you are Chekhov because you are eating sunflower seeds."

Chekhov came to us, bowed and said,

"Yes, it is I. I am Chekhov. I was invited to entertain you after your performances. Let me treat you to some sunflower seeds." With these words he stretched his hand out to me.

I said no but it was getting dark and we were going to the hotel. He got into the same cab with me, and cracking jokes and talking to me in a funny way, he treated me to sunflower seeds all the way.

In Odessa, I stayed in Room 48 of the Northern Hotel. Now this is a really historical place for me.

One night after the performance we were sitting in my room drinking tea and talking. All of a sudden, there was a knock at the door.

"Who is there? Come in please!"

We saw a long baguette being stuck through the doorway. Then the head of a dark-haired stranger appeared in the door.

"Who are you?"

"It is us," the man replied. We saw the very tall man with the dark hair come inside. He was accompanied by Anton Pavlovich Chekhov.

"Please excuse us, do not send us away, and treat us to some tea. This is bread, and here is some melon, sausages, and this is Mr. Sergeenko," said Chekhov. "He is a quiet man and he does not smoke." There was a pause.

"Put down your weapon," he said to Sergeenko, who was holding the long French bread as a soldier holds his rifle.

We did not know what to do with the bread. It was a huge piece of bread in a very small room with a tiny table, so we cut it into several pieces and put it on the newspaper that was spread on the table. Then we had more tea. Chekhov apologized for such a late visit again. He said,

"You theater directors invited me to spend some time with the theater. Yet, every time I come to see them, they are always busy counting the money, or their office is closed. So when I heard the noise through your door after the performance, I decided to say 'hello.' Maybe you could give me a warmer welcome."

We spoke until two or three in the morning. Sergeenko also remembered about our meeting late at night and called it "a talk between Anthony and Cleopatra."

I still remember Sergeenko. He was a very humble and quiet man, too quiet perhaps. He was the complete opposite of the joyful and talkative Chekhov.

On the next day, Chekhov gave me a volume of his *Stories*. I was very happy. He told me that since I had visited almost all the cities in central Russia and in Siberia, he made the following inscription on the front page of his book:

"To the great actress of the Russian land."

I told him, "Why are you making such an inscription? Now I cannot show this book to other people because they will start laughing at me. I am just an ordinary actress."

"Then, why do you call me a great author? If they have traveled across the country as much as you have traveled, then they can laugh."

Before he left Odessa, he gave me his photo with an autograph:

"For happy memories in room 48 in the Northern Hotel from a man who was visiting Odessa on a performance tour. A. Chekhov."

Every time I look at his portrait my heart beats faster, and I get emotional.

Konstantin Stanislavsky. "Chekhov and Artyom"

Only once did Chekov ever criticize his favorite actor, Artyom.

"My dear friend, you should not behave as if you are a Norwegian!"

The old man looked at the writer with eyes full of surprise. We had not said a word about Norway during our entire conversation.

Artyom did not understand anything. Finally, Chekhov cleared up what he wanted to say. Recently, Chekhov had seen Artyom perform in Ibsen's play, *The Wild Duck*. Ibsen was a Norwegian writer. They had performed Ibsen in a soft, realistic manner, and could not create the symbolic image of a half-crazed old man from Norway.

Chekhov continued, "Listen, you are a Muscovite, a Russian, and you have a guitar."

Alexander Rodionovich — Artyom — understood Chekhov's remark to mean that he never showed symbolism in his acting. Artyom was so upset and disappointed by this remark that he got sick. This worried Chekhov, because he was Chekhov's favorite actor. On his way from Moscow to Yalta, Anton Pavlovich wrote a letter to Artyom that said:

"I was very sad when I found out that you are sick. After finding out what kind of illness you have, I am calmer. This is nothing serious. Get well, get better, my dear friend. May God give you all the best."

From Yalta, Chekhov wrote to Vishnevsky and another actor who had visited Artyom.

"Pray tell me, how is the health of Alexander Rodionovich? Does he perform, or is he still at home?"

Artyom went on to play Akim in Tolstoy's *Power of Darkness*. Some actors and literary critics thought that this role was an immense success. However, Artyom was unhappy with his acting and he came to Stanislavsky, the actor and director. Artyom said,

"If you think that I am not a good actor, give this role to someone else."

Stanislavsky replied, "No. I will keep you in this role. I was about to replace you with another actor, but he plays badly."

"Whom do you mean?"

"Some actor named Stanislavsky," answered Stanislavsky himself.

Alexander Rodionovich remembered Chekhov. After the performance, Chekhov came down to the dressing rooms. [Rodionovich said to him,] "You know, I'm being criticized by theater critics."

Chekhov replied, "Please do not pay attention to the bad reviews. Put all the newspapers and magazines with your reviews in a pile. I do not read my book reviews until the summer. When summer comes, and the weather is beautiful, and the sun is shining, I sit outside in the sun, and I read these reviews. It is such a pleasure to read them scolding you. Do the same! Go to your summer cottage, wait for a nice summer day, take this mess of newspapers to a table outside, have some warm tea with milk, and read them little by little, one newspaper a day. The weather will be good, and it's always a pleasure to read them scolding you. This is how I read my critics."

Artyom said, "This is what Chekhov told me, and I followed his advice."

Artyom was very appreciative of Chekhov. He saw Chekhov as the founder of a new page in Russian theater. Most of all, he loved one of Chekhov's reviews of his performance of Mr. Firs from *The Cherry Orchard.*

Chekhov was very tired and sick. After all the ovations and celebrations, he came to the dressing room and whispered,

"You were wonderful." Chekhov's review consisted of only one very short phrase, but he had given a great gift to Artyom, a gift that would last a lifetime.

When Chekhov died in 1904, it was a huge blow for Artyom. The same year Chekhov's last play *The Cherry Orchard* started to blossom on the stage.

Nikolai Efros. "From the History of The Cherry Orchard"

When did Chekhov start writing his drama *The Cherry Orchard*? I cannot tell you the exact date. It was definitely after the first night of *The Three Sisters*, performed on July 1, 1901, that people began to ask him to write another play.

Sometimes, a few randomly said phrases that I heard from the people surrounding Chekhov shed light on the history of creation of his new play.

Once Stanislavsky carefully asked Chekhov about his next play and when it could be expected for the theater reading. Chekhov went over to his writing desk, pulled out a bunch of little notes with scribbles on them, and shook them in the air, saying,

"My entire new play is here, on these little notes."

Then, Chekhov returned all those notes back in the desk drawer. He did not speak of his future play again for a while.

We can say for sure, based on the letters and conversations with several people who surrounded Chekhov, that in the summer of 1902 Chekhov had created an outline of a future play, and even found its title.

In June of 1902, Chekhov's wife Olga Knipper was seriously sick. Chekhov stayed at her bed side for several days. In order to entertain her, and distract her from her illness, Chekhov asked her once,

"Would you like to know the title of my new play?"

He knew that this would lift up her spirits. He moved closer to Olga Leonardovna's ear and discovering there was no one else in the room at the time besides the two of them, he whispered quietly:

"*The Cherry Orchard.*"

That was the first mention of his new piece's title.

He always kept it a secret — the titles of his new works. He made absolutely sure that no one could find out about his title before the work was finished. Chekhov was kind of manic about this policy.

One day, later that year, his sister, Maria Pavlovna, visited Chekhov in Yalta. She asked him about the title of the new play. Anton Pavlovich suddenly looked very worried, and looked around the room. There was no one else except for him and his sister. The only other person in the house was their mother, who was in another room at the time. Even then, Chekhov did not dare to say the title of the new play out loud.

He thought for a little bit, looked around again, took a small piece of paper, wrote something carefully, folded it several times, and then gave it to his sister. She took it and read, *The Cherry Orchard.*

It took Chekhov a long time to actually start writing this play. At the end of the summer, he wrote to his wife from Yalta to Moscow,

"I will not write my new play this year, and even if I felt like writing, I will not do so now."

The next several letters mentioned that he was not going to start writing this play that fall, or even that year.

Savva Mamontov. "Two Meetings with Chekhov"

A rather sad event happened to the manuscript of *The Cherry Orchard.* Anton Pavlovich stepped out of his room for a few minutes, and left on his desk the loose sheets of paper covered with his small, neat handwriting. When he was away a sudden summer thunderstorm moved in. The wind scattered the pages of the Chekhov manuscript all over the garden.

After they collected the pages and brought them to Chekhov, he could not read a single word there. The rain washed away all the ink from those pages. People asked Chekhov, "Don't you remember what was written here?"

Chekhov answered with a smile, "I don't remember what I just wrote. I will have to rewrite all these scenes."

He never did. Thus, a whole scene from this great play has been lost.

Sergei Naidenov-Alexeev. "Chekhov in My Memories"

The first time I saw Chekhov was from a distance. In my notebook, dated September 21, 1901, I wrote the following: "Yesterday, I saw the best play ever onstage, *Three Sisters* by Chekhov. The playwright was present, which may be the reason that the actors were so inspired and vibrant.

It seemed to me that the story of those three sisters and the cruelty of life around them touched everyone. All who were present at the theater were inspired to ask themselves, "Why do we live in this world?" After watching this play, you wanted to do something good for others, to make a difference in someone's life.

After the performance, Chekhov stood on the stage, making clumsy bows to the public, clasping both hands to his chest. He seemed very close to those in the crowd.

I looked closely at his face. I believed I may have seen him earlier in the day at the Junker's Bank by Kooznetsky Bridge. No, I decided, maybe he was not the same man, I did not think the man at the bank could make such a wonderful and soft smile.

Someone sitting close to me in the theater told me,

"He is such a wonderful man."

That was the same time period when I was full of dreams and plans for the future. I bought myself a writing desk, an armchair, a lamp and a nice inkwell. I divided the inheritance I had recently received — 800 rubles per year — into monthly installments of 75 rubles per month. I decided to work at writing for one year. If nothing came of it, I would quit.

After several months, by the time the *Three Sisters* was being performed at the Moscow Art Theater, I had already written three plays. One of these plays, the *Children of Mr. Vanushin*, was on stage, had become a success, and was my saving grace. I made enough money to enable me to live comfortably for several years. I made connections in the literary word, but most importantly, this play of mine gave me an opportunity to see Anton Pavlovich Chekhov in person again.

Four months later I met him, in his Yalta home, after having seen him at the theater.

Chekhov himself came to the door, and greeted me, "Come in, come in. I have been waiting for you."

I found him a friendly and sensitive man, and understood how he had inspired the whole Art Theater.

Chekhov told me that in order to become a good literary artist, you have to write a lot, every day, over a long time.

I have to tell you how I decided to visit Chekhov, with the story beginning weeks earlier. I knew that I could not stay in Moscow in the cold spell we were having. I had to go south as quickly as possible. So I decided to ask the theater director, Fedor Abramovich Korsh, about possibly traveling south. He invited me into his study, and said, "Go to Yalta and rest. Chekhov lives there. He is a very friendly and genuine man. I am planning to stage his play, *Marriage*, and I need to ask his permission. Take this letter and bring it to him for me."

And so, I decided to go to Yalta. The next day, I was on the train for Yalta, with a letter from Korsh to Chekhov in my pocket.

Leonid Leonidov. *"Past and Present"*

I was readying myself in my dressing room for the final scene of the third act when I suddenly came across Chekhov, sitting on a small sofa under the wall clock in the spot where actors usually wait for their cue to enter the stage. I became numb. I thought that he was as worried as myself. However, he was in complete control, and he said some kind and supportive words to me:

"Listen, please do not worry. Olga is also worried."

After the third act was performed with great success, they pulled up the curtain. All of the actors stepped out for an ovation, bringing Chekhov out as well. A storm of applause greeted us, as all in the theater stood up. They welcomed the author with a long speech on behalf of the theater.

During his trips to Moscow, Chekhov often visited our rehearsals and performances. His remarks about staging his plays, or those of other playwrights, were always very short and to the point. For example, when we performed *In My Dreams* by Nemirovich-Danchenko, Chekhov came to see the performance. The author was very worried as he sat there anticipating Chekhov's remarks at the end of the performance. Chekhov kept silence. Then, all of a sudden, he said,

"Why do you have palm trees on the stage when you have a scene in the restaurant? You should remove the palm trees!"

That was it. He never said anything else about the play.

When I repeatedly asked Chekhov about how to perform Lopakhin, one of his major characters, he kept silence. After much badgering, he finally replied,

"How should you perform Lopakhin? In yellow shoes."

I remember that it was a precious gift for me to receive his autographed photograph, dated with the date of the first performance of *The Cherry Orchard*.

Stanislavsky told me once, when he was explaining one of his plays, that he could visualize a very tall mountain, and Chekhov on the very top. Little figures of people seemed to be very small in comparison with him. Chekhov found these people — Firs, Gaev, Lopakhin — grabbing them right in the midst of their lives. They sat beside him like inanimate puppets before he breathed life into them; then they started moving and he had to watch that they moved in the right direction, did not fall asleep, and made the right moves.

Another memory: it was July 1904, and I was at the Kiev Railway Station restaurant on my way to Odessa from Moscow. I saw a familiar face in front of me, and then I recognized the man as Henryk Sienkiewicz. He opened a newspaper, and we both read, "A telegram from Badenweiler: Chekhov is dead."

Viktor Troinov. "Meetings in Moscow"

Chekhov's literary fame grew.

The years of financial struggle and work with diminutive, obscure magazines were over. He was relatively well-off and could afford the fairly independent life of a well-known writer.

However, as his fame grew, his disease became more and more severe over the years.

He was a doctor by profession, and he had practiced in his younger years. Therefore, Anton Pavlovich was not ignorant of his own medical condition.

Chekhov spent the winter of 1903-1904 in Moscow. He always spoke of his illness in passing, as casually as possible. While he did not want to talk about his health, its condition revealed itself in his face. His face looked darker, his complexion was dull, and he had many fresh wrinkles on his forehead.

Worst of all was his deep, constant cough, the obvious and inescapable mark of the tuberculosis that had developed in his lungs for years.

Chekhov met Gorky in Moscow.

"The actors, they send me very warm regards."

Gorky was very interested in going to the opening performance of Chekhov's play *The Cherry Orchard*, and said repeatedly, "When will it happen?"

Chekhov replied, "I have no idea about the date. We've argued with Stanislavsky over it several times. He thinks that it's a lyrical drama. This is not true. I wrote it as a farce, a comedy, a true satire."

Chekhov stopped for a few moments, thought about something, and then continued,

"Perhaps Stanislavsky is right. But every time I go to the rehearsals, I'm in pain. Stanislavsky cuts out all the lengthy monologues from my play."

Chekhov's play was to be published with the publisher Znanie. Gorky suggested publishing it there in its original form.

"No, no," Chekhov shook his head in dissent. "We need to publish it exactly as Mr. Stanislavsky has produced it. This way, other theaters wishing to perform the play will do it in the same way. You know that Stanislavsky is far more knowledgeable about theatre than us."

As always, he ended the conversation with a brief joke, adding in a tragic voice,

"When you decide to stage Moliere's *Hypochondriac*, I shall not let you do it without me. I am a doctor, and this is the one play I do know how to produce."

"You know, my dear Mr. Gorky..." Chekhov once said in a very reassuring way. "Do you know that our Russian culture is still quite young? Three hundred years ago, the English had Shakespeare, the Spanish had Cervantes, and in France, Molière put on his comedies. Our culture and literature date back only a hundred years, to Pushkin. But now we are catching up to and even surpassing the world. Look at Dostoevsky, Tolstoy: they are read all around the globe. Now, our lives are surrounded by darkness and hardship, but our people are changing for the better."

Chekhov made a small pause and then added,

"I would like to live for another ten years, to see life get better."

CHAPTER SIX

Chekhov in Yalta: 1898–1904

Introduction

I am going to buy a nice property in Yalta, build a house on it, so that I can spend my winters there. My mother would live there with me. I am not going to design and built it by myself—everything will be done by an architect.

> —Anton Chekhov, "Letters." His letter to Mikhail Chekhov,
> October 26, 1898

I bought a piece of seashore, not far from the pier in Gruzuf. Now we are the owners of a small bay, which has space for a small boat.... The house is rather poor, but its roof is shingled, and it has four rooms and a spacious corridor.

> —Anton Chekhov, "Letters." His letter to Maria Chekhova,
> January 14–15, 1901

He liked to build, create, and plant gardens. He took very good care of the fruit trees in his garden. He used to tell me when we were in his house in Yalta,

"If every man who owns a piece of land could make it look nice, all our planet, our Earth would be such a beautiful place to live."

> —Maxim Gorky. "A.P. Chekhov"

While living in Yalta, Anton Pavlovich continued to have the same wandering spirit. Moscow still attracted him. From time to time, he made trips to the capital, especially after marrying Olga Leonardovna. But his health in Yalta did not improve. He went to the Ufa region to drink horse milk for medical treatment; shortly after, he went to a spa in Nice, France. But the lung disease continued to develop.

> —Maria Chekhova. "From the Distant Past"

[This is one of the last letters written by Chekhov before his death, from a spa in Germany.—P.S.] Badenweiler is a wonderful place. Warm and

Anton Pavlovich with his younger brother Ivan Pavlovich, in spring 1901, at the backyard of the newly built Chekhov house in Yalta.

pleasant for life. But three days from now, I will probably start thinking
about how to get out of here, to escape the boredom.

> — Anton Chekhov, "Letters." His letter to A. Kurkin,
> June 12, 1904

For many years, Chekhov was sick with a terrible disease *[tuberculosis —
P.S.]* which eventually killed him, but I want to ask you: Did Russian
readers hear any words of complaint from Chekhov? It was really amazing
to see the courage with which Chekhov fought his illness and then died.
Even when he had the most painful sufferings, no one would ever have
suspected this.

> — Ivan Bunin. "Chekhov"

I remember his funeral, as if all that was a dream. I remember his grave,
completely covered with flowers. The future generations will remember
his name with gratitude and with quiet sadness. He dreamt about happiness.

> — A. Kuprin. "Chekhov. In Memoriam"

Elena Shavrova. "A.P. Chekhov"

*[Elena Shavrova, an aspiring writer and translator, fell in love with Chekhov
when she was a teen-ager and he was a mature writer of short stories; one of the
Chekhov's best short stories about love, "A Lady with a Dog," is loosely based on
their love affair — P.S.]*

We went for a picnic outside of Yalta, on a nice sunny day.

"He has arrived! Chekhov has arrived!" Mr. Schmidt, a navy officer shouted
to us from a distance away, as he waved his hat in the air in greeting.

He continued, "He has been in our town for two days so far. He stayed
at the Farbstein Hotel. Today, he had coffee at the Welters Coffee House, and
had a dinner at the Central Park Restaurant. Oh, and all of you are invited
to have a picnic with him tomorrow!"

The next day, Chekhov, in the midst of a cluster of young writers, was
walking towards the Yalta suburbs to have a coffee with his new friend, a
Tartar merchant named Mr. Nuri. On the way, we saw a huge mansion right
at the outskirts of Yalta.

I told Chekhov, "Every time when I see such a beautiful big house like
this, my imagination whispers to me that very happy people must live there."

Chekhov did not say anything, but looked at me very carefully. After a
little distance away from the house, Chekhov drew close and whispered in
my ear,

"I think that you have made a wrong statement about this kind of house and the people who live there. It is simply because you are young and don't grasp the reality of life yet. Please remember that huge wealth cannot give people happiness. That is all."

We arrived at Nuri's home as it grew dark. The master was waiting for us at the front door, and he instantly put Chekhov at the head of the table, seated in the chair for the most respected of visitors.

Within a couple of minutes, Chekhov was conversing with Nuri as if he had known him for years, asking many questions, and showing great insight into the merchant's life.

The next day, Chekhov and I were sitting having a meal. I felt so shy and embarrassed that I was awkwardly burning my lips with hot coffee while fingering the cookie crumbs on my plate. Finally, I spoke to him.

"Anton Pavlovich, I would like to ask you for a favor. I have written a short story, called 'Sophie,' which is about life in the country. I wondered if you could take a look at it, and tell me if it's worth publishing."

Chekhov answered me with a charming smile on his face, "So, that is why you are here. You have written a short story, huh? Wonderful. Despite the fact it is too hot these days, I will read it. Then I will give you my opinion if you will have a future as a writer."

After this conversation, I met Chekhov almost on a daily basis: either in the city park, the waterfront alley, or at the local waterfall Urchin-Su. A few days later, Chekhov told me,

"People always seem to give me a lot of stories to read. Despite the fact that you are a very young lady and have not lived a great deal of life yet, your story is one of the best I have read while I have been here. If you wish, we can publish it. However, I made a few changes here at the end of the story, with a pencil. I wish you to grow and become a good writer, which is likely with such a good start."

Anton Pavlovich took my story with him and shortly left Yalta. My short story was later published in a major periodical, *The New Time.*

Daniil Gorodetsky. *"Memories of Anton Pavlovich Chekhov"*

The local newspaper that I used to publish at the time wrote that Chekhov came to Yalta on July 16, 1889. There was a section in the local newspaper that would list the people visiting Yalta. Chekhov was included in one of those lists. We could not resist the temptation and added the word "writer" next to his name. The ad read as follows,

"Chekhov, A.P., a writer, arrived in Yalta from Odessa. He is staying at the Farbstein Hotel."

Chekhov looked very upset when he came to our editorial office. He said,

"Why did you do this? Why did you say in your newspaper that I am writer? First and foremost, I am a doctor, not a writer."

A little earlier, before the Chekhov's arrival, I received a letter from P. Sergeenko that Chekhov was going to come to Yalta for a few months and was planning to stay for a while at a local spa. Sergeenko asked me to arrange Chekhov's accommodations.

At the time, Chekhov's popularity of was so huge that people of all ages wanted to make his acquaintance, whether men, ladies, young or old. I was kept busy with numerous requests: "Can I meet Chekhov in person?," or "Can you introduce me to Chekhov?," and so on. People were bothering me a lot, but they were bothering Chekhov himself even more.

Every time Chekhov went walking along the waterfront, people used to point at him and speak about him loudly behind his back. There would be crowds of people following him every time he went for a walk in the city park. Many people came uninvited to his hotel room to speak with him, or invite him to "appear at a charity concert," or "to go sea-fishing," or to go to "a very decent party."

How did Chekhov treat all those irritating visitors? Was he angry at them? On the contrary, he was always friendly and humorous. At the time, he was an always well-balanced and well-reserved man.

Once Chekhov came to my house while I was writing a short story for a small provincial newspaper, joking, "Are you working hard on a new masterpiece?"

I replied, "Yes, I am working hard on my creation. Yet I am sick and tired of all this."

Chekhov added, "Tell me about it! When I started my writing career, I wrote a lot of small pieces for all kinds of newspapers and magazines. If you want to become a writer, the first condition is that you have to write and write, without interruption."

I said, "You are absolutely correct, but not everyone can be a great writer like you, in the full meaning of this word."

Chekhov said, "But why should every person become a writer in the true meaning of this word? Recently, I received a manuscript to review. You know, on the very first page, I saw a quote that stated a writer should be ready to sacrifice his entire life and even his soul to become a real writer. I was touched by this. But then I thought, 'Why should one be a writer?' Our society needs all kinds of good professions. To be a good doctor, a good shepherd, a good soldier or a good farmer — all these professions should be as respected as being a good writer."

I. Gurland. "Memories of Chekhov"

I was a law school student at the time, accompanied by local journalist Gorodetsky — when we were meeting Chekhov when he arrived from Odessa to Yalta by ship on June 16.

The sea seemed to be rather quiet to us, but nevertheless Chekhov told us that he had developed seasickness. He told us the next day that he had felt as if the land was shaking under his feet.

Chekhov tried to make a joke on the next day:

"It seems to me that my work will never be finished here, after this bout of seasickness. First, it was my new play (*The Wood Spirit*) and then my new short novel (*The Dull Story*). Now bits and pieces of these two works are totally mixed up in my head!"

I was a student of the Yaroslavl University Law School at the time, and I remember this time very well, as it was a good period in Chekhov's life. In one of Chekhov's letters to me written much later, in 1892, I remember him writing this:

"There are many difficult moments in a life of every person, and those few happy days during our summer together that I spent in Yalta then were a real pleasure for me."

A.A. Kuprina-Iordanskaya. "From the Memories of Kuprin"

Every morning, at 9 A.M. sharp, I used to arrive at Chekhov's dacha in Yalta to work on my short story "In the Circus."

My financial situation was not very good. Just before I arrived in Yalta a few days earlier, I had several short stories published in the *Odessa News*. The expected royalty payments were late, so I was completely broke. This made it awkward for me to stay for dinner at the Chekhov's house. However, Anton Pavlovich, being a very observant man, somehow discovered my secret. Every time I planned to take my leave, I would tell Chekhov that my landlady was expecting me to return for dinner.

Chekhov used to say in a decisive way,

"Please, stay with me and let's share a meal together. When I was a young and a healthy man, I could easily have dinner twice a day, so I am sure that you can have three dinners during the same day!"

Chekhov liked my short story "In the Circus."

As a doctor, he gave me directions and explanations as to what symptoms circus athletes experience that should be paid special attention to by an author writing about them, namely me.

Chekhov said that the author should describe the symptoms in such a way that the readers would have no doubts about the nature of the illness. Chekhov was very involved in this, and even read me a short lecture about different heart problems and conditions. I understood that if Chekhov were not such a wonderful writer, he could have become an exceptional doctor.

Mikhail Pervukhin. "A.P. Chekhov and Yalta Residents"

In Yalta, Chekhov helped young aspiring authors on a regular basis. One day, when I was visiting Chekhov, I saw a huge pile of manuscripts on top of his writing desk. Chekhov told me,

"I am really tired now. I have read about five of these manuscripts today, and now I need a rest."

I asked him, "Are you reading this for the *Russian Thought* magazine?

Chekhov replied, "No, no. What are you talking about? These are all works by the up and coming authors who are bothering me these days."

I saw such manuscripts on the Chekhov's desk all the time. Once I looked at the manuscripts and noticed that they had all been read and thoroughly edited by Chekhov. There were margin notes throughout, with some phrasing having been corrected.

And from time to time, Chekhov would insert a few words, always in his beautiful style.

Lev Shapovalov. "Chekhov's House in Yalta"

In Yalta, there was a bookstore owned by Mr. Sinani, a local bookseller. This was a regular place for the local literary artists to meet. Anton Pavlovich used to go there almost daily to pick up new publications and forthcoming books.

Chekhov gave the impression of a very friendly, amiable and approachable person. Very soon, our casual acquaintance grew into real friendship. We spent a lot of time together. We used to walk around the streets of Yalta, visiting each other, and speaking about subjects that animated us.

During one of these conversations, Anton Pavlovich asked me to design and build a new house for him in Yalta. After several minutes of hesitation, I agreed. However, I felt the weight of the responsibility of building a house for one of our best writers.

Anton Pavlovich showed me his property in a distant Yalta suburb. I made a sketch of the future house, and shortly after this, Anton Pavlovich and Maria Pavlovna accepted it. Soon, they were both daily visitors to the construction site, supervising how the house was being built. At the same time, Anton Pavlovich planted his trees in the back field. He never trusted anyone with this particular job, so he planted his entire garden by himself.

About ten months later, the construction of the house was finished, and the Chekhovs moved in.

Anton Pavlovich presented me with his photograph and an inscription:

"To L. Shapovalov, with fond memories and gratitude for the house he has built for me, from Anton Chekhov. Yalta, December 16, 1899."

I remember this photograph and I have kept it carefully for nearly fifty years. It reminds me of the several years that I spent in Chekhov's company.

Maria Chekhova. "Chekhov Museum in Yalta"

The life of my brother, Anton Pavlovich Chekhov, can be divided into four periods — the Taganrog, Melikhovo, Moscow and Yalta periods. Our family has changed residences three times during those periods.

In 1897, Anton was admitted to the clinic of Professor Ostroumov, and I realized that drastic changes in our lives had to be made. So I made the necessary changes immediately. After discharging Anton Pavlovich from the clinic, the doctors told him to adjust his life into a more structured routine, and spend his winters in a southern climate.

Following their advice, Anton Pavlovich traveled to a resort in Nice, in the south of France. Life in our home in Melikhovo was dull and empty without him.

Upon his return in the spring of 1898, he was in much better health and spirits. Life at Melikhovo slipped back into its old routine, but despite his appearance, we had to consider the implications of the doctor's recommendations. Anton's health was now our first priority.

The summer of 1898 unfolded with poetic beauty in Melikhovo.

However, the seasons kept changing and with the arrival of fall, Anton Pavlovich was left with the dilemma of where to spend the winter. He felt out of place during his time abroad, and did not wish to travel again. He did not want to leave Russia, Moscow in particular.

In one of his letters to V. Sobolevsky, the editor of the *Russian News*, he wrote, "Being away from Russia will be bad for me, bad in every respect. I remember that the southern coast of Crimea was a good place. It was homey and restful in Crimea, and it is closer to Russia."

Anton Pavlovich decided to spend the winter of 1898-99 in Yalta.

In September of 1898, my brother Anton Chekhov left for Yalta with plans to stay there for several months. However, in October of 1898, our father, Pavel Egorovich, suddenly passed away.

This sad event pushed my brother to make the ultimate decision. Anton decided to move the entire family to Yalta. He went on his own, and found a plot of land for a reasonable price on the outskirts of Yalta, in the village of Alupka.

When I joined him in Yalta to discuss family affairs, the plot had already been purchased. On the day of my arrival, we went to see it together. Much to my disappointment, it was far from the seashore and on a steep mountain slope. It was located too close to a busy street, with absolutely nothing on it but an untidy vineyard, struggling in the hard, rocky soil.

Never being well off financially, with money being tight once again, Anton had to mortgage the plot right away.

At the beginning of 1899, he accepted an agreement with the publisher Marx, selling them all of his present and future works. Although the agreement was not very profitable for Anton, it offered us the chance to complete construction of our new home in Yalta.

Chekhov visited the construction site almost daily in the winter of 1898-99. That spring, Anton planted the first trees in the new garden. A great lover of nature, Chekhov wanted to turn his backyard into a blossoming paradise. Like he had done in previous years in Melikhovo, he spent entire days planting trees, shrubs and flowers. He upheld an extensive correspondence with several flower shops, ordering all kinds of seeds and gardening equipment. Roses were his favorite flower, and he cultivated a large variety of them in his Yalta garden, some being introduced to Crimea's climate for the first time. He tended the flowers himself, allowing no one else the privilege.

Kuprin, the novelist who often visited us in Yalta, later related that Anton wanted to see his backyard transformed into a natural wonderland. "Every tree has been planted in my presence, and so naturally, this garden is very dear to me," he told Kuprin.

Chekhov recollected aloud,

"When I saw our property in Yalta for the first time, it was an untouched heath in the wilderness, rampant with weeds and with wild thistle plants. I have tamed this wilderness, and turned it into a beautiful garden." These words expressed my brother's belief that "a few hundred years later, the whole earth will turn into a beautiful garden," and that as a result "life will be much easier and much more pleasant." He had this beautiful belief in a happy future for all mankind.

In the spring of 1899, Chekhov briefly returned to Melikhovo to make all the necessary preparations for moving the rest of the family to Crimea.

In September of 1899, my mother Evgenia Yakovlevna and I arrived there. Soon after, our entire considerable family moved in to our new house in Yalta. Then the final, last period of my brother's life began — the Yalta Period.

Living in Yalta, Chekhov greatly missed the Russian landscape that was so dear to his heart. He lived in Yalta apart from his regular circle of friends, writers, painters and theatrical figures; without his beloved Moscow, where he had been in regular contact with its many literary editors, bookshops, and theaters.

This does not mean that Anton Pavlovich disliked Yalta and the western shore of Crimea in general. To the contrary, in many of his letters he reflected positively about Crimea, which he particularly enjoyed in spring and autumn.

"Living out there, in Crimea, one must spend a couple of months per year in Moscow, not in the summer, of course, but in winter," he wrote shortly after moving to Yalta.

As soon as we moved to Yalta, many of his friends began to visit, helping him spend his forced retirement in a more pleasant way. During those years, our house received a whole slew of visitors, including the most prominent of Russia's personalities in literature, art and science.

First of all, I should mention Maxim Gorky. It was there, in Yalta, where their friendship began when Gorky spent several days in our Yalta home in 1901.

Among the frequent visitors to our home were writers Kuprin, Mamin-Sibiryak, Bunin, Teleshov, Gilyarovsky, and many others.

One particularly exciting event that I remember was the arrival of the Moscow Art Theater in 1900. The whole cast visited Yalta in order to show Anton Pavlovich the production of his plays, *The Seagull* and *Uncle Vanya*.

That year was a beautiful spring. The entire theater company, along with the directors Stanislavsky and Nemirovich-Danchenko, spent most days inside our house. During and after the performance, a large group of artists came to Yalta for the occasion. Also among our guests was Olga Knipper, Anton's future wife, one of the finest actresses of the company. Olga helped my mother and me receive our numerous guests. Anton Pavlovich was very happy and pleased. There were numerous captivating discussions about literature, art and theater which took place in both our house and garden.

Chekhov often visited Leo Tolstoy, or spoke to him over the telephone in the winter of 1901-1902, while Tolstoy was staying at Mrs. Panina's estate in Gaspra.

In 1902, another prominent writer from Moscow, V. Korolenko, visited our house.

The most frequent visitor to our house was Mr. Elpatievsky, the local doctor, who was very active in public town affairs. He quickly became one of our closest friends. Because of his poor health, Anton Pavlovich had to give up his medical practice, but he never failed to give his professional assistance to needy patients, whom he, as a doctor, received free of change. His stethoscope always lay in its usual place on his writing desk.

Vladimir Ladyzhensky. "Old Days"

Your face gazes at me from the photograph on my writing desk. My dear and precious friend! Our conversations and your laughter are forever imprinted in my memory. I believe that most of all, I shall remember your eyes — sometimes sad, and at times joyful, shimmering with the treasure of your wonderful humor.

One can write a great deal about Chekhov. I should have known this, and recorded all of his thoughts and our many talks, in order to assist the future biographer in his description of this Atlas of our literary world. So it stands to reason that these random and erratic notes do not pretend to give a general picture. I will only try to depict several brief impressions that this great artist made on me.

As far as I recall, I met Chekhov in St. Petersburg at the end of the 1880s. He was incredibly sad, since he had been forced to say goodbye to Moscow and Central Russia, which he loved, and move to Crimea for the winter.

He invited me to visit him in Crimea during the winter seasons, saying,

"It is a pity, but I cannot visit Moscow during the winter."

However, in the springtime he returned to Moscow, and was admitted to the hospital almost simultaneously with his arrival. He wrote to me that his health was poor, and that he had to sell his complete works to the publisher for only 75,000 rubles. This was not a profitable agreement for Chekhov, but unfortunately inevitable. He needed the money this contract would bring, to build his new home in Crimea. I am not sure if it was worth it, but his dacha in Crimea, near Yalta, was truly wonderfully built.

Both Chekhov and his sister, Maria Pavlovichna, put great care and thought into the design and construction of their new residence. However, it was impossible for Chekhov to accept the necessity of living so far away from Moscow.

Here are some lines from the letters he wrote me while building the dacha:

> Thank you for remembering me, and writing to me. It seems likely that I will make Yalta my permanent residence, so I am already building a comfortable abode for myself. I have invited some of my friends here, and I plan to start a vineyard, so that I can treat them with good red wine when they visit.
>
> During the winter I plan to live in Yalta, but I plan to live in Melikhovo, my estate near Moscow, in the summers.
>
> Please write me, and remember that I now live in a far-away place, one not of my own volition. I need at least some communication with my friends. I need it badly.

When I visited Chekhov in Crimea, he asked me, "Do you like my house and garden? Despite its unquestionable loveliness, this place is my prison."

With the passing of time, he liked his dacha, and took great care of it.

Chekhov told me once, sadly, "People get married in the same way that I ended up living in this cottage. At first, they do not like each other, but over the years, they become familiar and get used to each other."

In spite of his illness, and the fact that his health was deteriorating, Chekhov continued to work very hard.

Viacheslav Fausek. "My Meeting with Chekhov"

It happened in Yalta in 1893, when I still worked as a civil administrator. My meeting with Chekhov was totally unexpected, through his sister Maria. At the time, she was renting the apartment of a friend of mine.

One of the first things Chekhov asked me was,

"Do you write?"

I had published a few short stories in children's magazines, as well as several articles for the national newspaper, the *Russian Herald*, as their correspondent from Southern Crimea.

I think that my amateur writing was what really sparked our friendship. Chekhov welcomed both my writing and me in a simple and warm manner.

During our conversations, we found out that Chekhov had graduated from Taganrog High School; I had attended the same school. We spoke about mutual acquaintances, the school itself, and the teachers, all of which were constant sources of hilarity and wit. Chekhov spoke about his past with lots of energy and humor, and we spent most of the time laughing.

The Yalta waterfront in tourist season displayed the full range of visitors. You could chance upon pretty much any sort of person there. Chekhov had a habit of strolling the waterfront together with a Mr. Miroliubov, a singer from the Moscow Opera who had been sent to Yalta to improve his lungs. It was more likely than not to find them also accompanied by a group of writers. One day, Chekhov invited me to come along with them, and meet his friends. He did not object to having a drink, but we always drank in moderation. Even then, he complained about his weak heart. Nonetheless, Chekhov never refused to go to the Bolotnikov Pub for barbecue, or to one of the numerous wine cellars in Yalta for a glass of wine.

Sometimes, more people joined our company, and we had a really good time together.

As soon as we would run into a nice group of people, we would go into the nearest restaurant, move several tables together, and enjoy a lovely dinner. Then, we would travel out of town for a barbecue, or go to the Central Hotel for coffee.

Chekhov never left our company of close friends. That said, I don't think that he was very happy in our company. He always sat quietly, and pretended to drink wine. Maybe he was observing and making notes on the people who were drunk and talking too much. Was it true, or not? No one will know for sure.

Chekhov stayed at the Russia Hotel in downtown Yalta. One day, he said to me,

"Why don't you come and visit me at the hotel? Come over, and we will talk."

"What is the best time for me to come? What times are you not too busy, Anton Pavlovich?"

"You can come whenever you want. I am always busy, but I don't mind stopping my work for you. I like to relax and talk to people."

I began visiting the Russia Hotel on a regular basis. I remember those days.

A knock at the door.

"Can I come in?"

"Yes, come in, come in, please." Behind the door, you could hear the voice of Anton Pavlovich and the sound of a chair being pushed away from a writing desk.

Chekhov rose from behind the table. You could see the inkwell, the pen and pages of paper strewn across the desk. Whenever I came, he appeared to be in the midst of his work.

"I don't want to interrupt you. You were just writing when I came, am I right?"

"Oh, I don't mind at all! How are you? Please, take a seat. I told you, I write all the time," Anton Pavlovich told me with a smile.

I asked him, "Do you write after dinner?"

"Yes, even after dinner. I do not take rests. As soon as the post-dinner heaviness in my stomach goes away, I sit down at the table and resume writing."

Then he spoke about the process of writing,

"Sometimes I cannot write. Then I stop, and go for a walk and visit my friends, or go to a restaurant. In a short while, it gets better, and I fall back into my normal routine. Of course, sometimes my work does not progress as I want it to. I try to write, I cross it out, but no matter what I do, nothing good comes out. Then I have to stop.

"Whatever I have published in my life constitutes maybe half of what I have written. I have a whole suitcase of unfinished manuscripts, which I have started, crossed out and never finished — countless stories and novels."

One day, I asked Anton Pavlovich why he was so pessimistic in more recent short stories, and why he depicted Russian life in such dark colors. Chekhov replied to me,

"Now, listen. I wrote many things in a joyful and humorous way, and now it is time to get serious about life."

At the time, I had written a book about Yalta and its suburbs. It was published and sold in local bookstores. I asked Chekhov about his impressions regarding my book. He told me,

"The historical part of the book is very good. The factual part is too short. It should be two or even three times bigger."

I told Chekhov, "You know, I wrote this book all by myself, only from time to time. For a big work — something like the *Encyclopedia of Yalta* — we would need a group of people."

Chekhov interrupted me, "I cannot agree with this. I am very jealous of my own literary work, and I would never agree for even one person to be my co-author. I wouldn't even agree to publish something with another person. I like what I write, and I do not want to share my name with anyone. I like being successful, and I like to see other people's success. A journalist should write about everything."

I asked Chekhov, "What can Yalta, this small provincial town, give to a journalist to write about? It is a bustling railway station and resort in the summer and a tiny provincial town in the winter."

"But," Chekhov said, "you are mistaken. When you live in Crimea all the time, you are in very favorable conditions for writing. You are surrounded by so many different people, people like the Tartars. Every one of their small villages has its own legends and folklore."

"One needs to speak the Tartar language," I replied.

Chekhov agreed with me, saying, "You are right. But, for example, Mr. Z. knows the local Tartar language, and he could be useful to you. Why not try writing more journalistic essays?"

"I will try," I promised.

"Then, do it. I wish you luck."

Vladimir Posse. "My Life"

I spent about ten days in Yalta. I kept running into Chekhov everywhere: we used to meet in the city, or walking along the waterfront, or along the paths in the park. In the evening, Gorky and I used to visit his villa. Usually, Miroliubov and another writer accompanied us.

In Chekhov's company I felt comfortable and relaxed. He was a quiet, tender man who never put on airs. He was very sincere. He looked at you very carefully, but without intrusion. His eyes were at once sad and smiling. He was a sick man himself, and at the same time he was organizing a charity medical center for sick patients who did not have enough money to pay for proper medical treatment.

A couple of times, I spoke to Chekhov alone, without Gorky, Miroliubov or anyone else. I remember I was sitting at his desk, and he was sitting on his sofa at the back of his room. We were talking about life and literature. He spoke a little about his own personal life. We both fell silent for a while, busy with our own thoughts.

The silence was abruptly interrupted by Chekhov, catching me completely off guard: "Vladimir Alexandrovich, would you ever marry an actress?"

I responded indecisively, "Well, I don't know really. I might. I suppose I could."

There was a harsh note in his voice, a note that I had never heard before. I suppose he must have married Olga Knipper with a certain amount of hesitation. His personal, inner life is almost unknown. The letters that have been published so far reveal nothing about the life of his heart. Clearly, it was complicated. I can tell you for sure that before his marriage at the advanced age of 40, Chekhov was not only involved with women, but loved them passionately and certainly had a few affairs.

When I was going from Moscow to St. Petersburg, he asked me to bring some of his printed galleys to the publisher Marx. He told me that he had included some weak early stories in the edition of his *Complete Works* forthcoming in Marx. Chekhov said,

"Some of my early work is not good enough and I hope it will not be published again."

I met Chekhov later the same year, in Moscow.

He was accompanied by Gorky, at the performance of his play, *The Seagull*. Before this, I had neither seen nor read the play. During one of the intermissions, I came to Chekhov, who was standing in the lobby, supporting his back against a column, his head tilted slightly back. He looked a little sad somehow. I told him,

"Anton Pavlovich, I would like to thank you for this bold act of literary bravery, for having depicted such a great writer as Trigorin — maybe as great a writer as Turgenev himself— a mean and vulgar person."

I felt that I'd said something wrong. Chekhov grew pale and answered in a very dry voice,

"For this you will have to thank not me, but Mr. Stanislavsky, who has made a vulgar man out of a decent character. I did not make him a bad man."

Later on, I read the play, and understood that Chekhov created the character of Trigorin after his own image.

During the next intermission, Chekhov and I went backstage. Just before the bell to the third act, we saw Gorky at some distance, surrounded by a group of young admirers. Gorky addressed them loudly, and then there was a burst of laughter and applause. It turned out that on his way through the theater, a group of young men had recognized him and started applauding. Gorky thanked them, bowed, and said,

"Why should you stare at me, dear sirs? Am I a corpse or a dancer? You would do better to pay attention to this wonderful play that is being performed here tonight."

After this meeting, which happened around 1900, I never saw Chekhov again. He could no longer go to St. Petersburg because of his bad health. He wrote to me on March 3, 1901, with bitter irony,

"I have a bad cough and am feeling bad, but as for the rest I cannot complain."

His spirits were low at the time and he wrote to me,

"Please remember that I live like a hermit. Have mercy on me when you write, and include the following: First, what is happening in the civilized world? Secondly, where is Gorky and what is his correspondence address? Third — are you going to come to Yalta to visit me?"

He was always very friendly with Gorky and myself.

On April 21, 1901, Chekhov answered a brief letter I'd written to him as follows:

> Dear Vladimir Alexeevich,
>
> Your letter came to Yalta, and then was forwarded to me in Moscow, and that is why I was delayed and received it only yesterday. Please do not be angry for my delay answering you. Gorky is happy and full of life. I saw the doctor who examined him, and I saw Mr. Miroliubov who asked me to support Gorky, and they both say hello. My own health is not very well, and I have to go to a spa in the south to drink horse milk. I might as well be going into exile. It would be nice if you could send me two issues of *The Life Magazine* that you publish. I will send you my new address this Friday, and I will be very grateful to you. As well, I will send you my newly published short stories. Yours, A. Chekhov.

Ivan Bunin. "Chekhov"

After Moscow, we had not seen each other until the spring of 1899, when I came to Yalta for several days during that spring. I met him walking along the waterfront.

"Why don't you come and pay me a visit one of these days?" he asked me, and added, "Come to my place, really!"

"When?" I asked him.

"Tomorrow morning, let's say about 8 o'clock."

He must have observed the enormous surprise in my eyes, for he added, "We get up early as a rule. How about you?"

"Yes, as a matter of fact, I also get up early."

"Me too," he said. "So come over as soon as you get up tomorrow morning. We'll have coffee together. Do you drink coffee in the mornings? Mornings are for coffee, not tea. It's a wonderful thing. When I work, I drink nothing but coffee and chicken stock. Coffee in the morning, and soup at lunchtime."

We reached the waterfront in silence and sat on a bench.

"Do you like to look at the sea?" I asked him.

"Yes, but it is too empty for me."

"Actually, that's the best thing about the sea," I said.

"I don't know," he said, looking into the distance, distracted. He added, "I think it's good to be an officer, or a young man, or a university student, and sit at a noisy place, and listen to lively music."

In his usual way, he remained silent for a time, and then added without any obvious connection, "It's difficult to describe the sea. Do you know how I saw it described recently in the notebook of a junior school student? 'The sea is big.' That was it. I find this quite wonderful."

A few years back, in Moscow, I'd known him as a big tall man, friendly, kind, and energetic. He met me in a simple way. It was so simple, in fact, that I'd thought at the beginning that there was a coolness lurking beneath his reserved attitude and simple manners.

In Yalta, I discovered he had changed a great deal. He'd lost weight, his skin was darker, he moved much more slowly, and his voice was dull. His manners were the same, very friendly, but a little more reserved. He was talkative, but mostly in very short simple sentences. Even in conversation, he was distracted by other thoughts, sometimes speaking about things without any obvious connection and allowing his listener to make the connections in his flow of speech.

It was around four in the morning, as a rule, when Olga Knipper would come back, smelling of perfumes and wine. She would say to Chekhov, "Still awake, my darling? This is not good for your health. Are you are still here, my dear Mr. Bunin? Well, at least I know that you two were not bored all this time in each other's company."

At this point I would usually rise and take my leave.

Chekhov always liked to repeat that if a person does not constantly work, and does not live in an atmosphere of creative writing, then even if this person is as wise as Solomon, he would never be able to fully use his gift. Sometimes he accompanied this speech by pulling his notebook out of his desk, raising his head, and rapidly blinking his eyes behind his glasses as he waved this little notebook in the air.

"Look, I have exactly a hundred plots written down here. Yes, my dear sirs, I am not like you young men. I am a hard worker. Would you like me to sell you a couple of plots?" he would joke.

One day he told me, "You know, I am getting married."

Then he proceeded to joke about how very nice it would be for a Russian man to marry a Germanic woman [*Olga Knipper had a German background — P.S.*], because of how the Germans like to be so well organized. Any child of Olga's would not crawl around the house on all fours, beating frying pans and bowls with a big wooden spoon and causing a racket.

Obviously, I knew about his love affair with Olga Knipper, but I had no idea it would end in marriage. I was also friends with Olga, and I knew that she came from a completely different background than the Chekhov family.

I knew that it would be difficult for his sister Maria to get along with Olga when she became the mistress of the house.

Olga was definitely an actress to the bone, and she would not abandon her theater in exchange for family life. I knew that any strained relations between his sister and his future wife would have a negative effect on Anton's health. As is often the case in such situations, Chekhov would suffer no matter the outcome, regardless of whether he took his wife or his sister's side. I thought, 'For him, this will be like committing suicide or being sent to prison.' However, I chose to simply keep silent at the time, and did not tell him anything.

In September, Chekhov wrote to his wife, "Now I feel much healthier. Bunin visits me daily."

Thus I began my inexhaustible conversations with Chekhov.

When I went to visit him for the first time, he did not look good at all. He read me some of his earliest short stories. He was rewriting a few of them because, as he put it, some of them were wishy-washy. It seemed to me that even when Chekhov knew he occupied a prestigious position in the literary ranks, he did not fully understand how precious he was, that he truly was an exalted and gifted writer.

At the beginning of December, Anton Pavlovich returned to Moscow.

I planned to go abroad, and had applied to get my foreign passport and permission to travel. Every night, I would visit Chekhov, staying until 3 or 4 in the morning, until Olga would return home from the theater.

Most of the time, she would go to a play or sometimes a concert. Mr. Nemirovich-Danchenko would come to pick her up in a tuxedo, smelling of cigar smoke and expensive perfume. She always wore an evening gown, leaving the scent of her perfume trailing after her. This beautiful young woman would come to her husband with the following words: "Please don't be bored staying here all by yourself, my little boy. I know that you will be here with Bunin. Goodbye, my dear."

Next, she would turn to me, "Goodbye."

Then she would leave, accompanied by Nemirovich.

Chekhov never went to bed until she returned, and our midnight conversations were very precious to me.

Alexander Kuprin. "Chekhov. In Memoriam"

Chekhov's cottage was located outside of Yalta, on a country road that went to the village of Alupka. The road was covered with a thick layer of dust.

I don't know for sure, but I think that its architectural design made it the most interesting building in Yalta. It was asymmetrically constructed, without any obvious historical style; there was a little tower attached to the side, a glass veranda at the back, a huge deck, and lots of windows of all sizes and shapes. The flower garden was small and the fruit and vegetable garden was still immature. They had all kinds of trees: peaches, pears and almonds. During the last years, the garden produced a lot of fruit, and it was very touching to observe Anton's childish delight in it. His passion for gardening was not just the feeling of a man who owns a property, but something much deeper and stronger.

He once looked at his garden, winked at me and said,

"Listen, every tree in this garden was planted by my hands. Before me, there was just an empty place, a ravine covered with weeds and thistle. And now I've made it very cultured and beautiful, both my cottage and this lovely garden.

"You know what?" he continued, "In two or three hundred years, the whole earth will be turned into one huge, beautiful garden, and life will be very easy and pleasant for everyone."

This idea of the good life in the distant future appears in several of his major works, and it was one of his most powerfully held dreams. Perhaps he was contemplating mankind's future as he was cutting fresh roses still wet with morning dew.

Speaking of Chekhov's garden, I would like to add that there were huge swings and a bench at the back. Both were left by the actors of the Moscow Art Theater when they visited Yalta to perform *Uncle Vanya*. There was only one reason for the visit: they wanted to perform before Chekhov himself when he was too sick to come to Moscow. Chekhov was pleased and proud to have these objects in his garden, and he often mentioned his sincere admiration of the theater and his friendship with the actors of the Moscow Art Theater. It is also worth noting that those wonderful actors made Chekhov's last years much more enjoyable by expressing their respect for his work.

There were two dogs and a tamed crane in his backyard. I should mention that he loved all kinds of animals except for cats, which he loathed for some reason. He remembered his dogs Bromine and Quinine from his previous estate, Melikhovo, with kind words. He once said to me, in his usual joking way,

"Dogs are wonderful people!"

The crane was very suspicious of newcomers but was very friendly with the cook and the butler. It did not fly, but it liked to walk along behind the servants whenever they crossed the garden. One of the dogs was called Tusik. The other was called Kashtanka. That was one totally silly, lazy dog. It had light brown fur, big yellow eyes, and a perpetually stupid expression. It would bark at newcomers for the first few seconds, but as soon as you paid it a little bit of attention, it would fall on the ground, show its belly, and flirt with you. Anton Pavlovich would shove the dogs aside with his walking stick whenever they got in his way, and growl at them with pretended strictness,

"Get away, get out of here, you silly dog!"

Then he would look into his visitor's eyes, and smiling, he would joke,

"Do you like this silly dog? I can give it to you as a gift. You would not believe how silly this dog is."

I must emphasize again that both children and animals instinctively loved him....

Chekhov said to the beginning young authors, "All of you should be grateful to me in one respect: it was me who opened the editors' doors for the writers of short stories. Before, when you used to bring a short story to an editor's office, they did not even want to read it. They only looked at you with astonishment and disgust. 'What is this? Do you call it a literary work? This is smaller than a sparrow's beak. No, we don't want this.'

"But then I made a breakthrough, and paved the way for others. What do you think? Yes, they treated me badly sometimes. Yes, they made my name a generic one. Yes, they sometimes made jokes about me, calling other people, 'Hey, you, Chekhovs *[Chekhov-type men — P.S.]*.' Yes, they were joking like this, and maybe it was funny."

Ekaterina Peshkova. "Meetings with A.P. Chekhov"

[E. Peshkova was the wife of Russian novelist A.M. Gorky — P.S.]

On March 19, 1899, when Alexey Maximovich Gorky came to Yalta, he met Chekhov there. He wrote me, "Chekhov is a wonderful person. He is very soft, kind and attentive. People love him. He has crowds of friends, and someone is always striking up a conversation with him. I have never had such pleasure from a conversation as when I talked with him."

They met regularly during Gorky's stay in Yalta in 1899. As a rule, they met at the Sinani bookstore, which was a kind of club for visiting writers, artists and actors. One instance, they were sitting on a bench next to the store, admiring the sea.

In one of his letters to Yalta, Alexey Maximovich wrote, "Chekhov lives in solitude. People do not understand him. He has a great number of admirers, yet he has told me, 'I live in solitude, as if I were in a desert.'"

On his letter dated March 29, Alexey Maximovich wrote to me from Yalta, "I stayed at Chekhov's place all night, talking. He is such an interesting person to talk to! However, his health is bad, and is progressively getting worse. He does not know this, and has his heart set on going to Moscow for Easter, but his doctors will not let him go."

Alexey Maximovich was completely charmed by Anton Pavlovich, as was I. I met Chekhov in the spring of 1900, when together with Gorky I arrived in Yalta, and stayed in a hotel located on a street leading to the sea.

Anton Pavlovich came to visit us along with Bunin. I met Chekhov for the second time at his house, and was very embarrassed, and blushed all of the time.

Evgeniya Yakovlevna, Chekhov's mother, welcomed me in a very warm way. There were many literary writers who visited Chekhov's house that spring, including Mamin-Sibiryak, K. Staniukovich, A. Kuprin, Ivan Bunin, Evgeny Chirikov, Sergei Elpatievsky, along with their families.

Soon after, the Moscow Art Theater arrived on tour, and the quiet Chekhov house was filled with people from morning till night, overflowing out into the garden as well.

During our next visit to Yalta in 1901, we stayed at Anton's cottage. Anton Pavlovich walked to Gaspra by foot, to the house where Leo Tolstoy used to live.

For the second time, I met Anton Pavlovich in January 1904 in Germany, when he was on his way to meet Professor Evan. My children were under the weather so I stopped in Berlin on my way to Carlsbad. Olga Leonardovna encountered me in Berlin and invited me to their hotel, saying, "Anton Pavlovich is waiting for you." We came into their room, which had two windows facing the street, and a nice round desk in the middle along with a sofa and two armchairs.

Anton Pavlovich was sitting in one of the chairs. He stood up when I came in, and we greeted each other. Anton Pavlovich asked after my children and how their doctors were treating them. He said,

"I am a doctor, so naturally I am interested in the type of care you received."

I told him that the doctor told me to wrap a warm bed sheet around my son when he had a fever and red rash, which was most likely the measles. After this treatment, the boy promptly fell asleep and returned to full health.

Anton Pavlovich told me, "You need a strong heart for that kind of treatment, but it is not a bad thing to do."

Next, Chekhov discussed Berlin, how he felt everything was too comfortable for him and that local women had too long legs. He then added that there was a nice zoological garden there.

Anton Pavlovich was very thin, having lost a lot of weight, but was full of life in his shining clear eyes.

It seems to me that this trip to Badenweiler had given him hope for the future. There were some of his friends who mentioned in their memories that, before his departure from Moscow he felt that "he was on his way to face his death," but I had not noticed that.

To the contrary, he had lots of plans. He told me that after Badenweiler, he would like to visit the lake district of Italy.

Maxim Gorky. "A.P. Chekhov"

I have just been to Chekhov's funeral, and am very depressed. I cannot fully explain how deeply I am upset. Chekhov was a great person and a wonderful artist who fought his whole life against vulgarity. Yet, Anton Chekhov was brought to Russia in a railway car used for transporting fresh oysters and he was put in a grave next to the Cossack's widow Olga Kukarekina.

These are small things, but when I remember the oyster railway car, I am ready to cry from sheer anger. For him, there would be no difference if we brought his body back in a box of dry linen. As for Russian society, I cannot forgive such disrespect.

I would have preferred a personal private funeral, with only those in attendance who truly love him. Instead, there was a huge crowd of so called "public figures" and a huge mess of noisy, crowded and vulgar men and women.

There was not a single word spoken amongst the crowd about Chekhov. Instead they discussed the dresses and the celebrities they saw, including Shaliapin and me. Some people were climbing the trees to be able to see, and broke several branches. They were talking like this:

"Look, there is his wife!"

"And who is this?"

"Look, they are crying!"

"You know, he does not owe a single penny — everything belongs to his publisher Marx."

"You should not pity her, because she makes ten thousand rubles per month at the theater."

It was all extremely vulgar, intrusive and bold. I plan on writing an article about it, and a group of his closest friends such as Bunin, Kuprin,

Andreev and I are planning to contribute. We will write a book, *Memories of Chekhov.*

Alexey Pleshcheev. "Chekhov in Yalta"

We were taking a cab across Yalta. Chekhov was visiting the Black Sea, and he was trying to explain something to the Tartar driver in front of us. The man nodded his head in reply.

Chekhov told me that we were going to visit his little property. "You know what? I have a little property with a tiny house by the sea. It is my little secret — nobody knows about it. I bought this property so that I could have some solitude while I work, far from prying eyes. "It was the tiniest miniature house, as if from a fairy tale, with two tiny windows. It was close to a rock, on a small cliff, and right next to the sea.

It seemed to me that one could not enter it upright, needing to bend over to enter inside.

"Do not tell anyone about this little house. No one knows that I have property here," Chekhov told me. He wanted to show me the inside of this hut, but the man who was guarding it had left for a while with the key. Therefore, we could only peer inside through the small window. You could see that there was nothing but a writing desk and a chair inside.

Next to the hut, you could see the sea waves hitting a rock that used to be called the Pushkin Rock *[a great Russian poet was visiting Crimea many years ago, and according to tradition he wrote some of his poetry there — P.S.].*

One of the last photographs of Anton Chekhov, taken several months before his death in the winter of 1904.

Chekhov and I took a short walk along the seashore, and then parted. He was tired.

Soon I had to leave Yalta. We briefly met a few times later, in St. Petersburg and Moscow.

Lev Altshuller. "Memories of Doctor Altshuller's Son about Chekhov"

When Chekhov moved to Crimea around 1900, he met one of his friends and colleagues, the local physician, Dr. Altshuller, who later became his family doctor. Thus began their friendship, which lasted until Chekhov's death.

Chekhov often visited the doctor, and the doctor's family visited Chekhov in his house in Alupka.

I remember Anton Pavlovich very well. I remember his low and slightly hushed voice, his soft smile, and his pince-nez hanging on a string. Every time we visited him, Anton Pavlovich would greet us very heartily, treat us to chocolate, and invite us for long walks in his garden. Once he warmly presented us with one of his collections of short stories.

Isaac Altshuller. "About Chekhov"

I remember one day when I came to visit Chekhov. He was reading a review of one of his works. Lifting his face to greet me, he said,

"Here you go, my friend! I was not aware of this, but I am now apparently entering the third stage of my life."

Then, adjusting his glasses with a habitual gesture, he added,

"Until this morning, I had not had so much as even one period in my life, and now I've got three of them."

Personally, I don't know how many parts you could divide Chekhov's life and work into, but my own friendship with Chekhov began and developed during his last period. His life in Yalta lasted for the last five years of his life.

At the end of September of 1898, in an attempt to escape from the cold weather, I moved south to Yalta, a city I had never even visited before. I met with my friend Dr. Pivovarov, who introduced me to the local family physician, Dr. Elpatievsky. They both tried to convince me that I should quit my life in the North and retire permanently to Yalta.

One day, as we were strolling through Yalta's central park, we found

Chekhov sitting on one of the park benches with Dr. Orlov from the local hospital. We ended up walking and talking as a group for the rest of the day.

Chekhov had come to Yalta without any particular plan: he'd decided to move south and was looking for a cottage. One day, Dr. Orlov, who loved Chekhov and was worried about him, joked with him as we were all sitting at a park bench,

"We're all doctors here: let's all examine one another."

Chekhov softly declined the offer and said, "This is not a very good idea; let's just go for a nice long walk in the park instead."

By the fall of 1899, the cottage was complete and Chekhov moved into his study to resume his work. He was a very organized man. All the objects in his room and on his desk were put in a certain, very strictly maintained order. Each of the candle holders, inkwells, several china elephants, an *All Moscow* magazine published by Suvorin, a jar of mints and several other objects were always in the same places on his desk. I was surprised that he kept everything in such perfect order. I never saw anything untidy on his desk. He always dressed neatly and strictly, from early in the morning till late at night. In fact I never saw him dressed casually, never without a fresh white shirt and a tie. He was the son of a small grocery store owner who had spent his childhood in complete poverty, but he had acquired all the manners of high society. All of his habits were infused with noble manners, perfection-seeking and an internal grace.

The period from the spring of 1899 to 1901 was rather joyful. Chekhov moved to a new cottage as he was doing significant creative work including overseeing the productions of his two greatest plays, *Uncle Vanya* and *The Seagull*, by a major theater in the capital. The visit of the theater to Yalta, becoming the member of the Academy of Sciences, and receiving several major literary prizes — all of this had a positive influence upon his spirit.

The problem was that too many people wanted to visit him, interrupting his work and boring him to death.

Once, late at night, there was Chekhov's voice on the phone:

"Oh my dear, my brother, I just had to take a laxative again!"

"Why did you do that?" I asked.

"A young writer, Mr. N. has visited me again."

Chekhov liked Tolstoy very much. In 1901 Tolstoy was ill and living in Garspa, a small town near Yalta. Chekhov visited Tolstoy there on several occasions. Whenever Chekhov visited Tolstoy, the great novelist spoke to him in a very friendly and loving manner.

When I asked Tolstoy which of Chekhov's books he loved the most, Tolstoy answered,

"I live by Chekhov these days. I greatly admire and enjoy his works. He notices every little detail, which is amazing. His works are filled with great messages, and he has developed his own style; he does not imitate anyone, but he writes in his own way."

After a while, Tolstoy added, "Chekhov is such a wonderful man, but his plays are simply terrible."

Alexey Sergeenko. "Two Meetings with Chekhov"

Our father was journalist Pyotr Sergeenko. He and Anton Pavlovich Chekhov were childhood friends. They had gone to the same high school in Taganrog, and remained on friendly terms throughout their lives. On September 10, 1900, my sister and I, still teenagers at the time, accompanied our father on a visit to Yalta. The first thing my father did was to go to Anton Pavlovich's house, and get an audience with Chekhov. My sister and I remained at the hotel. This visit didn't take long, and our father soon returned to tell us that Anton Pavlovich had invited him to return for a longer stay the following morning.

On the morning of September 11, my father left for Chekhov's house, while my sister and I again remained at the hotel.

About an hour later, my father returned with Chekhov, who had come to see and examine my sister. Even though he was sick and it was a very hot day, he had decided to come and meet us. Along the way, Chekhov had asked my father questions about things such as our age, our names and our general health. When he entered our hotel room, I noted that Anton Pavlovich was a rather tall, pleasant-looking man. He appeared to be in his early thirties, even though he was really forty years old at the time.

He was dressed in a neat, respectable walking costume, and held a grey walking stick in his hands. He had a friendly smile, and open and kind eyes that squinted at us from behind glasses. I could not help but wonder if his flushed face was due to the fever that normally accompanied lungs as sick as his were rumored to be.

"Hello, dear children! Perhaps you have heard of me? My name is Anton Pavlovich Chekhov, and I am a doctor. Please, allow me to ask you some questions."

Then he directed several questions at my sister. She told him of the pains in her stomach, and in her side, and the unpredictable dizzy spells which had left her unconscious on several occasions.

Chekhov listened to all of this very carefully, and then said,

"Which side of your stomach is in pain?"

She showed him.

"And do you cough at all?" She answered yes. He told her that he coughed as well, and said that there was nothing wrong with having a cough. Then he asked her,

"Are you a vegetarian?"

She said, "Yes."

He said, "You know, I'm also a vegetarian. Do you live in the country?"

"Yes."

"And you are not bored there?"

"No."

"Do you think you'd enjoy a visit to the theatre?"

"I have never had the chance to go, so I wouldn't know."

"No matter; you are only 16, after all. You have to be joyful and enjoy life." Anton Pavlovich had been sitting in an armchair, and my sister had come to stand along the wall beside him. He stood up, and approached her. He noticed that she had a rose attached to her jacket.

"Who gave you this rose?" Chekhov asked her.

"It's from my father," she answered.

At first, my father and I could not understand why he had asked her about the rose. Later, Chekhov told us that it was his way of finding out if she was involved in a relationship with any young man. He made his diagnosis, and said that he would like to speak to my father in private.

When he was leaving, Chekhov told my father that his daughter did not have any serious illnesses. He said,

"She's just feeling unwell because she's a teenager. She will grow and it will all go away, and she will soon be healthy again."

Everything happened exactly as he had told us.

We left Yalta that very day, but two weeks later, I saw Anton Pavlovich for a second time. We had all come to see him with my father.

"Hello."

"Hello."

"Are you fourteen years old already? You look like your father! Please take seat here," he told me.

It was nice of him to pay me attention.

"And what about the Niva Publishing House?" he asked, turning to my father.

I knew that A. Marx was the publisher of the *Complete Works* by Chekhov, and that all of the negotiations had been arranged by my father. As they talked about publishing houses, I listened carefully to their conversation. Soon after

our visit, we had to leave Crimea. On our last day there, I was happily surprised to receive an autographed photograph from Chekhov.

Isaac Altshuller. "About Chekhov"

Anton Pavlovich married Olga Leonardovna Knipper in 1901, in secret.

On that day, his way of life changed completely. As Mr. Chekhov's family
physician, I can say that from a medical standpoint, this was not a change
for the better.

One of the French specialists who treated tuberculosis said people with
tuberculosis should forget about the laurels and glory. These words can be
proven by the life of Chekhov. His happiness turned into unhappiness, and
brought him to the end of his life; there were, in particular, two things: the
Moscow Art Theater and his marriage.

I remember how Chekhov was worried before the production and
rehearsals of his plays at the Moscow Art Theater. He was very upset after the
failure of *The Seagull* at the Alexandrinsky Theater, and happy with the new
performance by the Art Theater. Although he had promised everyone that he
would never write plays again, he was now writing plays specifically for this
theater, and the Art Theater became the Chekhov Theater, and made Chekhov
very popular at the end of his life.

When Chekhov was younger, he'd had several relationships with women,
and he would tell his friends about them when he was in a good mood. Yet,
I had never heard about any serious attachments previously. He got involved
with Olga Leonardovna after one of the rehearsals of the Art Theater. When
I read about their marriage in the newspapers, I immediately recalled one of
my visits to the Chekhov house in the year of 1900.

She was standing at the top of the stairs, and he stood at the bottom of
the stairs. She was dressed in a white dress, and she looked very happy, filled
with health and joy; she was a young woman in the prime of life, the leading
actress of the Art Theater, with great expectations for the future.

He looked different: extremely thin, weak with sallow skin, aging very
quickly, and hopelessly ill.

When they married their lives together, the fatal consequences came very
soon for Chekhov.

She had to stay in Moscow in order to perform at the theater, and he
could not leave his "warm Siberia," as he called Yalta, without great risk to
his health.

I knew Chekhov well, and I could predict the sad outcome. He started making frequent trips from Yalta to Moscow and back. Each time he returned from Moscow to Yalta, he would be suffering from serious throat bleeding, or coughing fits, or a fever. He tried to deceive himself by saying that he was feeling fine in Moscow, but got sick when he came back to Yalta.

He spent most of the winters of 1901-02 and 1902-03 in Yalta. He felt bad. At the end of this period he had changed. His face was very pale, his lips were bloodless, he'd lost a lot of weight, and his hair was gray. All the symptoms of the tuberculosis were progressing rapidly. He was out of breath, and he had catarrh of the bowels.

In the spring of 1903, on the recommendations of Professor Ostroumov, he decided to spend the next winter in Moscow. By the fall of 1903, he was feverish most of the time and his bowel troubles were back.

However, the Moscow Art Theater had its own interests. They wanted new performances, and were pushing him to complete his next play, *The Cherry Orchard*.

More and more frequently I found Chekhov sitting in an armchair, or lying down on the sofa without any books or newspapers in his hands. For the first time in his life, he was complaining about his work. He said that he was writing and re-writing the play, but that he could do it only from time to time when he felt a little better. In October, I tried to tell him the whole truth; I tried to save him, telling him not to kill himself, not to go back to Moscow because it was complete insanity. Yet, he decided to go to Moscow in December. You know what happened next.

This was inevitable.

Chekhov attended the rehearsals of his play in a state of great excitement, and he had lots of visitors, since it was in the middle of the theater season.

On January 17, 1904, *The Cherry Orchard* opened, and practically all of Moscow was celebrating and congratulating Anton Chekhov.

He could hardly stand on the scene; he was coughing all the time. I met with him after these events. He spoke about the celebrations and the numerous gifts he had received. One of the gifts was a very handsome 18th century inkwell. I told him that it was very nice, but Chekhov hated antiques. He said,

"You know what? If you like it, I'll include it in my will, and they'll give it to you after my death." He looked sick and he was feeling bad, but I still could not believe at that time that in less than six months, that inkwell would be in my possession.

He stayed in Yalta until the end of April, and then he planned to go to the Russian-Japanese war as a doctor because a doctor could get a much closer view of the action.

At the end of April he went to Moscow, and then to Badenweiler in Germany. Olga Leonardovna told me later that on the way to the spa, the famous physician Dr. Evald examined him in Berlin. He looked at Chekhov, said nothing, shrugged his shoulders and left. It was not polite — but probably he gesticulated like this in confusion — why would they take such a sick person for a trip somewhere?

As for me, even when I knew that his end was near, I was struck as though by lightning when I read the telegram about his death.

Sergei Elpatievsky. "Anton Pavlovich Chekhov"

Anton Chekhov finally returned to Moscow. He'd been living in Yalta for several years due to illness, but now he had returned. I remember when he came back, he was upset over the bad weather, but he told me that he was really happy to be back in Moscow.

Moscow occupied all his thoughts, and it was truly the promised land for him. Everything that was good, pleasant and nice for Chekhov was connected with this city. I met many people who were patriots of their own cities — they were men from Saratov, Poltava, and Siberia — but I have never met anyone with such a passionate love for this city. Nothing could compare to Chekhov's love for Moscow.

We both knew Moscow very well, as we both studied at Moscow University. When Chekhov was in a good mood, he would remember the famous street vendors selling cakes with onion and pepper, "stuffed with dogs' hearts," as he used to say. These cakes were made in a dirty small lane named the Mokhovaya Street. They were probably made for us, medical students who studied nearly, at the autopsy theater and the science lab.

He often remembered the small streets of the old Moscow: the Patriarshy Pond, Bronnaya and Kositskaya Streets.

He liked everything about the city: the people, the streets, the churches, and the classic Moscow cabmen.

He would go to Yalta for a few months, and then he would always want to return to Moscow. In his play *Three Sisters*, the characters kept coming back to the same theme in different ways: "We are going to Moscow! To Moscow!"

Yet, it was Anton Pavlovich himself who wanted to return to his favorite city.

However, his illness continued to grow worse, and eventually, it cut his life short.

Solitude. He lived in solitude. He was surrounded by family and friends in Yalta, but he felt as if he lived in solitude. He missed the busy literary life of the capital with its glittering parties and vibrant intellectual life. In his personal life, Chekhov was a very quiet, well-mannered and tolerant man, maybe too tolerant; yet he was very strict in his literary judgments when he was talking about other people's writing, perhaps too strict at times.

Nikolai Garin-Mikhailovsky. "In Memory of Chekhov"

Anton Pavlovich Chekhov never told us what a character should become.

He simply depicted people in different circumstances for us. He was brilliant at describing very dull people without exaggeration, people who all lived in our times and existed in real life. He worked with an enchanted chisel, this great sculptor of literature. Chekhov was the best short story writer, the best of his genre.

I met him for the first time in Crimea, where I used to work with his brother-in-law, K.L. Knipper. I met Anton Pavlovich and his family in April 1903, at his cottage in Yalta. He appeared extremely tired, but he was oblivious of the approaching perils.

"Do you know what I am working on right now?" he asked me in a jovial way. "In this little notebook I have put many plots, ideas and expressions. It is enough to write new works for the next ten years. My original, pencil handwriting has faded, and so I am tracing the pencil lines with ink. As you can see, I have almost completely rewritten it."

He affectionately thumped the small notebook with his hand and added,

"I have hundreds of printed pages of writing material in here. If I were to ever finish writing all of this, why, my family should be pretty well off."

As we know, the publisher Marx had bought all his works for only 75,000 rubles. Anton Pavlovich spent all of this money on the purchase of his new residence, and even then he needed more money to keep it. As a result, his family lived very modestly, having to account for every dime.

In Moscow, he had a flat on the third floor with no elevator. Whenever he visited Moscow, he had to walk all the way up in a warm and heavy winter coat. He used to take a couple of steps and wait for a while, completely out of breath.

If he'd had the means, he could have lived longer and given people more literary treasures, the seeds of which he took with him to the grave.

The Polish people gave their national poet Senkiewicz a wonderful, comfortable estate where he could live until old age. However, we did not give anything of the sort to our genius.

When we parted with Chekhov, he told me that he would like to visit me in Manchuria, just north of China.

"I will come and visit you soon," he promised, and then repeated in a stubborn way, "I will come to visit you. I will see you again."

However, I was left with the premonition that this was to be our last meeting in life.

Vikenti Veresaev. "A.P. Chekhov"

I met Chekhov in Yalta in the spring of 1903. It was Gorky who brought me to his home. Chekhov's house was located on a small, very dusty street in Alupka, a distant Yalta suburb. A tamed crane walked along the steep, hilly backyard, with stunted trees marking the edge of the property.

I was invited into the study of Anton Pavlovich. It had a large writing desk, and an enormous sofa behind it. There was an unpretentious side table attached to the desk, littered with postcards from writers and actors, all of them autographed. On the wall hung a warning sign to all who came within, "No smoking please."

Chekhov lived a very humble life; I believe a far too humble one.

He was constantly coughing and spitting blood into a small glass container.

Anton Pavlovich told us that he had recently received a letter from the father of a big family from Odessa. The letter told of his daughter, a young lady who recently met with Chekhov while traveling by boat from Sevastopol to Odessa. The letter from her father read like this: "You, Mr. Chekhov, write many beautiful short stories.... But being such a good writer, how could you make advances on a young lady with such indecent proposals?"

Chekhov laughed heartily at this letter as he told us that he had never in his life traveled by sea from Sevastopol to Odessa. There was a smile on his face, and his eyes danced with mirth. But I felt the impression that, inside, he was melancholy.

Several days later I came to see him and say goodbye. Again, he appeared sad. At the time he was packing his suitcase for Moscow to see his wife Olga Leonardovna, an actress there. He loved Moscow, and spoke about Moscow as if he were a student going on vacation to his favorite town. It was obvious that his health was very bad, and he would not live long.

He asked me, "Have you ever been to Italy?"

"Yes, actually, I was there last year," I replied.

"Have you tried their famous wine, Chianti?"

"Yes, I have."

"It was always my dream to go to Italy and drink Chianti there," he said.

Vladimir Knipper-Nardov. "Memories of A.P. Chekhov"

I met with Anton Chekhov in 1904, in Berlin, when he stayed with my sister *[his wife Olga Knipper — P.S.]* on his way to Badenweiler. I had just come to Germany to study acting in Dresden with Professor J. Miller. It was a large upheaval in my life, since I was separated from my first wife, and I was very emotionally unstable.

Anton Pavlovich was a sensitive man and as soon as we met, he noticed that something was the matter. He asked me about what had happened to me. I tried to reply with a joke. Until this time, I had never gotten any letters from him. Then, a few days later, he sent me a postcard. The most important part of his postcard was the last phrase, "Be more joyful."

I remember my first, and last, meeting with Anton Pavlovich.

I thought over his words for a long time, and was struck by the strength of his ability to express every detail of a person's innermost emotional state.

Mikhail Pervukhin. "From My Memories of Chekhov"

Chekhov used to give the following advice to us literary artists:

"As soon as you can afford it, please, run away from Yalta. Do not live here! Escape it as soon as you can!"

"Why should we do this, Anton Pavlovich?"

"Yalta is not a place for a literary artist. Here, we live in a kind of vacuum. A writer should have close contact with life, with people from the masses, so to speak. And the writer lives and thrives on the nectar he gets from this everyday life. He should know and see the human mind working around him, and he should be involved in human processes. Nothing is happening here in Yalta, and therefore, writers should be banned from living here under threat of capital punishment."

Chekhov noticed that I made a slight smile, and he began smiling as well.

"Yes, yes, you can start laughing at me and teasing me, asking 'Why did you buy a house here?' Then I will answer you. First of all, this so happened because of my illness, and secondly, because of the weakness of my character. Yes, I wanted to buy a house, and this was my weak point. You should take into consideration that I wanted to be a landlord, a house owner, from my youth. And here, in the city of Yalta, I had the chance to fulfill my dream. This is how I became a man with property."

I heard some sad tones in Chekhov's voice. He continued,

"But I bought my house ahead of time. I was in a rush. I should have waited for some time, say, a hundred years. Then, in the future, people would have flying machines that could move at a hundred — no — a thousand kilometers per hour! One day, we will have whole railways flying through the air. Then you could get up early in the morning in Yalta, have your breakfast in St. Petersburg, fly to Moscow to have your tea, and in the evening on the same day, you could fly back to Yalta.

"And at night, in the same day, real people from Moscow or from St. Petersburg could visit you for a few hours, and then it would make perfect sense to live here in Yalta. Otherwise, it does not make any sense to live here at all!

"You know who should be allowed to live in Yalta among the writers of our time? Historical novelists, such as Salinas. Do you know that a few days ago, Salinas himself visited Yalta and stayed in the Grand Hotel? They say he was accompanied by a beautiful French lady."

One of the people amongst our company humbly said that there were a couple of serious literary journals here in Russia — *Vestnik Evropy* [*Messenger of Europe*] and *Russkaia Mysl* [*Russian Thought*].

Chekhov answered,

"It is not important how many literary journals we have, but their quality. Let us look at these magazines. Their total circulation could be a maximum of fifty thousand copies. And this is in Russia, with a population of 150 million people. It means that three thousand people could read one copy of a literary journal! There are entire cities in this country that do not subscribe to a single literary journal. Yes, they all have their intellectuals, but they're busy playing cards. Yes, you know, whole railway containers filled with playing cards arrive there all the time. You should remember, dear gentlemen, the people who read these literary journals are mostly intellectuals. Simple people such as peasants and workers do not read them. However, intellectuals make up a very thin layer of the population, a sometimes barely visible layer in the crowd of people around us. These intellectuals — what have they read? I can tell you. Recently, I visited a typical provincial town. It had a commerce center, a boulevard where high school students walk across the city. I went to the public library and got my hands on a copy of a literary magazine. I noticed that it had never been opened before.

"No, no, my dear gentlemen, you should not start this enterprise, a new literary magazine. Nothing good would come out of it, especially if you do it outside of the capital, St. Petersburg. And if you do it in the capital, do you know how much start up money you will need? At least three hundred thousand! And then, you will have to get another two hundred thousand to stay afloat. How can you find enough subscribers? Without enough subscribers, all your work and money starting your journal will have been in vain."

The people who asked this question about publishing a literary journal, after hearing of these huge sums of money, always grew embarrassed, and instantly retired from our party.

Still, Chekhov was interested in developing this topic. He coughed a couple times, and then continued,

"In spite of all its difficulties, we do all need a new literary journal. It would be fantastic. You know, this really is a great idea. I even have a title; it should be called *The Russian Archive*."

Year after year passed, but Yalta did not have even the smallest drama theater.

Chekhov was very disappointed by this. He said,

"It is very difficult to live here. I wish we could have any theater, even one of the worst quality, so that at least a few good actors could visit and perform here from time to time. Life without a theater is very difficult!"

After living his boring time in Yalta, as he said, "without a gulp of fresh air," Chekhov took a leave and visited the city of Moscow, which he loved. When he left, it seemed that he looked much younger and healthier, full of energy. When he returned, he was very tired, very sad and gloomy.

The saddest I ever saw him was when he left Yalta for the last time to head to Badenweiler, the sanitarium in Germany where he died.

After Chekhov died, people in Yalta spoke about erecting a monument to Chekhov. Nothing came of these conversations except a few empty words about monuments.

The poet Nadson died a few years earlier in Yalta. I met Chekhov on the way to paying my last tribute to him. Chekhov told me,

"I just visited the Nadsons' house. You know, people read his poetry and almost every year, there is a new edition of his poems published. But people cannot even make a small bust of this poet here in Yalta. Think about this. We are all such swine, you know."

Chekhov's phrase, "We are all such swine," echoed in my head for a long time.

Natalia Gubareva. "Memories of A.P. Chekhov"

I met Chekhov in 1899, when I spent the winter in Crimea, in Alupka. I heard from the local pharmacist that Anton Pavlovich Chekhov was in Yalta. There were very few familiar people there — and now I had a chance to see a new face, Anton Pavlovich himself!

I discovered his address and went to visit him. I knew that Yalta would be foreign to him as a new arrival. Everyone, however, in Yalta already knew of him and were talking about him. Women were following him in droves, attempting to get his attention to try and talk with him, even going so far as to throw bouquets of flowers into his room through the window! As soon as he appeared at a concert or in the city park, females flocked about him, writing him notes, talking to him, and only he was paying no attention to any of it. He was sick with tuberculosis at the time.

My female friend shared all of this when I arrived in Yalta.

After all these stories, I was wondering if he would find time to talk to me. As I drew closer to his house, I felt awkward. I was invited in, and finally a servant addressed me:

"Could you please wait in the living room?"

I waited for about an hour.

Then a man entered whom I had never seen before, with a very pale face that looked like a parchment paper. He stood in the middle of the room, hesitated for a little while, and then said,

"Oh, well. I did not want to meet you. I knew that you would remind me of my youth." Then he started coughing.

I was embarrassed. He took me by the hand and said, "Hello, nice to see you again."

Then he closed his face with his both hands, was quiet for a little, and said, "You remind me of those happy days in the Babkino cottage."

I was upset and did not know what to do. Then I said, "Anton Pavlovich, I do not understand."

Without taking both hands away from his face he said, "Yes, maybe you do not know this, but it was us who wanted to examine the young lady who came to visit us for the first time. So my brothers and I went one by one under your deck, pretending that we wanted worms for fishing, but we wanted to take a good look at you."

I laughed out loud.

He looked at me and said, "Are you feeling unwell?"

I replied, "Yes, I had several inflammations of the lungs, five in a row to be exact, and the doctors recommended Yalta for my recovery."

He waved with his hands in the air. His eyes were shining, and he looked like a sick man. Then there was silence for some time.

"You have a pretty nice house here is Yalta," I said.

"Yes, and I have another, smaller house close to Gurzuf," he replied.

I said, "I have been there a couple of times earlier horseback riding. The road was so narrow that it was difficult to go there even by horse, but there was nothing there, except for a very tiny house at the very edge of the sea."

"That is exactly the place that I bought," he replied.

"Are you really going to live there, in that solitude?" I asked him.

"Yes, I was going to live there."

"But there were no roads there. You could hardly get in there."

"That is exactly the reason why I like it! I am going to furnish it with a bit of furniture and a tea set very soon. When faced with the possibility of losing your life, perspectives change and you can behave strangely. It feels like a candle burning at both ends."

He started coughing very often, and then said, "If you are going to visit me again, please come to my little cottage."

I replied, "Yes, I will."

As I left Chekhov's house, I had tears in my eyes. I never saw Chekhov again.

Boris Lazarevsky. "A.P. Chekhov"

Chekhov lived in Yalta, and I lived not too far away from him, in Sevastopol. I used to buy books at Mr. Viaznov's bookstore, where I met a young man, a shop assistant named Mitya Kamyshov, who loved my short stories.

One day he told me, "You know what, Lazarevsky, your stories are not any worse than others. I know of a good publisher in Moscow, and we can publish them."

Mitya somehow knew Chekhov and with his help, my first volume of short stories was published in 1903. I published about 5000 copies and made nearly 200 rubles. All the major literary journals wrote favorable book reviews, and several major newspapers ran reviews as well.

The most precious review arrived in the form of a letter from Anton Pavlovich Chekhov. It was very friendly, tender and supportive.

"I liked your story, most of all because your characters speak as if they are people in real life. You should write a play."

I did not listen to the advice. I did not feel like writing a play in the future — but this is how I became a professional short story writer.

Maxim Gorky. "A.P. Chekhov"

He was a very simple man, and he loved everything that was simple, truthful and sincere.

One day, he was visited by three ladies dressed in formal evening attire. They filled the room with the rustle of their silk skirts and scent of their perfume. They sat around Chekhov in a serious way, pretending that they were interested in politics and asking him questions:

"Anton Pavlovich, what will be the outcome of the war?"

Chekhov coughed a couple of times, thought for a little while, and then answered in a soft and serious voice, "It will probably be ended with a peace treaty."

"Yes, you are right, but who will win — the Greeks or the Turks?"

"Whoever is stronger."

"Yes of course, you are right, but who do you think is stronger?" the ladies went on asking him.

"The people who eat better and who have a better education," Chekhov answered.

"Oh, this is so witty," one lady said.

"And which do you prefer — the Greeks or the Turks?" the other lady asked.

Chekhov looked at her sympathetically and answered with a friendly smile, in a soft and gentle voice,

"I like marmalade. Do you like it?"

"Oh, we all like it very much," the first lady exclaimed.

"And it tastes so good," the other lady added. Then all three ladies launched into an extremely busy conversation, showing their deep knowledge on the subject of marmalade. It was obvious that they were satisfied, well-nigh delighted, to abandon the pretense that they were interested in politics and the Greco-Turkish War, which had never crossed their minds before their visit to Chekhov.

When the ladies were leaving, they told Anton Pavlovich, "We will send you the best marmalade!"

As soon as they left, I told Chekhov, "You are a wonderful conversationalist."

Anton Pavlovich smiled quietly and said, "You should talk to people in their own language."

One day, I met the Assistant Prosecutor in Chekhov's office. The man was young and had only recently graduated from law school. He stood before Chekhov, gesticulating wildly, and pronounced the following question in a very officious way,

"Anton Pavlovich, you pose us all a very serious question with your short story, 'The Evildoer.'

"If we agree that Denis was an evil man and that he committed this crime with criminal intent, then I should send Denis to prison without any hesitation, in the interests of society. Yet, he is a person without any education and he was apparently acting without fully understanding the consequences of his acts. In this case, I should take pity on him. Yet, if I take pity on people like him, how can I guarantee that Denis will not repeat the same crime again? This is the question that needs to be answered. What should I do?"

He stepped back, folded his hands on his chest, and pierced Anton Pavlovich with his glance. He looked both very serious and professional and rather stupid. His eyes were shining.

Chekhov answered, "If I were a judge, I would say, 'Denis, you should go home.'"

"On what basis?" the prosecutor asked.

Chekhov said, "I would tell him, 'You are not a criminal, Denis. Go home now.'"

The prosecutor laughed for a few seconds and then became serious. He said,

"No, Anton Pavlovich. This question can only be resolved in the interests of society, and I am called to defend these interests. Perhaps he is a wild savage with no education, but Denis is a criminal, and this is the truth."

"Do you like gramophones?" Chekhov suddenly asked, without any connection to the previous conversation.

"Oh yes, I love them," the young man answered innocently.

"I hate gramophones," Anton Pavlovich said.

"Why?"

"Because they sing or speak without understanding anything; they are just repeating. It seems to me that they are dead. And do you like photography?"

It turned out that the young prosecutor was a passionate photographer. He discussed his hobby without interruption and at length. He was not interested in gramophones, but his constant and mechanical conservation reminded me of one.

When the young man left, Anton Pavlovich said gloomily, "Look, people like that can determine a man's life."

Then, after a small pause, Chekhov added, "Prosecutors like fishing; they go for pike."

When I came to Yalta, Chekhov invited me to go with him to the village of Kuk-Choi, where he had a small house.

He spoke with excitement, "If I had a lot of money, I would have built a sanatorium for sick teachers here. You know, I would build a large building, with huge windows and huge rooms. I would have a large library, a vegetable garden and an orchard. There would be lectures on history, literature, and mythology. Teachers must know something about everything — everything, my dear fellow!"

He coughed suddenly, looked at me out the corner of his eyes, then smiled one of those charming smiles that attracted me so irresistibly to him and made me listen carefully to all he said.

"Does it bore you to listen to my fantasies? I like to talk about them. If only you knew how badly the Russian villages need good teachers. Now, come inside, I will give you a cup of tea as a reward for your patience."

That was so characteristic of him — to speak of serious things with sincerity, and then suddenly change the topic and finish with a joke. He had the gentle smile of a man who knows the value of words and who knows how to dream dreams.

We walked in silence to the house. It was a hot, clear day, very sunny. Far below, a dog barked guardedly.

Chekhov took my arm, bowed to the dog and said quietly, "It is sad but true: there is many a man who envies the life of a dog."

Then he added immediately, with a laugh, "Today, I can only make weak speeches. This means that I am getting old."

He would often tell me something like, "You know, there is a teacher, he has just come to Yalta. Could you do something for him? So far, I have been making arrangements for him."

He would say, "Listen, Gorky, there is a teacher here who would like to meet you. However, he is too sick and he cannot come to you. Could you go and talk to him? Please do it for me."

Sometimes, I would see such "teacher" visitors at Chekhov's house. Usually, a teacher would sit carefully on the edge of a chair, in a very awkward way, trying to speak wisely and in an "educated" way, all the while making an effort not to look stupid in the eyes of a famous author.

Sometimes, a "teacher" would simply make Chekhov so tired that it was impossible to answer them at all. Chekhov would listen carefully to the long and incoherent speech, a smile would appear on his face, and a small wrinkle on his forehead, and then with his soft voice, Chekhov would speak nice, simple and homely words; words that would make all conversation very simple once more.

The teacher would stop attempting to be "very educated" and would suddenly become a real person.

Anton Chekhov and Olga Knipper. "Letters"

[At the age of 39, Anton Chekhov started corresponding with Olga Knipper, a leading actress of the Moscow Art Theater, whom he had met at a rehearsal of his play The Seagull. *Their correspondence lasted until the writer's death five years later, and included more than 800 letters.*

After his marriage to Olga in 1901, Chekhov was persuaded by his doctor to take up residence in Yalta, a southern spa on the Black Sea, on account of his illness.

Olga decided to remain in Moscow to continue her career. Several times a year, each traveled from Moscow to Yalta or from Yalta to Moscow to see the other, a distance of over 500 miles, and wrote each other passionate letters during the time they were apart.

Anton's letters to his wife are written in a very typical "Chekhovian" manner, in which passionate declarations of love, and serious thoughts about art, life and theatre are couched in a playful, jovial style.— P.S.]

I became so happy that I even laughed from happiness, when I received a letter at the post office. I had thought that the writer Chekhov would not forget about the actress Knipper, and you did remember me. Thank you.
— Anton Chekhov. "Letters." From Olga Knipper to Chekhov, June 22–23, 1899

Yes, you are right: the writer Chekhov did not forget about the actress Knipper. Be healthy, joyful and happy; work, jump around, fall in love, sing, and, if possible, don't forget about a retired writer and your passionate admirer, A. Chekhov.
— Anton Chekhov. "Letters." His letter to Olga Knipper, September 3, 1899

Dear Actress,
How are you? As you see, I write to you almost every day. When an author writes to an actress so often ... well, my pride might suffer. Writers should keep actresses in a strict discipline, instead of writing letters to

them. Sometimes I forget that I am the coordinator of actresses. Be healthy, dear actress.

> — Anton Chekhov. "Letters." His letter to Olga Knipper,
> October 4, 1899

Good morning. How are you, my darling? How did you spend the night? I just got up, washed my face, had a cheap coffee, and started writing this letter.... Let's try to spend the next summer together, in the North.... I am kissing your clever head, please feel my hot kiss. Adieu, my academician. Love me and write to me, Your actress.

> — Anton Chekhov. "Letters." From Olga Knipper to Chekhov,
> August 6, 1900

Why don't you come here, Anton? I heard that you plan to go abroad.... What do you mean by this? It was warm and nice up here [this last summer] and you could have had a nice life here, and we could have loved each other and gotten close to each other.... You have a warm and loving heart. Why do you force it to be cold?

> — Anton Chekhov. "Letters." From Olga Knipper to Chekhov,
> September 24, 1900, Moscow

My dearest Olya, my dear little actress... You write that I "have a warm and loving heart, but I force it to be cold." How did I show this to you? My dear, I always loved you, and I never tried to hide it away from you.... You expect a lengthy conversation, with serious faces and serious consequences: but I don't know what else should I tell you except for one thing, which I have already told you 10,000 times, and which I will keep on telling you for a long time to come — I love you, and that is all. And if we are not together now, we have to blame those devils who put a virus into me and the love of art into you.

Adieu, my dear old woman, and let holy angels guard you. Write to me. Yours, Antoine.

> — Anton Chekhov. "Letters." His letter to Olga Knipper,
> September 27, 1900

You know, Anton, I am afraid to dream too much. I mean to tell you about my dreams, but it seems to me that something good and strong will grow from our feelings. And when I start to believe in this, my soul gets warm, and I want to live and work, and don't talk about the routine trifles of everyday life.

> — Anton Chekhov. "Letters." From Olga Knipper to Chekhov,
> December 11, 1900

My darling,

I kiss you, my treasure, I kiss you with warm, strong, and tender kisses, the ones you like. Don't be sad, my dear. We will have a good life ahead of us. Don't be angry with me, and don't stop loving me. Your dog.

> — Anton Chekhov. "Letters." From Olga Knipper to Chekhov,
> September 18, 1902

My dear,

You write to me that you are tormented by your conscience that you don't live with me in Yalta, but live in Moscow. What can we do, dear? Just think about it: if you live in Yalta in winter, your life would be ruined.... I knew that I married an actress, and when I married, I understood it very clearly that in winter you would live in Moscow. Your husband, A.

> — Anton Chekhov. "Letters." His letter to Olga Knipper,
> January 20, 1903

You must love every word, every thought, every character, every soul you create, and you must know that people need all this. There is no other writer like you, and therefore, don't close yourself off and isolate. People await your new play like a manna from heaven. I kiss you. I kiss your hands, and I pray to God that you feel better. Do you receive my letters? Yours, Olya.

> — Anton Chekhov. "Letters." From Olga Knipper to A. Chekhov,
> September 24, 1903, Moscow

I am all impatient for the moment when I will meet you, my joy! I live a dull life without you. A day without thoughts, without desires, just a pack of playing cards, and pacing across the room.... Don't forget about me and think sometimes about the man you married some time ago. I scratch your shoulder, your back, and your neck, and I kiss you my darling.... I embrace you and pull your leg. Yours, Someone.

> — Anton Chekhov. "Letters." His letter to Olga Knipper.
> April 10, 1904, Yalta

Olga Knipper-Chekhova. *"About A.P. Chekhov"*

Everyone experiences certain important and decisive moments in life. For me, that moment, that year, was 1898. I had just graduated from the Moscow Drama Theater Studio and had become an actress. The same year, I met Anton Pavlovich Chekhov. This was the beginning of years of creative work, filled with excitement and faith in what the future held.

That day, the founders of the newly created Moscow Art Theater had their first meeting with our favorite writer, a man whom we all admired. I will remember that moment forever. I can recollect everything that happened down to the smallest detail. We all met Chekhov for the first time on September 8, 1898.

I will always remember my excitement upon receiving a brief note from Vladimir Nemirovich-Danchenko saying that Chekhov was going to come to the rehearsal of *The Seagull*.

I shall always remember the moment I first met with Chekhov face to face. We all were charmed by his personality, by his simplicity, and by his ability to talk with people. His character didn't permit him to teach people, or to show them how to perform his plays, or to lecture the actors in any way. We did not know how we should speak with him, and so we all felt embarrassed when we met him for the first time.

He looked at us actors in a rather serious way, smiling from time to time as we looked at him. He did not tell us how to act and answered all our questions in a joking manner. Barely a serious word came from his lips. He did not come to the second rehearsal since the weather was rainy; instead he went south to Yalta, which he disliked.

A few weeks later, we held the first performance of his play *The Seagull*. It was December 17, 1898.

Our new theater was half full. As we performed, we were very nervous.

At one particular moment, we ended up with our backs to the public. After the third act, complete silence reigned for several seconds. Then something strange happened. For some time, we did not understand what was going on. The theatre descended into chaos, everything around us was resonating with deafening ovation and celebration. The entire theater, both the public and the actors on stage, were united as one. No one left the stage; we all stood there, puzzled, before beginning to embrace and kiss each other....

Then we all decided that we had to write a telegram to Yalta. *The Seagull* was a huge success.

In the summer of 1904, Anton Pavlovich accompanied me to Germany, and from there, he departed quietly for a better world. He woke in the middle of the night, and for the first time in his life, he asked to send for a doctor. I tried to calm myself. I remember the terrible moment when people came to the door, and went rushing off for the doctor, leaving me in solitude for some time. I remember very well the sound of their fading footsteps.

The doctor came, and he asked me to give some champagne to the patient. Anton Pavlovich sat up in his bed, and with a very strange and meaningful smile told the doctor, "I have not had champagne for a long time."

He downed the glass, and said in German, although he had never spoken German before — "Ich sterbe." *["I am dying."—P.S.]*

He calmly lay down on his left side, and then he was quiet forever. The doctor left and suddenly, a terrible silence filled the night. The only sound was that of a big, black moth that had flown into the hotel room, and was beating against the electric bulb on the ceiling.

I felt completely alone.... I knew that I had just lost a wonderful, irreplaceable man. In the morning, the first of many visitors began to arrive in my rooms. I had stood the entire night on the balcony, looking at the first rays of the rising sun, at all the world awakening, and especially at the serene and slightly smiling face of Anton Pavlovich. For me, all that happened that morning was part of a huge mystery. I will never experience such a moment again as long as I live.

Nikolai Ulianov. "The Portrait of Chekhov"

I met Anton Pavlovich Chekhov in 1904, in his Moscow apartment. I came to talk with him about our future sessions of painting his portrait.

We sat in the dark room, and suddenly I had the idea of painting him sitting in half-darkness. I understood that in order to depict the true inner world of Anton Pavlovich on canvas, there was no need for bright colors or cluttered, elaborate backgrounds.

Anton Pavlovich agreed to sit for me, but we could not find the proper time, and postponed it altogether.

He died over the summer of the same year.

Our painting session never took place, but I, nonetheless, decided to make his portrait based on his photographs.

You could not find any particular, dominant feature in his face. There was some kind of tenderness in his face, which escaped you because his expression was constantly changing.

V. Serov, a famous painter, told me the same thing. He said that he had also admired Anton Pavlovich, and even done a pencil sketch of him much earlier. Serov added,

"I could not make an oil portrait of Chekhov. He truly was a great man, but his face.... Its countenance was always changing, and we had a hard time depicting his likeness."

The Lifetime of Anton Chekhov

1860

January 17. "Anton Pavlovich Chekhov is born in the city of Taganrog, in the merchant Gnutov's House, in Politseyskaya Street" (*Official Birth Record Book*, RGALI — Russian State Archive of Literature, Chekhov, File 1, p. 472). Yet, in his letters Chekhov referred to January 16 as his birthday: "I am already 38" (to Maria Chekhova, January 16, 1898); "Today is my birthday. I am 39" (to Maria Chekhova, January 16, 1899).

1863

July 31. Maria Pavlovna Chekhova, Anton's younger sister, is born.

1868

August 23. Anton is enlisted in the Taganrog City School.

1873

Fall. Anton visits his first theater performance; he starts doing this on a regular basis, and takes part in the amateur plays.

1874–75

Anton's father starts the construction of a new house. His grocery store does not bring sufficient income, and financial bankruptcy follows.

1875

August 10. Alexandr and Nikolai, two elder brothers, move to Moscow to enter the university and the Moscow Art School.

1876

April. Pavel Chekhov, the father of the family, secretly goes to Moscow to live with his sons, and to escape the debtor's prison.
July. Evgenia Chekhova, the writer's mother, moves to Moscow.
July. Anton, after his mother's departure, lives in the merchant G.P. Selianov's house.

He pays for the rent and food by tutoring. He even sends some money to Moscow to support his family.

1877–78
Anton Chekhov writes two plays, *Without a Father* and *Contradictions*, and a vaudeville, *A Chicken's Song, or Chirp*. He reads a lot of books at the city public library.

1879
May–June. Anton's graduation exams at the Taganrog City School.
August. Anton moves to Moscow to join his family. They live for several months in the damp basement of St. Mikhail's Church in the Grachevka District.
September. Anton enters the medical department of Moscow University.

1880
January. Anton Pavlovich publishes his first short story, "A Letter to an Educated Neighbor," in *The Dragonfly Magazine*.
March 9. Two of Chekhov's short stories are published in the *Dragonfly Magazine* No. 9.
May 11. "You Can't Kill Two Birds with One Stone," a short story by A. Chekhov, is published in *The Dragonfly* No. 18.
May–June. Exams at Moscow University in June, July, August, November, and December: *The Dragonfly* publishes several short stories by Chekhov.

1881
September–October. Short stories by Chekhov start to appear in the *Spectator [Zritel]* magazine.

1882
January. The Census Committee of the city of Moscow enrolls Anton Chekhov as a census officer in the 2 Division of the 5th neighborhood.
February–December. Short stories by Chekhov appear in the Moscow humor magazines *Dragonfly*, *Spectator*, and *Alarm Clock*.

1883
The end of the year. A collection of short stories, *At Leisure Time [Na dosuge]*, is prepared for publication, and illustrated by Nikolai Chekhov, the writer's brother. It is not published due to the lack of funding.

1884
May. Chekhov prepares to publish the first collection of his short stories, *Tales of Melpomena*.
June. Anton Chekhov graduates from the medical department of Moscow University.
June 18. Chekhov writes a formal request letter to grant him permission to practice medicine in Voskresensk, Moscow Region.

August 4. The first installment of the novella *Drama at Hunt* [*Drama na Okhote*] is published in the *Daily News* [*Novosti dnia*].

September–December. Chekhov starts practicing medicine as a family doctor.

1884

Chekhov works on his PhD thesis, *History of Medicine in Russia*. He reads several dozens of books on history and on medicine.

1885

February–March–April. Chekhov continues a column in *Fragments* magazine, titled "The Fragments of the Moscow Life."

1886

St. Petersburg Newspaper (No. 1, 1886), a prominent daily, publishes a short story, "Dressed for Halloween."

March 8. Chekhov receives the printed galleys of his first book of short stories, *The Blunt Stories* (*Pestrye Rasskazy*).

March 25. Elderly novelist D. Grigorovich, a friend of Dostoevsky, Turgenev and Tolstoy, writes a lengthy letter to young Chekhov, admiring his talent.

April 24–May 10. A trip to St. Petersburg. Chekhov visits the editorial offices of several major periodicals, meets prominent writers D. Grigorovich and A. Suvorin.

July 25–28. Chekhov goes to Zvenigorod, Moscow Region, to temporarily replace his friend, Doctor S. Uspensky.

August 27. Chekhov moves to a new apartment on Sadovo-Kudrinsklaya Street in Moscow, the house of J. Korneev.

October–November–December. Chekhov submits short stories to different periodicals on a daily basis, writing to support his family.

1887

January 4–11. Chekhov visits the Second National Congress of the Russian Doctors.

February 2. Chekhov is elected a member of the Moscow Literary Fund, a charitable organization that supports beginning writers.

March 9–14. Chekhov goes to St. Petersburg and meets with several prominent writers and journalists, among them A. Suvorin and D. Grigorovich.

March 18. Eighteen short stories are sent to Suvorin for the second collection of stories. The original working title is *My Stories*.

April 4. Chekhov goes to Taganrog, the town of his childhood. He meets with his uncle and other distant relatives, then visits the church and his old friends.

April 19–20. Peter Tchaikovsky reads Chekhov's short stories in *The New Time*, and writes him a letter of admiration. This starts the friendship between two great artists.

June–July. About twenty short stories are written and published during this period, a story every two or three days.

October 5. Chekhov completes his play *Ivanov*, which he writes in less than two weeks.

October 6. Chekhov visits the Korsh Theater and gives his play, *Ivanov*, to the actor V. Davydov to read.

November 19. The first night of the play *Ivanov*. The public and the theater critics have completely opposite opinions of the play: from hatred to adoration.

1888

January 1. Chekhov starts his work on his novella *The Steppe*.

March, the beginning of the months. *The Steppe* is published in *The Northern Messenger*. Huge success among literary critics and the reading public.

March 14–21. Chekhov makes a trip to St. Petersburg, and meets there with his colleagues and friends, Suvorin, Pleshcheev, Leskov, Polonsky and Leontiev.

December 19. The Alexandrinsky Theater in St. Petersburg, one of the oldest and biggest Russian theaters, starts rehearsals for the play *Ivanov*.

1889

January 31. The play *Ivanov* is a huge success. Numerous positive reviews appear in the media.

March, the beginning of the month. Chekhov starts working on the play *The Forest Spirit* [*Leshyi*]. He reads works by Dostoevsky.

June 17. Nikolai Chekhov dies. It is a very tragic event for the writer, because he was very close to his brother.

July 5. Anton visits Odessa, at the invitation of the Odessa Drama Theater.

July 16–August 9. The writer's first trip to Yalta, a spa town in the south, at the Black Sea.

September 4. Chekhov returns to Moscow from a lengthy trip south.

October 14. Peter Tchaikovsky visits Chekhov in Moscow. The writer asks for permission to dedicate his new collection of short stories, *Gloomy People* [*Khmurye liudi*], to the great composer. Tchaikovsky invites Chekhov to write a libretto for his new opera.

1890

January 28. Chekhov outlines his trip to Siberia. He compiles a list of literature to be read before the trip.

March, the end of the month. The collection of short stories *The Gloomy People* is published by A. Suvorin. It is dedicated to Peter Tchaikovsky.

April 21. Chekhov's departure to Saklhalin. From a letter to A. Lensky: "I am leaving today. The Yaroslavsky Railway Station, at 8 pm. The Chekhovs, Kuvshinnikovs and Levitan will see me off to St. Trinity Church."

April 21–July 10. Chekhov's trip to Sakhalin via Volga, Perm, Tiumen, Tomsk, Krasnoyarsk, Irkutsk, and Khabarovsk. He writes a diary and a series of traveler's sketches, *From Siberia,* which are published in A. Suvorin's periodical, *The New Time.*

July–August–September. Chekhov visits numerous settlement prisons, talks to people, and collects materials for the census of the Sakhalin population.

October 13. Chekhov visits the Southern Sakhalin.

October 17–December 8. A trip from Vladivostok to Moscow via Japan, Hong Kong, Singapore, Ceylon, Suez, Constantinople, and Odessa.

December 8. Chekhov arrives in Moscow. The family moves to a new rented apartment, the Fairgang House on the Little Dmitrovka Street.

1891

January 1. Peter Tchaikovsky highly praises Chekhov's new story "Gusev" in a letter to his brother, Modest.

January 5. Chekhov starts work on his new novella, *The Duel*.

March 19–April 27. Chekhov goes for a trip abroad, to visit Vienna, Venice, Florence, Rome, and Paris. He visits several major art museums, Vesuvius and the French Parliament.

May–June–July. Chekhov moves to a dacha Bogimovo, in the suburbs of Moscow. He works on his book *The Sakhalin Island*, and works at his novella, *The Duel*. Several close friends visit him briefly at the dacha: L. Misinova, I. Levitan, A. Suvorin, and N. Lintvareva.

1892

January 10. Chekhov returns to Moscow.

March 1. The Chekhovs move to Melikhovo, their new country estate. Chekhov works at his story, "Ward No. 6," and enjoys life in the country.

April 15. A trip to Moscow. Chekhov brings the manuscript of "Ward No. 6" for *The Russian Review* [*Russkoe obozrenie*].

July–August–September. Chekhov works as a doctor at fighting with the cholera epidemics, near Melikhovo. This medical activity takes much time and effort, and literary work is temporarily stopped.

1893

July 10–28. Chekhov writes the novella *The Black Monk*.

November 25–December 19. A trip to Moscow. Chekhov makes an agreement with the publisher I. Sytin for the publication of his selected short stories in a book form.

1894

February 16. In a letter to A. Suvorin, Chekhov discusses his plans to go to Yalta, Crimea: "I am in a hurry, because I am tormented by cough. There is nothing serious so far.... It is, so to speak, a mechanical cough."

March 2. Chekhov leaves Melikhovo for Crimea.

March 5. Chekhov arrives in Yalta and stays at the Russian Hotel. Meetings with the local writer V. Tausek, actress A. Medvedeva, and doctor L. Sredin.

April 2. In his conversation with G. Rusanov, Leo Tolstoy highly praises *The Steppe* by Chekhov.

April 3. Chekhov leaves Yalta for Melikhovo.

June 26. A small summer cottage is built in Melikhovo. Chekhov starts his work on a new play there.

1895

January 2. Levitan arrives in Melikhovo to see Chekhov after a long absence.

April 9. Chekhov sends his story "Ariadna" to V. Lavrov, the publisher.

May, the end of the month. *The Sakhalin Island* is published as a separate book.

August 8–9. Chekhov visits Leo Tolstoy in Yasnaya Polyana. From a letter to Suvorin: "I spent with him 1.5 days. What a wonderful feeling. I felt very easy, as if I were at home."

August 9. Chekhov admires the Tolstoy novel, *The Resurrection*, after a family reading.

September 4. Leo Tolstoy writes a letter to his son Lev, and mentions Chekhov: "He is a gifted man, and has a kind heart."

December 3–6. Chekhov reads *The Seagull* to actors, L. Iarovskaya, and V. Nemitrovich-Danchenko.

1896

February 15. Chekhov visits Leo Tolstoy in Moscow. They discuss Tolstoy's recent novel, *The Resurrection*.

April 6–8. Chekhov has serious bleeding in the mouth.

July 29. Chekhov completes his novella *My Life*.

October, before 7. Chekhov sends three plays to A. Suvorin, to be published in a book form: *Ivanov, Uncle Vanya,* and *The Seagull*.

October 12–16. Chekhov and Potapenko visit the rehearsals of *The Seagull* at the Alexandrinsky Theater.

October 17. The first night of *The Seagull* is a failure. Very disappointed, Chekhov leaves during the second act for his cottage in Melikhovo.

October 22. A telegram from Potapenko: "The second performance of *The Seagull* was an absolute success."

1897

March 25. A strong throat bleeding. Chekhov spends several days in the Ostroumov Hospital in Moscow.

March 28. Leo Tolstoy visits Chekhov at the hospital. They talk about literature for several hours.

April 10. Chekhov leaves the hospital and goes home to Melikhovo.

April 15–16. A group of university students visit Chekhov at his estate in Melikhovo.

May, the end of the month. Numerous positive book reviews on the story "The Peasants," in all major newspapers and magazines.

September 1. Chekov goes abroad to France.

September 4–6. A trip to Paris.

October–November. Chekhov visits Nice and Monte Carlo. He slowly recovers from his illness.

1898

April 14. Chekhov goes to Paris with M. Kovalevsky.

April 25. Nemirovich-Danchenko asks Chekhov for his permission to stage *The Seagull* in the newly created Moscow Art Theater.

May 2. Chekhov leaves Paris for St. Petersburg.

May 5. Chekhov returns to Melikhovo.

December 17. The Moscow Art Theater performs *The Seagull*. The first night is a great success.

December 18–20. Numerous telegrams to Chekhov from Moscow on the success of his play.

1899

January 1. From a letter to P. Sergeenko, in which Chekhov suggests publishing his works at the Marx Publishing House: "I don't mind selling him my works."

January 20. Chekhov sends a telegram to P. Sergeenko that he agrees to publish his *Complete Works* for 75,000 rubles.

April14. Chekhov brings his *Uncle Vanya* to the actors and directors of the Maly Theater.

May 7. Chekhov goes to Melikhovo. Before his departure he meets with Olga Knipper, an actress of the Moscow Art Theater, who later becomes his wife.

June 28. Chekhov meets with the painter, Janov, who agrees to buy his Melikhovo estate.

July 6. Chekhov travels to Moscow. He meets with Olga Knipper.

July 20. Chekhov travels with Knipper from Novorossiisk to Yalta. He checks the construction of his new house.

August 5. Chekhov arrives in Moscow to visit his publisher Marx.

August 27. Chekhov arrives in Yalta; he lives in the newly built house.

September 30. Chekhov receives a telegram from the Moscow Art Theater. The actors and directors congratulate the author with the beginning of a new theater season.

October 26. The first night of *Uncle Vanya* at the Moscow Art Theater.

October 27–29. Telegrams to Chekhov and numerous positive reviews in the press on his new play.

December, the end of the month. "A Lady with a Dog" is published in *The Russian Thought*, No. 12.

1900

January 8. The Russian Academy of Sciences elects a group of outstanding Russian writers as honorary members, among them Leo Tolstoy, Anton Chekhov, Vladimir Korolenko, and Alexander Koni.

January 16. The Division of Russian Literature at the Russian Academy of Sciences sends an official letter to Chekhov stating that he has been elected an honorary member of the Academy.

March–April. Several young writers visit Chekhov in Yalta and stay there for several days, including M. Gorky, V. Posse, and A. Kuprin.

April, 7. The Moscow Art Theater arrives in Sevastopol, the biggest city in Crimea, for a tour of four productions, two by Chekhov (see below). Maria Chekhova, the writer's sister, and Olga Knipper, the leading actress and his future wife, arrive two days earlier: "The dacha construction was coming to an end, the garden was being planted." Olga makes friends with Chekhov's pets: two stray dogs and a crane who live at the dacha.

April 8. Chekhov is seriously ill with tuberculosis, and bleeds profusely in his throat.

April 10. Chekhov arrives in Sevastopol, about 100 kilometers from Yalta, to see the performance of his latest play, *Uncle Vanya*.

April 23. The last performance of the Moscow Art Theater in Yalta is a huge success. Chekhov, a shy man, tries to escape but is not allowed. He is called repeatedly to the stage, receives a laurel and a letter of congratulations signed by 180 people, among them many leading Russian intellectuals, such as the novelist M. Gorky, the painter A. Vasnetsov, the composer and pianist Sergei Raklunaninov, and others. Maria Chekhova writes that she "never saw such a triumph in the theater hall."

April 24. The actors of the Moscow Art Theater leave Yalta, and present Chekhov with a gift: a garden bench and swings used in their production of *Uncle Vanya*.

July–early August. Olga Knipper visits Chekhov, who is alone in Yalta, while Chekhov's family (his mother and sister) are in the summer cottage in Gurzuf.

August 3. In Gurzuf, Chekhov meets Vera Komissarzhevskaya, a leading Moscow actress. They discuss new stage productions. Chekhov gives her his photo, with the inscription: "To Vera Fyodorovna Komisarzhevskaya, August 3, on a stormy day when the sea was violent, from a quiet person: Anton Chekhov."

August 5–8. Olga Knipper leaves Yalta; Chekhov sees her off to Sevastopol.

August 8. Meeting with Stanislavsky, the artistic director of Moscow Art Theater, during which Chekhov makes a promise to complete a new play by September 1.

During August–September, 1901, Chekhov writes his play *Three Sisters*.

October 23. Chekhov arrives in Moscow and a few days later reads his new play to the actors of the Moscow Art Theater.

October, the end of the month. Chekhov and Gorky visit different Moscow theaters practically every day, meeting actors and writers.

December 14. Chekhov arrives at Nice from Vienna. He instantly starts working at the new, revised version of the third and fourth acts of *Three Sisters*.

December 29. Chekhov and Nemirovich pay a visit to Professor M. Kovalevsky in Beaulieu. On the same day, Stanislavsky writes to Chekhov from Moscow, after one of the final rehearsals of *Three Sisters:* "We often remember you and admire your sensitivity, and your knowledge of the theater, the kind of theater about which we are dreaming."

1901

March 30. Knipper arrives in Yalta.

April 14. Knipper leaves Yalta for Moscow.

April 26. A letter from Chekhov to Knipper: "I am ready to marry you on the first day of my arrival in Moscow, but only if you promise me that, until that day, not a soul in Moscow will know about it. Somehow, I am terribly afraid of the wedding ceremony, and the champagne you have to hold in your hand, with an enigmatic smile on your face."

May 25. Wedding of A.P. Chekhov and Olga Knipper in Moscow, in the Church of the Ascension on Plushchikha, with only four witnesses present, and no guests. After the wedding, the newlyweds visit Knipper's mother and then immediately leave for Ufa, to a spa resort in southeastern Russia.

Chekhov sends a telegram to his mother: "Dear Mother, I am getting married, please bless me. Everything [in the family] will remain the same as it was before."

June 2. A letter to his sister Maria: "You know I am a married man. I think this action will change neither my life, nor the atmosphere in which I have lived. Mother probably says otherwise, God knows what, but please tell her that there will be absolutely no changes in our lives."

July 1. Chekhov and Knipper leave Ufa for Yalta, via Volga, Samara, Tsaritsyn, and Novorossiisk.

August 3. Chekhov writes his will:

> To Maria Pavlovna Chekhova,
> Dear Maria, according to my will, I leave you for life my dacha in Yalta, my money and all income from my dramatic works; and I leave to Olga Leonardovna [Knipper], my wife, my dacha in Gursuf and five thousand rubles. If you wish, you can sell the estate.... Help the poor. Save our mother. Live in peace.
> Anton Chekhov.

August 9. In his conversation to O. Sadovskaya, a Moscow actress, Chekhov promises to write a new play for her future anniversary: "Let me express hope that, if circumstances are favourable, and if I am in good health, I will write a play which I will send to you."

September 12. Chekhov visits Tolstoy in the village of Gaspra in Crimea.

September 15. Chekhov leaves for Sevastopol by ship, and then the same day, for Moscow by train.

September 16. Tolstoy discusses Chekhov's stories with his friends and assistants. Some of the stories are read aloud. Tolstoy says: "He is a very unusual writer: it seems that he throws words at random, but they create a living picture. And so much intellect! He never uses unnecessary details, every detail is either necessary or beautiful."

September 18. Rehearsal of *Three Sisters,* with Chekhov's participation. The actor Luzhsky remembers: "He went to several rehearsals of the play in the fall, and gave very detailed comments concerning the production. For example, he himself staged the scene of the fire in the Third act ... he had rehearsals personally with me, each at least an hour long."

September 21, 24. Chekhov is present at the two first performances of *Three Sisters,* which receives a standing ovation and a most warm reception by the audience: "*Three Sisters* is a great success, it is performed better than the play is written. I made several producer's remarks, gave some author's advice to some actors, and they say that the play is being performed much better than last season."

December 9. Dr. Altshuller pays a visit to Chekhov in Yalta and examines his tuberculosis. Chekhov's health is rapidly deteriorating.

End of 1901. A letter to Sergei Raklunaninov: "Today I visited Tolstoy. We had a very interesting conversation which lasted about two hours."

1902

January 11. The Moscow Art Theater presents Chekhov's play *Uncle Vanya* for the Pirogov Congress of the Doctors. The members of the congress sends a telegram to Chekhov: "The members of the 12th Pirogov Congress of the Russian Doctors extend their wishes of health, and express deep respect for their beloved author and dear colleague."

March 16. A letter to Knipper: "I am not writing a play, and I do not want to write one, because there are too many playwrights these days, and the work becomes too tedious and boring and mundane."

June 9. Nemirovich writes to Stanislavsky saying that Chekhov has assured him that he will be able to complete his new play by August 1.

June. Chekhov, at the invitation of the millionaire and art patron Morozov, leaves for the Urals, through Nizhny Novgorod, Volga, Kama, and Perm, to Morozov's estate.

August 14. Chekhov moves to Yalta.

September 15. Tolstoy reads the Chekhov story "Little Darling" to his family: "He laughed until he had tears in his eyes."

December 18. K. Stanislavsky sends a telegram to Chekhov about the huge success *of At The Bottom*, the latest play by Gorky.

1903

January 1. A letter to Knipper about the new plays of the Moscow Art Theater for the future season: "There is not a single outstanding play, though all of them are good.... All the plays are good literature though."

January 3. Chekhov asks his family to rent a dacha so that he can escape from his numerous visitors, and sit in silence, concentrating on writing a new play.

January 15–16. Chekhov falls ill, with running temperature and constant coughing. His lung disease is getting worse.

February 2–14. Chekhov works at his short story, "The Bride."

February 20–23. Chekhov has another serious fit of his lung illness and cannot work at all.

March 15. Dr. Asltshuller examines Chekhov and does not allow him to travel to Moscow because of his lung disease.

End of March. Numerous meetings with young writers in Yalta: Gorky, Bunin, Kuprin, and Fedorov.

April 1. At a literary party in his house, Chekhov tells his colleagues that it was he who insisted that his wife should not quit the theater, though it was difficult for him to live in Yalta without her.

May 13–14. A trip to St. Petersburg. Chekhov speaks about the termination of his agreement with Marx, who has bought the copyright to all his works for 75,000 rubles.

May 24. Professor Ostroumov, a leading Russian doctor, examines Chekhov's lungs and finds his disease very serious, "emphysema in the lungs and catarrh of the bowels."

May 25. Leo Tolstoy, on Chekhov's request, compiles a list of the best short stories by Chekhov. He lists 15 stories, out of almost 600.

May 29. Chekhov visits his friend Yakunchikova in the distant southeastern suburbs of Moscow. He rents a separate summer cottage and works there for two weeks on his new play, *The Cherry Orchard*: "I sit in front of a big window, and work little by little."

September 15. A letter to M. Lilina: "I almost finished my play, but eight to ten days ago I started coughing, and became weak again.... It has turned out to be not a drama but a comedy, in some places even a farce."

September 26. A telegram to Knipper: "Four acts are ready. I am revising the final draft. I will send them to you soon."

September 30–October 1. Dr. Altshuller examines Chekhov and finds his health very unsatisfactory. The doctor does not allow the writer to go to Moscow due to his poor health.

October, first half of the month. Another three-week delay in completing *The Cherry Orchard* due to poor health and numerous visitors.

October 18–19–20. The directors of the Moscow Art Theater read *The Cherry Orchard* to the actors. Stanislavsky cries out loud during the reading.

November 9. The Moscow Art Theater has the first rehearsal of *The Cherry Orchard*, with casting and first discussion.

November, the end of the month. Chekhov edits numerous manuscripts of the beginning writers who ask for his advice.

December 2–4. Chekhov goes to Moscow.

December. Chekhov attends the rehearsals of *The Cherry Orchard*, which are held at the theater practically every day, making numerous remarks about the production, and making changes in the text of the second act. At night, as a rule, he goes to see other plays being performed.

December 11. Chekhov refuses to become President of the Society of Lovers of Russian Literature due to poor health.

1904

January 17. The first night of *The Cherry Orchard* in the Moscow Art Theater. The play is interrupted after the third act with an ovation. Chekhov receives numerous congratulations from his colleagues, from other writers, and from actors and audience members. Chekhov attends the official dinner after the performance.

February, the beginning of the month. Chekhov attends literary Wednesdays at the home of N.D. Teleshov, where questions of literature are discussed.

February 15–17. Chekhov goes from Moscow to Yalta.

February 27. A letter to Knipper: "I live a boring, uninteresting life. The people around me are completely uninteresting, indifferent to everything."

April 24. The Moscow Literary Society elects Chekhov its honorary member.

May 1–3. Chekhov goes to Moscow.

May 3–19. Chekhov has serious problems with his health; constant coughing with hemorrhage; the writer stays indoors for almost two weeks.

June 2. The writer N.D. Teleshov visits Chekhov in Moscow: "Anton Pavlovich was thin and exhausted; I could hardly recognize him. I could not believe that he could change so much. He stretched his weak hand to me on which I did not dare to look, looked at me with his tender eyes which were not laughing any more, and said, 'I am leaving tomorrow. Goodbye. I am going to die.'"

June 5. Chekhov arrives in Berlin, accompanied by his wife.

June 9. Chekhov arrives in Badenweiler, a spa resort in Germany.

June 20–27. Chekhov has a constant fever and stays indoors.

June 28. A fit of illness: weakness of the heart and problems with breathing.

July 2. 1 A.M. Chekhov wakes up and complains to his wife that he cannot breathe.
2 A.M. A German doctor comes to see Chekhov; he gives the writer a glass of champagne and a camfora injection. Chekhov's pulse weakens. Chekhov sits up in bed, and says to the doctor in German: "Ich sterbe" ("I am dying" — he could hardly speak German); then he looks at his wife, has a drink, lies down on his side and is silent. Chekhov dies in the presence of his wife and the German doctor.

Annotated Bibliography

Altshuller, Isaac. "About Chekhov." *Sovremennye zapiski* [*Contemporary Notes*] (Paris) 61 (1930): 470–485. Also in: *Russkie vedomosti* [*Russian Herald*] 151 (July 2, 1914). A family doctor recollects Chekhov's life in Yalta in 1899–1904, including the history of the writer's illness, his family life, his last literary works, and his meetings with the local journalists who interrupted him from his writing.

Altshuller, Lev. "Memories of Doctor Altshuller's Son about Chekhov." *Literary Heritage* (Moscow), vol. 68 (1960): 691. The son of the Chekhovs' family doctor remembers the warm friendly relationships between his father and Chekhov.

Artyom, A.R., and S. Durylin. "Chekhov's Favorite Actor." *Teatr* [*Theater*] 2 (1935): 23.

Avdeev, Jury. *V chekhovskom Melikhove* [*Chekhov in Melikhovo*]. Moscow: Moskovskii Rabochii, 1953. The director and the founder of the Chekhov Museum in Melikhovo interviews Chekhov's sister Maria, who recollects their life in Melikhovo.

Avilova, Lydia. "A.P. Chekhov in My Life." In: *Chekhov v vospominaniiakh sovremennikov* [*Chekhov in the Memoirs of His Contemporaries*]. Moscow, 1947: 323–395. Avilova recollects her love story with Chekhov. They first meet in 1889 at a literary circle in St. Petersburg, when both he and she were beginning short story writers. Later, she visits him twice at the hospital, and then during the performance of his play *The Seagull*. Avilova insists that she was a prototype of Chekhov's characters. Leo Tolstoy meets Avilova and expresses his admiration of Chekhov.

Belousov, Ivan. "Chekhov as a Fisherman. From the Memoirs." *Tridtsat' dnei* [*Thirty Days*] 7 (1929): 78–79. A writer colleague recollects Chekhov's passion for fishing.

Belousov, Ivan. "About A.P. Chekhov." *Moskovsky ponedelnik* [*Moscow Monday*] 2 (June 26, 1922). Anton Chekhov makes hard choices working as a doctor.

Braz, Ilya. "New About Chekhov. Memoirs." *Krasnaia panorama* [*The Red Panorama*] 16 (1927): 12. A good friend, who is working on Chekhov's portrait, goes fishing with Chekhov at a nearby pond.

Bunin, Ivan. "From the Notebook. Chekhov." *Russkoe slovo* [*The Russian Word*] 297 (1904). Originally published in: *Sbornik Znanie* [*Collection of Knowledge*]. St. Petersburg: Znanie, 1905. Also in: Ivan Bunin, *Sobranie sochinenii* [*Works*]. St. Petersburg: Marx Publishers, 1915. A lengthy book of memories by Chekhov's closest friend, a prominent Russian writer and Nobel Prize winner.

Chaikin, A. "Anton Chekhov: My Travelling Companion." *Literary Heritage* (Moscow), vol. 68 (1960): 288–229. Originally published in: *Prikamie Almamnach* 28 (1960): 55–56. An actor and journalist from the town of Perm, Mr. A. Chaikin meets Chekhov on a train traveling to Sakhalin Island.

Chekhov, Alexander. "From Chekhov's Childhood Days." In: *Chekhov v vospominaniiakh sovremennikov* [*Chekhov in the Memoirs of His Contemporaries*]. Moscow, 1960: 25–65. Originally published in: Alexander Chekhov, *Detskie gody A.P. Chekhova* [*From Chekhov's Childhood Days*]. St. Petersburg, 1912. Anton's brother recollects their early childhood in the city of Taganrog in the 1860s.

Chekhov, Anton. "Letters." In: Anton Chekhov. *Polnoe sobranie sochinenii i pisem v 30 tomakh* [*Complete Works and Letters in 30 volumes*]. Moscow: Nauka, 1974.

Chekhov, Ivan, and Leonid Sulerzhitsky. "Memories of Chekhov." *Shipovnik* 23 (1925). Chekhov's brother and friend reminisce about Anton's childhood years.

Chekhov, Mikhail. *Anton Chekhov and His*

Plots. Moscow: Academia, 1923. Anton Chekhov's brother recollects their childhood.

Chekhov, Mikhail. "A.P. Chekhov and Mongooses." *Krasnaia panorama* [*The Red Panorama*] 28 (July 13, 1929). Anton Chekhov brings home several exotic animals from his trip to Sakhalin and Sri Lanka.

Chekhov, Mikhail. "Anton Chekhov During His Summer Vacations." In: *Chekhov v vospominaniiakh sovremennikov*. [*Chekhov in the Memories of His Contemporaries*]. Moscow, 1960: 66–88. Anton Chekhov visits his friends in the city of Taganrog during his summer vacations.

Chekhov, Mikhail. *Vokrug Chekhova [Around Chekhov]*. Moscow: Academia, 1933. Originally published in: *Chekhovsky sbornik* [*Chekhov Collection*]. Moscow: Chekhov Society Publishers, 1929. A detailed 220-page-long book of memories about Anton Chekhov's childhood and teenage years, written by his brother.

Chekhov, Pavel Egorovich. *Dnevnik [Diary]*. Moscow: Nauka, 1995. Anton's father wrote in his diary daily for almost twenty years.

Chekhova, Maria. "From the Distant Past." In: Maria Chekhova. *The Chekhov Museum in Yalta*. Simferopol, 1954. Chekhov moves to Yalta and his friends and family follow him there.

Chekhova, Maria. "My Memoirs." In: *Muzei A.P. Chekhova v Yalte [A.P. Chekhov Museum in Yalta]*. Moscow, 1949: 5–25. Anton's sister remembers their family life and Chekhov's work habits in the 1870s–1900s.

Chervinsky, Fyodor. "Meetings with A.P. Chekhov." *Ponedelnik narodnogo slova [Monday Edition of the People's Voice]* 4 (May 13, 1918). Chekhov listens to a boring musical comedy, then makes funny jokes.

Chitau, Maria. "A.P. Chekhov." *Zveno* (Paris) 210 (1926). An actress explains why the first night of *The Seagull* by Chekhov was a failure.

Chlenov, Mikhail "A.P. Chekhov and Culture." In: *Chekhov v vospominaniiakh sovremennikov*. [*Chekhov in the Memoirs of His Contemporaries*]. Moscow, 1960: 640–642. Chekhov possesses a lot of inner grace and culture.

Dolzhenko, Alexei. "Memoirs about Anton Chekhov." In: *A.P. Chekhov. Sbornik statei i materialov*. [*A.P. Chekhov. A Collection of Articles and Memoirs*]. Rostov, 1959: 335–345. Chekhov's cousin remembers their big family in the 1860s–80s.

Drossi, Maria, and Alexander Roskin. "Chekhov's Young Years." *Priazonskaya Rech* 41

(1910). Anton Chekhov's friends and neighbors recollect childhood years spent together.

Drozdova, Nina. "From Memoirs about Chekhov." *Novy Mir* [*The New World*] 7 (1954): 211–222. A female painter, Chekhov's friend, describes his writing habits during his life in Yalta.

Efros, Nikolai. *From the History of "The Cherry Orchard."* Petersburg: Soltse Rosii Publishing House, 1919: 65–67. Moscow actor and theater director Efros recounts the history of the creation of a Chekhov play.

Elpatievsky, Sergei. "Anton Pavlovich Chekhov." In: *Blizkie teni* [*Close Shadows*]. St. Petersburg, 1909. A family doctor remembers Chekhov's life in Yalta.

Ezhov, Nikolai. "Humour Writers of the 1880s." *RGALI Archive*, File number 189, 1–2, p. 19. A popular journalist describes Chekhov's life in Moscow in the 1880s.

Fausek, Viacheslav. "My Meeting with Chekhov." *Utro* [*Morning*] (Kharkov) 781 (July 2, 1909). A newspaper journalist becomes Chekhov's good friend.

Fedorova, Lydia. "About A.P. Chekhov." In: *Pamiati Chekhova* [*Dedicated to Chekhov's Memory*]. *Vestnik Manchurskoi Armii* [*The Heralds of the Manchuria Army*] (Laolian) 22 (July 22, 1905).

Fidler, F.F. "Literary Sketches." *Novy Mir* [*The New World*] 8 (1914): 35.

Fidler, Fyodor. "Mister Golikov." *RGALI: Russian State Archive*, File 19, pp.108–110. Chekhov is introduced by his friend to a famous poet A. Polonsky.

Garin-Mikhailovsky, Nikolai. "*Pamiati Chekhova*" [To the Memory of Chekov]. *Vestnik Manchurskoi Armii* [*The Heralds of the Manchuria Army*] (Laolian) 22 (July 22, 1905). A popular novelist remembers Chekhov's last years.

Giliarovsky, Vladimir. *Moskva i moskvichi [Moscow and Moscovites]*. Moscow, 1959: 347–373. A famous Moscow journalist describes his close personal friendship with Chekhov that lasted for many years.

Giliarovsky, Vladimir. "Optimistic People." *Chekov in Memories of His Contemporaries*. Moscow, 1960: 119–121. The Moscow journalist and Chekhov friend remembers visiting Chekhov on numerous occasions.

Glama-Meshchcerskaia, Alexandra. *Vospominaniia [Memoirs]*. Moscow, 1937: 257–260. A prominent Russian actress recollects Chekhov's remarks about theater.

Goldenveiser, Alexander. *Vblizi Tolstogo*

[*Around Tolstoy*], vol. 1. Moscow, 1922: 70, 79. Chekhov meets Tolstoy, and they talk about literature and music.

Gorky, Maxim. "A.P. Chekhov." *Chekhov v vospominaniiakh sovremennikov* [*Chekhov in the Memoirs of His Contemporaries*]. Moscow, 1947: 7–20. Originally published in: *Beseda* [*Conversation*] (Berlin) 2 (1923). One of the best Russian writers of the time is dearly admired and loved by Chekhov as they spend a lot of time together in the 1890s.

Gorky, Maxim. "Leo Tolstoy." In: *Zhizn insskustva* [*The Art Life*] 241–242 (1919–1920): 13–14 October.

Gorodetsky, Daniil. "Memories of Anton Pavlovich Chekhov." *Russikaia Pravda* 91 (July 3, 1904). A publisher of *The Yalta News* newspaper meets Chekhov at the seaport on his arrival from Odessa.

Gubareva , Natalia. "Memories of A.P. Chekhov." *Literaturnoe nasledstvo* [*Literary heritage*]. (Moscow) 68 (1960): 557–574. Chekhov plays a lot of practical jokes as a young man; yet 20 years later he looks very sick and tired.

Gurland I. "Memories of Chekhov." *Teatr i iskusstvo* [*Theater and art*]. 28 (1904): 520–521. A law student meets Chekhov at the seaport upon his arrival to Yalta from Odessa.

Kachalov (Shverubovich), Vasily. "From My Memoirs." In: *Shypovnik* [*Rosehip*] 23 (1914). Chekhov meets with theater directors and actors in the early 1900s.

Karpov, E.P. "My Two Last Meetings with Chekhov." In: *Chekhov v vospominaniiakh sovremennikov* [*Chekhov in the Memoirs of His Contemporaries*]. Moscow, 1947: 570–577. A theater director describes the first night of *The Seagull*.

Katargina, N. "Memories of A.P. Chekhov." *Literaturnoe nasledstvo* [*Literary heritage*] (Moscow) 68 (1960): 575–586. A famous actress meets Chekhov in Odessa and has a party at a local hotel.

Kazanin, A., and E. Vakulov. "Encounters with Chekhov." *Sovetskaia derevnia* [*Soviet village*] (January 8, 1929). Chekhov sponsors free lunches for needy village children at a local school.

Khotiaintseva, Alexandra. "Meetings with Chekhov." *Literaturnoe Nasledstvo* [*Literary heritage*] (Moscow) 68 (1960): 605–607. A female painter and admirer becomes the object of Chekhov's practical jokes.

Knipper-Chekhova, Olga. "About A.P. Chekhov." In: *Chekhov v vospominaniiakh sovremennikov* [*Chekhov in the Memoirs of His*

Contemporaries]. Moscow, 1947: 472–480. Chekhov's wife recollects the last five years of Chekhov's life.

Knipper-Nardov, Vladimir. "Memories of A.P. Chekhov." In: *Chekhov v vospominaniiakh sovremennikov* [*Chekhov in the Memoirs of His Contemporaries*]. Moscow, 1986: 611. Originally published in: *Literaturnoe nasledstvo* [*Literary heritage*] (Moscow) 87 (1970): 302–303. Chekhov's brother-in-law is one of the last persons who saw him alive, on his trip to Germany.

Komissarzhevskaia, Vera. "Memoirs." *Teatr i dramaturgiia* [*Theater and Theater Studies*] 2 (1935): 29–30. A famous Russian actress meets Chekhov in Crimea in 1896 to discuss future roles in Chekhov's plays.

Koni, Anatoly. *Izbrannye proizvedeniia* [*Selected Works*], vol. 2. Moscow, 1959: 340–348. A Moscow lawyer meets with Chekhov and other writers in the late 1890s.

Korolenko, Vladimir. "Anton Pavlovich Chekhov." In: *Russkoe bogatstvo* [*Russian wealth*] (Moscow) 7 (1904). A major Russian novelist becomes Chekhov's close friend.

Korovin, Konstantin. "My Meetings with Chekhov." *Rossia i slavianstvo* [*Russia and the Slavic World*] (Paris) 33 (July 13, 1929). A famous painter admires Chekhov's intellect.

Kovalevsky Maxim. "A Speech about Chekhov." *Rech'* [*Speech*] 301 (1915). Also published in *Birzhevye vedomosti* [*Stock market news*] (Moscow) 15185 (November 2, 1915).

Kuprin, Alexander. "To Chekhov's Memory." In: *Chekhov v vospominaniiakh sovremennikov* [*Chekhov in the Memoirs of His Contemporaries*]. Moscow, 1947: 132–161. Originally published in: *Sbornik Znanie* [*Collection of Knowledge*]. St. Petersburg: Znanie, 1905. A major Russian short story writer recounts details of his friendship with Chekhov and his life in Yalta in the 1900s.

Kuprina-Iordanskaya A.A. "From the Memories of Kuprin." *Ogonek* 38 (1948). The wife of Alexander Kuprin depicts the writer's visits to the Chekhovs' house in Yalta.

Ladyzhensky, Vladimir. "Old Days." In: *Rossiia i slavianstvo* [*Russia and the Slavic World*] (Paris) 33 (1929). Originally published in: Vladimir Ladyzhensky, *Pamiati Chekhova* [*To the Memory of Chekhov*]. Moscow, 1910. A literary artist describes how Chekhov was embarrassed by his popularity.

Lazarev-Gruzinsky, Aleksander. "A.P. Chekhov." In: *Chekhov v vospominaniiakh sovremennikov* [*Chekhov in the Memoirs of His Contemporaries*]. Moscow, 1947: 132–161. Originally published in: *Russkoe slovo* [*Russian word*] 151 (July 2, 1914). Detailed memories about Chekhov's life in Moscow in the late 1880s.

Lazarevsky, Boris. "A.P. Chekhov." *Russkaia mysl* [*The Russian Thought*] 11 (1906): 91–99. A meeting between a journalist and Chekhov in Yalta in 1903. Chekhov criticizes numerous literary movements and circles, and supports young literary artists.

Leonidov, Leonid. "Past and Present. From the Memoirs." [*Ezhegodnik MKHAT. The Annual Moscow Art Theater Book*], vol. 1. 1946: 463–464. The actors of the Moscow Art Theater pay a visit to Chekhov to discuss his new play, *The Cherry Orchard*.

Leontiev-Shcheglov, Ivan. "Chekhov." *Niva. Literaturnoe prilozhenie* [*Niva. Literary supplement*] 6–7 (1905). A popular short story writer becomes Chekhov's best friend in the 1880s.

Luzhsky, Vasily. "From the Memoirs." *Solntse Rossii* [*The Russian Sun*] 228 (June 25, 1914). An actor admires Chekhov's plays.

Maklakov, V.A. "Memoirs about Chekhov." *Rannee utro* [*The Early Morning*] 201 (1909). The journalist and senator recollects the warm personal friendship that existed between Chekhov and Tolstoy.

Mamontov, Savva. "Two Meetings with Chekhov." *Literaturnoe nasledstvo* [*Literary Heritage*]. (Moscow) 68 (1960): 542–543. Part of the manuscript of a Chekhov play is lost during a storm.

Melkova, A. "Tatyana Tolstaya and Chekhov." *Yasnopolyansky Sbornik*. Tula, 1974: 210. The daughter of a famous novelist falls in love with Chekhov.

Meyerhold, Vsevolod. "Diary." In: Vsevolod Meyerhold. *Nasledie. Dokumenty.* [*Inheritance. Documents*]. Moscow: OGI Publishers, 1998: 550–650.

Naidenov, Sergei (Alekseev). "Chekhov in My Memoirs." *Teatralnaia zhizn'.* [*The Theater Life*] 19 (1959): 25. Chekhov attends a performance of his play *Three Sisters* in Moscow.

Nemorovich-Danchenko, Vladimir. *Iz proshlogo* [*From the Past*]. Moscow, 1938: 185–189. Two chapters are dedicated to Anton Chekhov: "Chekhov" and "The Birth of a Theater." A Moscow theater director recollects his lengthy friendship with Chekhov during the 1880s–1890s–1900s.

Nesterov, Mikhail. *Davnie dni* [*The Old Days*]. Moscow, 1941: 79. Chekhov pays a visit to his sick friend Isaac Levitan, a painter.

Novikov, Ivan. "Two Meetings with Chekhov." In: *Kievskie otkliki* [*Kiev Response*]. 183

(1904). A popular journalist meets Chekhov at the end of his life.

Panov, Nikolai. *K portretu Chekhova* [*About Chekhov's Portrait*]. In: *Chekhov v vospominaniiakh sovremennikov* [*Chekhov in the Memoirs of His Contemporaries*]. Moscow, 1984: 607–609. Originally published in: *Zhivopisnoe obozrenie* [*Art review*] 40 (1904). Chekhov is depicted as always friendly and open to aspiring authors.

Pervukhin, Mikhail. "A. P. Chekhov and Yalta Residents." *Vselennaya Magazine* [*Universe*] 5 (1910). Chekhov has a lot of friends in Yalta. Yet, some visitors come and distract Chekhov from his literary work.

Pervukhin, Mikhail. "From My Memories of Chekhov." In: *Chekhov v vospominaniiakh sovremennikov* [*Chekhov in the Memoirs of His Contemporaries*]. Moscow, 1960: 606–639. Originally published in: *Russkoe slovo* [*Russian word*] 85 (March 29, 1905).

Peshkova, Ekaterina. "Meetings with A.P. Chekhov." *Literaturnoe nasledstvo* [*Literary heritage*]. (Moscow) 68 (1960): 613–621. Gorky's wife recollects the close personal friendship that existed between two great Russian writers.

Pichugin, Zakhar. "From Meetings with A.P. Chekhov." In: *Literaturnoe nasledstvo* [*Literary heritage*]. (Moscow) 68 (1960): 542–546. A friend visits Chekhov at the beginning of his writing career. Chekhov likes to play cards and make jokes.

Pleshcheev, Alexander. "The Staging of *Ivanov*." In: Alexander Pleshcheev. *Chto vspomnilos* [*What I Remembered*]. Paris, 1931: 179–195. The famous poet, writer and editor recollects the staging of several major plays by Chekhov.

Pleshcheev, Alexander. "Visiting A. Chekhov." *Peterburgski dnevnik teatrala* [*The Petersburg Theater Diary*] 1 (1904). Chekhov visits rehearsals of *The Cherry Orchard* at the Moscow Art Theater.

Pleshcheev, Alexey. "Chekhov in Yalta." *Literaturnoe nasledstvo* [*Literary heritage*] (Moscow), 68 (1960): 296–308. Chekhov supports aspiring authors.

Plotov, Mikhail. "A Big Heart." *Komsomolskaya Pravda* 164 (1944). Chekhov works as a doctor in his estate in Melikhovo.

Podiachev, Semyon. *Moia zhizn'* [*My Life*] Moscow, 1934: 100–102. An editor remembers the beginning of Chekhov's literary career in the early 1880s.

Pomerantsev, Aleksandr. "Memories about A.P. Chekhov." In: Maria Murzina. *Chekhoviana*.

Moscow: Nauka, 1996. Three journalists, including Chekhov, visit the shelters for homeless in Moscow; they meet again a few years later, and notice that Chekhov looks very sick.

Posse, Vladimir. *Moi zhiznenny put* [*My Way of Life*]. Moscow-Leningrad: Academia, 1929: 170–177.

Potapenko, Ignaty. "Interview." *Odesskie novosti*. [*The Odessa News*]. 8018 (1904). A popular journalist recollects his friendship with Chekhov in the mid-1890s.

Repin, Ilya. "About my Meetings with Chekhov." In: *Chekhov v vospominaniiakh sovremennikov* [*Chekhov in the Memoirs of His Contemporaries*]. Moscow, 1947: 99–100. A painter works on a famous Chekhov portrait.

Roskin, Alexandr, and Maria Drossi-Steiger. "Young Chekhov." In: Alexandr Roskin, *Antosha Chekhonte*. Rostov: The Rostov Book Publishers, 1939: 34–36. A Chekhov schoolmate and childhood friend recollects his childhood in Taganrog.

Rossolimo, Georgy. "Memoirs about Chekhov." In: *Chekhov v vospominaniiakh sovremennikov* [*Chekhov in the Memoirs of His Contemporaries*]. Moscow, 1947: 461–471. Memories of a Chekhov friend about the years of 1879–1904 spent in close personal friendship with the writer.

Semenov, Sergei. "Chekhov Meets Leo Tolstoy." *Peterburgski kurier* [*The Petersburg Courier*] 159 (1914). A French translator remembers Chekhov's visit to Tolstoy.

Serebrov-Tikhonov, Alexandr. *O Chekhove* [*About Chekhov*]. Moscow, 1931. Chekhov pays a visit to the huge estate of Savva Morosov, and then goes fishing.

Sergeenko, Alexander. "Two Meetings with Chekhov." *Literaturnoe nasledstvo* [*Literary heritage*] (Moscow) 68 (1960). Originally published in: *Russkoe slovo* [*Russian Word*] 279 (December 2, 1908). A journalist's son remembers Chekhov's friendship with his father and the publication of Chekhov's works.

Shapovalov, Lev. "How They Built Chekhov's House in Yalta." In: *Chekhov v vospominaniiakh sovremennikov* [*Chekhov in the Memoirs of His Contemporaries*]. Moscow, 1960: 648–672. An architect tells how the Chekhovs' house in Yalta was built.

Shavrova-Just, Elena. "A.P. Chekhov." In: *V strane minuvshego. Vospominania ob A.P. Chekhove* [*The Land of the Past. Memories of A.P. Chekhov*]. Taganrog: Sbornik, 1935: 271–276. A female short story writer explains how Chekhov assisted in starting her career.

Shchepkina-Kupernik, Tatiana. *Junye gody. Moi vstrechi s A.P. Chekhovym* [*Young Years: My Meetings with A.P. Chekhov*] Leningrad: Academia, 1925: 217–251. A prominent female poet and novelist becomes Chekhov's close friend for many years.

Simov, Vladimir. "From Memories about Chekhov." In: *Chekhov v vospominaniiakh sovremennikov* [*Chekhov in the Memoirs of His Contemporaries*]. Moscow, 1947: 93–98. A set designer works in close contact with Chekhov at the set design of his plays.

Sobolevsky, Sergei, and A. Less. "A Portrait." *Moskva* [*Moscow*] 1 (1960): 186–187. A university professor gives Chekhov more material for his literary work.

Stanislavsky, Konstantin. "Chekhov and Artem." In: Konstantin Stanislavsky. *Sobranie sochinenii* [*Works*], vol. 5. Moscow, 1958: 229–360. Chekhov loved the actors and, as a doctor, was happy to treat them.

Stanislavsky, Konstantin. "The Moscow Art Theater in Yalta." In: Konstantin Stanislavsky. *Sobranie sochinenii* [*Works*], vol. 5. Moscow, 1958: 229–360. The Moscow Art Theater visits Crimea to meet Chekhov and other writers.

Stanislavsky, Konstantin. "My Life in Art." In: Konstantin Stanislavsky. *Sobranie sochinenii* [*Works*], vol. 5. Moscow, 1958: 229–360. A major Moscow theater director maintains a close professional and personal relationship with Chekhov in the 1880s–1900s, staging for the first time most of Chekhov's plays. Several articles by Stanislavsky include his memories of Chekhov.

Stanislavsky, Konstantin. "A Trip to Crimea." In: Konstantin Stanislavsky. *Sobranie sochinenii* [*Works*], vol. 5. Moscow, 1958: 229–360. Stanislavsky and his theater go to Yalta to pay a visit to Chekhov and perform his plays.

Sulerzhitsky, Leonid, and Vasily Kachalov. "Interview." *Russkoe utro* [*The Russian Morning*] 5 (1909). A theater director and literary critic write about Chekhov and Gorky.

Sumbatov (Juzhin), Alexander. "Three Meetings." In: Alexander Sumbatov, *Zapisi. Stat'i. Pisma.* [*Notes. Articles. Letters.*] Moscow, 1951: 427. A literary artist meets with Chekhov and Tolstoy in Yalta.

Suvorin, Alexey. *Dnevnik* [*Diary*]. Moscow-Petersburg, 1923: 36, 80–82, 121–128, 150–1665, 294–197. A famous journalist, writer and publisher works closely with Chekhov in 1893–1902 on the publication of his works.

Suvorin, Alexey, and Anton Chekhov. "Works. Letters." In: Anton Chekhov. *Works in 35 volumes,* Vol 1. Moscow: Voskresenie Publishers, 2009. The newly published collection of works and letters reveal a previously hidden side of Chekhov's life, especially his interest in women. In particular, Chekhov describes his numerous secret love affairs in his letters to Suvorin.

Tan-Bogoraz, B. "At Chekhov's Hometown." *Chekhovsky iubileiny sbornik [Chekhov's anniversary publication].* Moscow, 1910: 480–485. Memories of a schoolmate about his childhood years together with Chekhov.

Teleshov, Nikolai. "A.P. Chekhov." In: *Chekhov v vospominaniiakh sovremennikov [Chekhov in the Memoirs of His Contemporaries].* Moscow, 1947: 162–181. A writer's memories about Chekhov as a doctor in the countryside.

Tolstoy, Lev. *Polnoe sobranie sochinenii [Complete Works].* Moscow, 1953. Vol. 53: 51–52, Vol. 54: 113, 191, 293–294. Chekhov meets Leo Tolstoy in 1901–1903 in the Crimea, and they talk about literature and life.

Troinov, B. "Meetings in Moscow. From the Memoirs." *Literatura i iskusstvo [Literature and Art]* 29 (July 15, 1944). Several brief meetings with Anton Chekhov in Moscow at the end of his career.

Ulianov, Nikolai. "Chekhov's portrait." *Izvestiia literaturno-khudozhestvennogo kruzhka [The Bulletin of the Literary and Artistic Circle]* (Moscow) 3 (1914). A painter makes several attempts to make a portrait of Chekhov, admiring his face as well as his intellect.

Varlamov K. "Meetings with Varlamov." *Petersburg Newspaper* 6 (January 17, 1910). An actor likes the sound of Chekhov's voice and gives him advice about singing on stage.

Veresaev, Vikenty. "A.P. Chekhov." *Krasnaia panorama [The Red Panorama]* 23 (July 13, 1929). Chekhov dies at a rather early age, and is admired by all of his friends and readers.

Volkov, Nikolai. *Meyerhold: A Biography.* Moscow: Academia, 1924: 125. A theater director develops a very special friendship with Chekhov.

Yakovlev, Alexei. "A.P. Chekhov." *Russkie vedomosti [Russian herald].* 190 (July 2, 1906). A group of university students pays a visit to Chekhov in his Melikhovo estate.

Yakovlev, Sergei. "Memories of A.P. Chekhov." *Russkii listok [Russian leaflet]* 201 (July 22, 1904). Chekhov works as a home tutor during his school years; later he is helping young authors with words of encouragement.

Yasinsky, Evgeny. *The Novel of My Life.* Moscow: Academia, 1925: 268–270. Chekhov supports young and aspiring authors by editing their manuscripts.

Zelenin, Peter. "About A.P. Chekhov and his Family." *Pridneprovsky krai [The Pridneprovsky Region]* 5177 (July 2, 1914). A Moscow doctor, escorted by Chekhov, pays a visit to a Moscow public house to study the social roots of prostitution. Chekhov works as a village doctor of the Moscow region in the mid–1880s.

Index

death 2, 31, 40, 49, 52, 54, 59, 83, 91, 96, 100, 123, 146, 168, 170, 171, 175, 176, 187
directors 6, 67, 108, 111, 112, 119, 122, 131, 133, 139, 155
Dmitrovka Street 51, 60, 76
doctors 21, 30, 33, 46, 49, 54, 55, 75, 84, 90, 113, 131, 153, 167, 171, 183
dogs 68, 95, 165, 166, 186, 188
Dolzhenko, A. (Chekhov's cousin) 17
Dostoevsky, F. (novelist) 78
dressing room 114, 116, 125, 136, 140, 143
Drossi, M. (childhood friend) 15
Drozdova, N. (friend) 62
"Dull Story" 151

editors 8, 9, 21, 22, 23, 25, 42, 45,48, 65, 69, 84, 87, 101, 102, 118, 154, 155, 166
Efros, N. (actor and theater director) 140
Elpatievsky, Dr. S. 25, 111, 136, 156, 167, 170, 176
estate 21, 46, 51, 52, 53, 54, 55, 56, 59, 60, 65, 66, 68, 76, 80, 82, 85, 86, 91, 93, 97, 156, 157, 165, 178
expressiveness 39, 50, 57, 62, 74, 75, 117, 119, 132, 165, 191
Ezhov, N. (writer) 115

Fausek, V. (journalist) 157
Fidler F. (writer) 87
Fish-Tank Theater 88
fishing 2, 14, 17, 18, 26, 46, 58, 59, 60, 74, 86, 94, 95, 126, 150, 182, 186
Flaubert, G. (writer) 63, 67
flower 154, 165
flying machines 180
Fragments Magazine 26, 101, 118
France 59, 70, 103, 145, 146, 153
friend 3, 15, 21, 22, 23, 27, 28, 35, 36, 42, 43, 44, 48, 49, 54, 55, 56, 58, 59, 61, 64, 67, 68, 72, 87, 92, 98, 112, 114, 139, 148, 156, 157, 170, 182
funeral 148, 168

garden 13, 53, 55, 57, 58, 63, 70, 71, 76, 79, 85, 91, 96, 103, 108, 134, 141, 146, 153, 154, 155, 156, 157, 165, 167, 168, 170, 186
gardening 2, 76, 154, 165
Garin-Mikhailovsky 177
Gaspra 81, 95, 96, 156, 167
geisha 3, 8, 73
general store 15, 16, 18
Germany 31, 40, 75, 90, 126, 146, 167, 175, 179, 181, 190
gift 17, 26, 42, 50, 65, 96, 117, 140, 143, 163, 166
Giliarovsky V. (newspaper journalist) 38, 47, 90, 116

Glama-Mesherskaya, A. (actress) 112
"The Gloomy People" 57
Gogol, N. (novelist) 23
Goldenweiser, A. (pianist) 25, 95
Golike, R. (editor) 87, 88
Goltsev (literary artist) 83
Gorky, M. (novelist) 3, 6, 7, 8, 43, 69, 78, 79, 81, 83, 89, 96, 100, 103, 110, 111, 124, 125, 126, 129, 134, 136, 144, 145, 146, 155, 160, 161, 162, 166, 167, 168, 178, 184, 186
Gorodetsky, D. (publisher) 149, 151
Greco-Turkish War 184
Greece 40
Grigorovich, D. (writer) 20, 23, 26, 34, 38, 40, 101
Gubareva, N. (Chekhov's friend) 46, 182
Gurland, I. (law student) 151

happiness 63, 79, 126, 128, 148, 149, 174, 187
health 6, 22, 25, 31, 51, 59, 61, 64, 65, 71, 75, 84, 90, 111, 121, 123, 127, 132, 139, 144, 146, 153, 156, 157, 161–164, 167, 172, 174, 178
hermit 161
high school 12–14, 18, 19, 26, 47, 134, 172, 181
highway 54, 75
Hong Kong 72
hospital 21, 22, 26, 33, 51, 52, 56, 68, 156, 171
hospitality 32
hotel 3, 28, 32, 48, 49, 72, 88, 92, 98, 132, 133, 137, 150, 158, 167, 172, 190
humor 19, 23, 34, 41, 66, 83, 90, 97, 99, 101, 156, 158
hunting 66

inscription 113, 138, 153
Italy 168, 178, 179
Ivanov 5, 108, 118, 119

Japan 3, 8, 73, 175
jokes 11, 40, 42, 46, 47, 48, 55, 60, 67, 68, 73, 77, 79, 86, 88, 90, 99, 102, 120, 125, 131, 134, 135, 137, 145, 151, 163, 166, 179, 186
journalists 7, 42, 67, 90, 102, 151, 159, 172

Kachalov, V. (actor) 98, 124, 125
Karpov, E. (theater director) 88, 119, 121, 122
Katarygina, K. (actress) 137
Kazan 3
Kazanin, A. (student) 60
Khotaintseva, A. (painter) 76
kindness 65
kiss 12, 187, 188, 189, 190
Knipper, O. (actress and Chekhov's wife) 4, 5, 87, 120, 121, 124, 131, 140, 156, 160, 163, 174, 177, 179, 187–189
Komissarzhevskaya, V. (actress) 75, 88, 89, 103, 121, 122, 123